THE CULTURAL POLITICS OF MARKETS

THE CULTURAL POLITICS OF MARKETS

Economic Liberalization and Social Change in Nepal

KATHARINE NEILSON RANKIN

DISCARD

University of Toronto Press

TORONTO AND BUFFALO

First published in North America in 2004 by
University of Toronto Press Incorporated
Toronto and Buffalo

National Library of Canada Cataloguing in Publication
Rankin, Katharine N.
   The cultural politics of markets : economic liberalization and social change
in Nepal / Katharine N. Rankin.

(Anthropological horizons)
ISBN 0–8020–3929–4 (bound).—ISBN 0–8020–8698–5 (pbk.)

   1. Newar (Nepalese people) 2. Sankhu (Nepal) 3. Culture—Economic
aspects—Nepal—Case studies. 4. Community development—Nepal—Case
studies. 5. Social change—Nepal—Case studies. 6. Nepal—Economic
conditions. 7. Nepal—Economic policy. I. Title. II. Series.

HN670.9.A8R36 2004   306'.089'95   C2003–907500–1

ISBN   0–8020–3929–4 (cloth)
ISBN   0–8020–8698–5 (paper)

Printed on acid-free paper

Designed and produced for Pluto Press by
Chase Publishing Services, Fortescue, Sidmouth, EX10 9QG, England
Typeset from disk by Stanford DTP Services, Northampton, England
Printed and bound in the European Union by
Antony Rowe Ltd, Chippenham and Eastbourne, England

CONTENTS

LIST OF MAPS

ACKNOWLEDGEMENTS

In Nepal many friends and teachers helped make my time productive and enjoyable. Thanks go especially to Madan Gopal Shrestha for research assistance and to Beku Laksmi Shrestha for ongoing commentary on Newari culture. The households of Hari Gopal Shrestha and Basu Dev Joshi welcomed me with particularly generous hospitality, and Bindra Joshi offered sisterly companionship. Bal Gopal Shrestha and the late Bert van den Hoek provided intellectual companionship during the research and commented extensively on the ethnographic chapters here. Sri Laksmi Shrestha and Bina Pradhan contributed especially thoughtful insights on the perspectives of Newari women and possibilities for a feminist consciousness among them. Surendra Rajopadhyay and the late Panchalal Joshi gave generously of their vast knowledge of the religious and ritual dimensions of Newar society. Sarla Shrestha, Pratima Shrestha, Madan Gopal Shrestha, Raju Shrestha and Dhana Prasad Panday assisted with transcriptions and translations from oral and archival sources.

The research was supported by a Fulbright grant from the US Education Foundation in Nepal, as well as two short-term grants from the Mario Einaudi Center for International Studies at Cornell University and an 'Assistance for New Researchers' grant from the Social Sciences and Humanities Research Council (Canada). An earlier version of Chapter 2 has been published in *Progress in Human Geography* (as 'Anthropologies and Geographies of Globalization', 27(6): 708–34); and parts of Chapter 5 appear in *Gender, Place and Culture* (as 'Cultures of Economies: Gender and Socio-spatial Change in Nepal', 10(2): 111–29). In both cases the editor has granted permission for reprinting.

I have benefited from critical readings by colleagues in Ithaca and Toronto, and co-panellists at conferences of the American Association of Geographers, including Stuart Corbridge, Amrita Daniere, Katherine Gibson, Kanishka Goonewardena, Ben Kohl, Vicky Lawson, Lauren Leve, Margit Mayer, Norma Rantisi, Susan Ruddick, Gavin Smith and Kathy White. Meric Gertler offered invaluable advice about the publication process. Banu Oja and Shambhu Oja provided many years of Nepali instruction and friendship that crucially underpin the research. Leah Birnbaum and Chris Cavanagh provided editorial assistance, and the index was compiled by Alan Yoshioka. Over the years my doctoral committee members gave just the right balance of support and criticism: thanks go to Susan Christopherson for sustaining my interest in market structures; to Lourdes Benería for encouraging me to keep a gender analysis at the forefront of my work; and to Kathryn March for inspiring me with her incomparable commitment to ethnographic methods and cross-cultural study. At Pluto, Julie Stoll consistently offered prompt, friendly and always-exactly-right advice for which I am very grateful. Virgil Duff at University of Toronto Press provided useful last-minute suggestions about the orientation of the introduction. Both found wonderful reviewers whose comments enriched the manuscript enormously.

Zachary Thomas was with me for part of the field research; I thank him for his steady stream of fresh insights, as well as for all his support and companionship then and since, which have played a major role in the production of this book. I dedicate the book to my parents, Mary Louise Backus Rankin and Douglas W. Rankin, among whose many contributions was a pressing impatience to see it done. They also donated last-minute editing services – and, of course, bear full responsibility for everything contained herein!

GLOSSARY OF NEWARI AND NEPALI TERMS

Note that Nepali words are denoted by (Nep.)

adhiyā	Form of rent, amounting to half of the summer rice crop
aṅgsa	Inheritance, patrilineal
argha	Conch-shaped vessel used for offering oblations to the deities
asānti	State of disorder
bāgya	luck, good fortune
bahā	Buddhist monastery
baji	Beaten rice, considered 'safe' for consumption among mixed-caste company, as it does not bear ritual pollution
bañjāri	Middleman, wholesaler
bejat	Shame
Bhā	Funeral priest caste
bhalādami	Gentleman
bhiksu	Buddhist monk; in Vajrayana Buddhism, priests are householders, but *Pancadana* is the only occasion among Newars when they assume the posture of monks – priests who have renounced this-worldly obligations and beg for alms.
bhvay	Feast
birtā	Land allocated by the state to remunerate local functionaries for carrying out administrative duties
bodhisattva	One who has reached nirvana and returned to the world of suffering in order to assist others in reaching the goal of enlightenment
bumbhāri	Local functionary charged with monitoring and resolving disputes over land – a position that was abolished after 1951 with the end of Rana rule
caitya	Small, domed shrine
camkha	Clever
cānakya	Newari book of proverbs

cheṃbhāri	Local functionary charged with resolving disputes surrounding the division of household property – a position that was abolished after 1951 with the end of Rana rule
Chipā	Dyer caste
choke byāj	Local interest rate paid in kind, commonly Nrs 0.02/Nrs 100/month
cipa	Ritually polluted, leftover food
Citrakār	Painter caste
dāijo	Nep., dowry
Dakṣiṇapatha	Ancient trade route traversing from the Gangetic plain south to the Deccan plain
dakṣiṇā	Cash payments made to priests as remuneration for service
dalah pau	List of dowry items received during marriage rites
dām	Coin; four *dam* is the equivalent of one paisa; there are 100 *paisa* in one *rupee*
dāna	Gift, presented to a ritually designated recipient, that enables the donor to alleviate misfortune or sin by ritual means
Danya	Caste serving as death specialist, barber and funeral priest for the *Jogi* caste
daśa	Inauspiciousness, misfortune
desa	sacred realm, country
dharma	Worship, religious practice, right action
ḍhiḍo	A thick cereal made from winter crops – wheat, corn or millet – and considered to be low-status food
ḍhikuṭi	Nep., treasury; a bidding game, or a form of rotating credit group
dhyāke byāj	local interest rate paid in cash, commonly Nrs 1/Nrs 1,000/day
dhvākā	Gate, door
digu dyo	Lineage deities, associated with each Newar lineage group
digu dyo guthi	Local association through which members of a lineage group organize the worship of lineage deities
Dom	Drum player caste, duck raisers
duāre	Local functionary, appointed to collect taxes and administer local justice – a position that was abolished after 1951 with the end of Rana rule
Duiṃ	Palanquin carrying caste, trumpeters
galli	Laneway

Gathu	Gardener caste
ghiu khāne	Nep., supplicatory gifts offered to a money-lender
goṣṭhī	Ancient Indian common interest group and precursor to Newar *guthi*
Gubhādyo	Deities of the Forest Monastery, *Gum Vihara*
Guṃ Vihāra	Forest Monastery, ancient Buddhist monastery located on the hillside north of Sankhu
Guruju	Colloquial for Buddhist priest
guthi	Place-based associations, primarily organized by lineage, or around the worship of a particular deity or obligations to perform death rituals
hulāki	Postal service associated with the Tibet trade – a system that was abolished after 1951 with the end of Rana rule
hundi	Foreign exchange service organize to finance Tibet trade
ihi	Girls' initiation rite
ijāra	Form of commission awarded to local functionaries for performance of governmental duties – a system that was abolished after 1951 with the end of Rana rule
ijat	Honour
isṭa mitra	Nep., friends and relations
jāgir	Form of land grant assigned by the state in lieu of a cash income as salary for its employees or functionaries – a system that was abolished after 1951 with the end of Rana rule
jajamāna	Patron (of other castes)
jajmāni	Patron–client system
jap	Telling the beads
jāti	Caste
jeṭhi	Eldest daughter or daughter-in-law
jhāra	System of corvée-like compulsory labour dating from Malla and Rana periods
jimiwāl	Local functionary, overseeing the collection of taxes on state-owned land
Jogi	Death specialist caste, midwife caste, musician caste
Jogi bva	Share of a feast set aside for consumption by Jogi caste, as an incarnation of a deceased ancestor
Jośī	Astrologer and Saivite Tantric priest caste
Jyapu	Farmer caste
karma	Fate
kasto kāl āyo	I had a brush with death
kātro	Nep., white cloth used to cover the body of the deceased

Kau	Blacksmith caste
kuśa	Grass considered to be ritually purifying
kvasah	Dowry, women's own property
lākhā	Gifts of bread or cash from the groom's family to the bride's family
lākhāmari	Sweet bread, exchanged during marriage rituals
lāy	Investment
Mahāsāṅgik	Buddhist monks who in the early centuries of the Christian era formed a dissident sect, later known as *Māhāyana,* and some of whom took up residence at *Guṃ Vihāra* near Sankhu
mhyāy masta	Married daughters, married sisters and their husbands and children
muri	Measure of weight; one *muri* is equivalent to approximately 50 kg.
Nau	Barber caste
Nay	Butcher caste
Newār bigriyo bhojle	Nepali proverb, Feasting has ruined the Newars
pacay yaye	To digest
Pañcadāna	Festival during which householders offer *dana* to Buddhist priests
Pāni patia	mandatory ritual purification taken upon re-entry into Nepal *desa* following travel beyond its borders
pāp	Sin
pāthī	Measure of weight; one *pathi* is approximately 3.6 kg.
pāti	Public resting shelters
pewa	Nep., women's own property
pharmaisi birtā	Land allocated to *duare* – a system that was abolished after 1951 with the end of Rana rule
phuki	Ancestor
pīṭha	Shrine to the mother goddess
pitri	Ancestor
Po	Untouchable caste, sweepers, fisherman, beggars, guardians of mother goddesses
prêt	Ghost
punya	Merit
Pvaḥyā jaḥle nya keni, sakwamiyā jaḥle manu keni	
	Fish get caught in the nets of fisherman, humans get caught in the nets of people from Sankhu
rāj guthi	Both a form of land tenure and a system for organizing the worship of important public deities and the execution of important public festivals

Rājopādhyāya Brahman	Hindu priest caste
rakam	Land grants issued by the state to remunerate agents of specific governmental administrative tasks
ratha jātrā	Chariot festival, the largest of which in Sankhu propitiates the goddess Vajrayogini
ropāni	Unit of land measurement, equivalent to one-eighth of a hectare.
Sakva	lit., 'below Tibet', Newari name for town of Sankhu
Śākya	Buddhist goldsmith caste
sāpati	Nep., small, short-term, interest-free loan
sati	Widow immolation
sāu	shopkeeper
sāu mahājan	Council of local merchants which assisted the *duare* in administering justice – a system that was abolished after 1951 with the end of Rana rule
Sāymi	Oil presser caste
sī guthi	Local association through which participating members organize the performance of obligatory mortuary rites
sīkāḥbhvay	Ritual during which the head of an animal sacrificed for a feast (usually a goat) gets divided into eight parts and distributed among senior men of a lineage in rank order by age
śrāddha	Mortuary site
Śreṣṭha	Merchant caste
surwāl kurta	Indian dress for unmarried women
thakāli	Leader; here in reference to groups of Newari traders residing in Lhasa
tilak	System for accruing dowry gifts, deriving from India, whereby groom's family requests specific dowry items and amounts from bride's family
tvaḥ	Neighbourhood centre, courtyard, quarter
udhāro	Credit, as in 'buying on credit'
Uttarāpatha	Ancient trade route linking the Gangetic plain with the Near East
Vajrācārya	Buddhist priest caste
vaidya	Traditional healer
vaṃśāvalī	Ancient chronicles recounting Newar history in oral and written form
vihāra	Buddhist monastery

INTRODUCTION

The practice of planning and international development has shifted decisively in the last two decades from state-led to market-led approaches. Markets have emerged once again as the dominant mechanism for achieving not only economic growth and efficiency, but also political freedom and social justice. As *The Economist* put it recently, revitalizing a tenet of classical liberalism, '[t]he point of a liberal market economy is that it civilises the quest for profit, turning it, willy-nilly, into an engine of social progress' (2001: 4). Markets are thus seen as aggregates of self-seeking buyers and sellers whose individual pursuits to achieve financial gain generate optimal social outcomes. With the post-Cold War reorganization of production and finance across national borders, this neoliberal vision has assumed a political force of international, indeed global, dimensions. And the discipline of debt regimes has by now brought even the post-colonial Third World and former socialist states within neoliberalism's ideological grip.

As a contribution to the critique of neoliberalism, this book explores how economic liberalization articulates with local social structures and cultures of value through an ethnographic study of the social embeddedness of markets. Given the variability of these relationships, market-led development will not necessarily expand opportunity, as the ideology of the 'free market' would have it; rather it may deepen existing injustice and inequality. The potential for exacerbating inequality increases, moreover, when planners eager to implement market-led approaches rely on a notion of 'social capital' – community solidarity and relationships of exchange and trust – to expand poor people's access to the market. For the idea of social capital, as it has been taken up in mainstream development circles, relies on naively idealistic understandings of the ways shared community values structure social life. Using the example of a 'traditional' (and ancient) Newar market town located in Nepal's Kathmandu Valley, the book shows how the 'value' ascribed to honour and social prestige intersects with economic opportunity. Special focus is given to two kinds of hierarchical rifts in this society particularly relevant for development planning: ideologies of caste and ideologies of gender, both of which shape opportunities unevenly for people in different social locations. These findings contest the relationship imputed in neoliberalism between market access and social opportunity, and demonstrate instead the significance of cultural ideology and cognitive structures in reconfiguring structures of inequality through market relations. It is shown that those in subordinate social positions have the capacity for critical reflection on inequality and domination that can become a foundation for more progressive notions of development, should planners learn how to recognize the critical resources within culture.[1]

The book blends the ethnographic approach of anthropology with the comparative and normative thrust of geography to draw conclusions about the practice of planning and development. The ethnographic content of the book, presented in Chapters 3–6, is based on fieldwork in the merchant community of Sankhu populated by people of the Newar ethnic group. Beginning with the town's role as a commercial centre on the ancient Asian overland trade routes, these chapters demonstrate how large-scale political economic currents shape the town's market culture and give it varying senses of locality over time. At the same time, locality does not emerge in a determined fashion, but is also produced by the agency and worldviews of people residing in Nepal.

Within Nepal, Newars have historically been associated with commerce and long-distance trading, and are known for their dense social networks and associational life, forms of 'social capital' that planners now widely promote as a foundation for economic growth. While Newar society is stratified by an elaborate caste system, its attitudes toward women's participation in commerce are relatively liberal.[2] Today the residents of Sankhu feel strongly the transition to 'open market' policies – especially through the emerging labour and commodity markets these policies generate – but the structuring force of caste and gender ideologies still prevails, shaping the experience of macroeconomic change. The ethnographic chapters document how historical processes of place-making have given shape to contemporary practices of accumulation – of symbolic capital (through gifting, feasting and other 'social investments') as much as of financial capital (through money-lending and land tenure). They situate these practices within the key anthropological debates about 'exchange' and 'hierarchy' in South Asia and emphasize the significance of cultural ideologies for creating and maintaining structures of inequality through market relations.

The purpose, however, is not, in the end, to resolve anthropological debates but rather to use theoretically informed ethnography to lay the groundwork for a critique of neoliberal ideology, and to contribute to a progressive theory of planning and development. To do so, the book relies on the application of 'practice theory' (elaborated in Chapters 1 and 2 with due reference to Bourdieu and Gramsci) to understand the social organization of economic practice. Thus the 'markets' to which the title of this book refers encompass transactions not only in land, money, labour and commodities, but also in honour and other forms of 'social investment' that comprise local 'economics of practice'. The focus is on the cultural meanings that surround markets as a form of social production, not merely on the mechanics of supply and demand. The expression '*cultural politics* of markets' signals the intention here to explore markets in material and symbolic goods as a locus for inequality maintained not just through uneven distribution but also through cultural ideologies. A focus on the politics of culture suggests that, while social change certainly requires material redistribution, it also necessitates the mobilization of 'political consciousness' through which subordinate groups recognize the established order as an arbitrary human construction and fashion alternative moralities. It is in this domain of cultural recognition that we can begin to detect some clear, if controversial, imperatives for the content and process of planning – to be explored in the final chapter of this book.

It must be noted at the outset that this book is not about the *implementation* of market-led development projects; indeed Sankhu lies within the Kathmandu Valley, virtually the only area of Nepal that has *not* historically been the object of aggressive (and capricious) donor-driven development schemes.³ There are some credit facilities available for 'small farmers' and I have noted in Chapter 4 how those facilities geared to leveraging local entrepreneurship in practice often become appropriated for 'social investments' within the Newar moral economy. The objective here is rather to bring findings about local 'economics of practice' to bear on a critical evaluation of the epistemological frameworks informing market-led approaches to development (and microfinance is the particular focus of discussions about development in Chapter 7). Newar society in particular has been selected because of the significant ideological space that exists within it for women (who are conventionally the focus of microfinance programmes) to accumulate and invest private wealth. If, even in the most permissive South Asian cultural contexts, women are shown to face ongoing constraints to entrepreneurship, then planners might be persuaded to rethink fundamental assumptions embedded in market-led approaches about the relationship between credit and opportunity. The Newar case also illustrates well the challenges for 'women's empowerment' posed by the present macroeconomic context. For here new patterns of commodification are playing a role in transforming gender ideologies in ways that diminish the scope for women to acquire and invest private wealth. In practice, development programmes often operate at the margins of these broader cultural-economic shifts.

CROSS-DISCIPLINARY LOCATION

Of course, the book reflects a journey across cultural boundaries – and the politics of positionality and 'epistemic privilege' raised when cross-cultural interpretations are committed to text. It also expresses the theoretical and political quandaries that have arisen over the course of cross-*disciplinary* travel, from an undergraduate anthropology department, to an applied professional Masters and doctorate in city and regional planning, to my current academic appointment in a geography department. Quite unexpectedly, the latter form of (disciplinary) travel has come to predominate the organization and central concerns of this book. The cross-disciplinary focus results in part from having brokered a peace with myself concerning the politics of representation by the time of this writing. I had already been travelling and working in Nepal for over 15 years, first as a student on an undergraduate exchange programme, then as an intern with a Nepalese institution researching women's economic roles, and finally in 1993–95, 1996 and 2000 as an independent scholar conducting the dissertation and follow-up research for this book. Having been deeply troubled in the midst of these experiences by the reflexive turn in anthropology, I had already worked my way into and then out of the authorial paralysis that comes with postmodernist anxieties over speaking on behalf of others – abandoning cross-cultural work altogether for a number of years in favour of activism and community organizing in my home town of Washington, DC. When I wrote the book, then, I had already settled on a politics of ethnographic re-engagement: on doing fieldwork as a means to unearth the perspectives of those not conventionally empowered to represent their culture and on interpreting those perspectives from the vantage point of a western feminist scholar interested in the cultural politics of social change.

The ethnographic voice developed in this book emerged, then, as much through cross-disciplinary travel as through cross-cultural travel. Anthropology has been the starting point, the home base, with its commitment to taking the perspective of people in places and cultures other than the hegemonic West. I have always been compelled by the role of anthropology in the major debates animating social science – about legitimacy, progress, meaning, development. Its role, as Clifford Geertz put it, has been:

… to make available to us answers [about our deepest questions] that others, guarding other sheep in other valleys, have given, and thus to include them in the consultable record of what man [sic] has said. (1973: 30)

Yet however much anthropology has contributed to 'reduc[ing] the puzzlement' and 'clarify[ing] what goes on' in 'other' places and cultures (Geertz 1973: 16), I have also felt that on the whole it suffers from a kind of relativism. Anthropologists' powers of description arising from long-term, qualitative, highly participative fieldwork have been primarily committed to rendering the unfamiliar 'recognizably human' (Rosaldo 1989: 40) and thus to asserting the equality of cultures. Even when those powers have been committed to chronicling the dialectics of domination and resistance, anthropologists tend to refrain from making normative judgements about the societies they study or to extend their analysis to evaluating the epistemological frameworks for policy making. In my view the act of reporting what goes on without taking a position on what is good and just amounts to a political indifference that can border on complicity with oppression.

With its emphasis on the spatial and scalar manifestations of culture, geography offers a comparative perspective from which to develop a normative dimension of cross-cultural research. Its record of documenting patterns of inequality over time and space in relation to macro political-economic processes places geography on solid political ground for articulating a *critique* of culture. Through the ethnographic evidence presented here, I choose to share this political ground. I do believe that a synthesis is necessary, to bring the ground-level insights deriving from ethnographic analysis to bear on a critique, not only of macro political-economies and the assumptions of neoliberalism, but also of local cultural ideologies maintaining systems of subordination and oppression. This book aims to achieve such a synthesis.

The field of planning has brought out the optimist in me. It offers a disciplinary location from which to ask: what is to be done? I read and teach and, through ongoing research, participate in the important work of documenting development as a neocolonial project, maintaining imperial and regional balances of power and impoverishing rather than empowering the poor. But I also view planning – the activity that development *does* – as a contestable terrain, one well worth struggling over in the classroom as much as in research. And I find in the perspectives of low castes and women presented in the book considerable cause for optimism about the capacity of those in subordinate social locations to recognize the arbitrary foundations of domination and to develop locally situated critiques of power. We need anthropology to help recognize the critical capacities of people and geography to place local struggles in a regional and global perspective, but it is in the domain of planning that we can imagine how to mobilize those local critiques as a challenge to dominant cultural ideologies from the grassroots.

SOCIAL EMBEDDEDNESS OF RESEARCH

A few words now on my hosts and how I went about this research. I was introduced to Sankhu through the brother of the mother of a close friend and former colleague at the research institute where I had formerly worked (such as many alliances are brokered in Nepal). Early visits were graciously hosted by Krishna Shrestha, a Merchant-caste carpenter whose home was already bursting beyond capacity with a growing extended family. I soon hooked up with Madan Gopal Shrestha, a committed researcher and practitioner of development with graduate training in demography, who agreed to serve as my research assistant in the afternoons, evenings and on holidays when he was not teaching. This introduction was made through his elder brother, Bal Gopal Shrestha, an anthropologist (cited frequently in these pages) also developing a research project in Sankhu, who holds an appointment at the Centre for Nepalese and Asian Studies, Tribhuvan University, through which my Fulbright fellowship had been organized. And I rented a room in the home of Basu Dev Joshi, a close friend of Madan Gopal's family who lives one minute up the street from Krishna. Throughout the research I took many meals at these three households, exchanged *tika* blessings on various festival occasions with the brothers, sisters, mothers, fathers I acquired by association, lounged over idle conversation as well as discussed and debated my observations about Newar culture.

These details are important for several reasons. First, they illustrate that I was already socially embedded in a particular way before I even began taking fieldnotes – 'she eats with a local political party leader', 'she goes around with the brother of a big businessman', 'she's the sister of the one who stays inside all the time', were the among the countless ways I was 'placed' through my early relationships. Clearly the relationships I brought to the fieldsite shaped my encounter with people in Sankhu and the findings recorded here – sometimes in ways I could not always be conscious of. Obviously the representations of Newar cultural economies in this book are my own, not some kind of objective truth, and they derive from a partial view of Newar society, however much I attempted to solicit a range of perspectives in my fieldwork. My social embeddedness also enabled me to undertake 'participant observation' as a primary research method. Through those three host families I participated in the public and private dimensions of town life as much as my time and energy, and as much as their capacity and willingness to include an uninitiated outsider would allow – in weddings and death observances, private meals and public festivals, the planting and harvesting of rice. The extended relationships forged through these activities made it possible for me to move iteratively between formal, semi-structured interviews recorded on audio cassette and the informal, unstructured and unrecorded encounters over meals, in tea shops, at the market where I could develop an understanding of the context within which the formal interviews took place. Of course, social embeddedness carries with it obligations and limits that became onerous to me at times when I sought perspectives, especially those of low castes, not likely to be encountered in the daily rounds of my closest hosts. Thus I conducted interviews with low castes later in my stay in Sankhu, when I could be confident that my relationships with my hosts would survive the stigma of my associating with their status inferiors and when I was known well enough to be able to move about independently, without reproach and without the escort usually expected of both a stranger and a woman. The shorter duration of my contact with low castes meant that opportunity for participant observation in their quarters was much diminished.

Second, the hospitality extended to me by these families and their close associates was limited neither to the routine afternoon snacks, the evening meals, and occasional feast nor to the much-needed companionship – in invitations to tarry for a while watching television or to run up to the hillside temple for morning exercise. The hospitality extended as well to the long, patient hours my companions spent impressing their views of Newar culture on me, not just fielding my relentless and undoubtedly tiresome questions, but also working to see that I understood in the right way the kind of society they lived in. In some cases these exchanges burgeoned into enduring friendships, but I always appreciated the opportunity to learn how people found meaning in their lives and chose to represent their practices and traditions. This is important to stress because I do not want the critique of culture in these pages to be confounded with

judgement of individual lives. On the contrary, I *liked* my Newar hosts
and I recognized the virtues people found in caste patronage relations
and ideologies of women's seclusion – as elements of *dharma* (religious
duty) or *ijat* (honour) – even as I was critical of their effects on low castes
and women. As Parish writes of the structures of thought and feeling
underlying practices of caste domination:

… [cultural ideologies] exist not only as systems of power and domination,
but also as systems of meaning and practice that nurture and guide actors, that
give meaning and significance to their actions and existence … Reaching for
the American dream, or seeking to live as moral Hindu householders, people
can sometimes participate meaningfully in social practices that oppress others,
perhaps even themselves. (1997: xvii)

Nor do I wish to reduce Newar culture (or any other culture, for that
matter) to practices of domination and oppression, even as I am compelled
in these pages to explore the dominating effects of cultural ideology.
Here again Parish's interpretation of *Hierarchy and its Discontents* is
illuminating:

What matters most, I think, is the politics that grows out of cultural life, not as an
expression of a primal impulse to dominate others, reflecting some transcultural
will-to-power, but as a constructed sense of reality that endows social relations
with a particular felt significance. (1997: xviii)

That is, how do people find meaning in practices that have oppressive
consequences for others – in my own culture as much as Nepal's?

Finally, readers may note that my preliminary contacts with Sankhu
came primarily through high-caste (or dominant-caste) men, for they
occupied the same social and professional networks as me. When I
presented my interest in understanding 'the local economy and culture',
moreover, I was routinely introduced in the early stages of my research
to male informants: the Vajracharya, Brahman and Joshi priests who
could apprise me of any of Sankhu's numerous festivals and other public
rituals; local elected officials who could provide me with data on the
town's households and commercial enterprises; representative heads-
of-households who could explain the workings of *guthis* (death and
lineage association), and the basics of the household economy. Men's
official stature and legitimacy notwithstanding, I soon recognized a
special significance of women informants for my research, beyond a
merely additive gendered perspective that men could not offer. The
first has to do with *my* gendered position: being a woman I experienced
directly practices that were responses to my social location as female,
culturally coded as dependent and vulnerable; for example, I was often

assigned an escort for travel in the public domains of the town. Yet as an ethnographer and a traveller of the world, I was also accorded the respect and deference of a prestigious professional and honoured guest. Negotiating these contradictions enabled me to bring into especially clear focus the importance of gendered opportunities and constraints on other people's lives.

Second, while men were officially vested with the authority to represent Newar culture and economy, in some important respects they also had a narrower range of experiential knowledge on which to draw than women. Patrilocal residence patterns and patrilineal modes of social organization ensure that men's views of social reality are shaped over the course of their lifetime largely by experiences in their natal household and lineage. Women's social location *in between* their natal and marital households, on the other hand, requires that they move regularly between two social worlds; this provides a wider experiential repertoire from which to interpret aspects of Newar culture having to do with household economies and their interface with wider Newar society. As a result of intersubjective access grounded in shared experiences (especially experiences of surveillance and 'protection') and women's more comparative perspective on household economies, I increasingly came to rely on women informants to build an interpretation of Sankhu's cultural economy and local capacities for critique of dominant ideologies.[4]

NOTE ON METHODS, TRANSCRIPTIONS AND ETHNOGRAPHIC VOICE

The bulk of my ethnographic data consists in observations and informal conversation made possible by long-term residence in Sankhu, as well as semi-structured interviews on various aspects of local economic practices – including such standard domains as money-lending, commerce and land tenure, but also other dimensions of 'economies of culture', like religious and caste patronage, the renowned Newar festivals and various means of defending one's honour. While doing the interviews, I sampled for diversity, speaking with as many people as possible from different class, caste, age, gender and occupational backgrounds, and working with them to find issues of particular relevance to their experience within a broad set of topical questions. Most of the interviews were conducted in the company of one of two Newari research assistants, both residents of Sankhu and both members of the Merchant Shrestha caste.[5] For discussions with low castes, who were unlikely to discuss their experiences in the presence of my higher caste co-workers, I often returned to their homes individually for social visits and independent interviewing after initial, formal introductions.

Most interviews cited here were recorded on audiotape. I indicate in the text where I cite from unrecorded interviews, to clarify that such citations represent my written notations at the time of the interview and not direct, unabridged quotations. Recorded interviews were transcribed and translated with assistance as necessary from a native speaker and appear in the text as direct quotations. I conducted interviews primarily in Nepali, not the Newari mother tongue, except when discussing Newari concepts not directly translatable into Nepali (for example, the Newari *kvasah*, women's own property, has a significantly different meaning than the Nepali *dāijo*). I chose Nepali as the primary medium of communication simply because, while I started studying Newari during the research, I was never fully conversant and because most informants spoke fluent Nepali. My research assistants provided translation from Newari to Nepali as necessary when informants expressed discomfort speaking in Nepali. The Newari has been transliterated according to the conventions of Manandhar (1986) and the Nepali according to the conventions of Turner (1931).

Anonymity has been preserved through the use of pseudonyms and by a more frequent practice of referring to informants by their subject position – for example 'a Butcher-caste married woman' – in order to emphasize a politics of social location. I follow the convention in anthropology of using the 'ethnographic present' (Tsing 1993: xv), except when I want to emphasize processes of social and cultural change, and the historically specific moments of articulation with macro political-economic processes. Obviously, there have been many important developments since the research for this book – most significantly the current Maoist movement and the government's military solution transpiring now in the context of the US 'war against terrorism' – that have had direct implications for Sankhu's cultural economy but that cannot be analysed extensively here.

After six months of residence in Sankhu I conducted a 150-household random-sample survey dealing with credit, investment and other business practices in Sankhu – to which I refer occasionally when its findings elucidate the substance of my interviews and observations. Finally, research on the historical construction of markets was accomplished both through focused interviews with the few remaining residents of Sankhu who had been directly involved with the Tibet trade and, mostly, through references to local economic history obtained from the handwritten notes of the Regmi Research Collection (archived on microfilm at the Nepal

National Archives) and from handwritten records at the archival branch of the National Guthi Association.

OUTLINE OF THE BOOK

Two theoretical chapters preface the ethnographic content of the book. Chapters 1 and 2 lay the theoretical ground for examining respectively the cultural dimensions of markets and exchange, and the articulation of local cultural economies with wider macroeconomic processes. Both chapters draw on major currents in the fields of anthropology and geography to develop the normative position advocated here and to build a foundation for challenging neoliberal orthodoxy in economics.

Chapter 1, 'Cultural Politics of Markets', introduces the neoliberal economic philosophy underlying market-led approaches to development, including its origins in the opus of Friedrich von Hayek and the recent embrace of 'social capital' resulting from the 'information-theoretic turn' in economics. In these views, culture is considered only insofar as it introduces more or less 'friction' to the efficient functioning of markets. Economic anthropologists and geographers have recently weighed in on debates about economic development, by revealing the cultural determinants of economic growth and by illustrating the range of non-capitalist 'alternatives' in our midst. The chapter reviews these arguments, noting their challenge to neoliberalism, but also their tendency to reify culture and harbour nostalgic expectations about the capacity for cooperation in non-capitalist contexts. I advocate an approach that emphasizes the cultural embeddedness of markets (*à la* Karl Polanyi), also one that is rooted in the more practical political orientation of 'cultural politics'. In particular, I engage Pierre Bourdieu's notion of the 'economics of practice' to develop a framework for exploring how cultural values underpin the production and exchange of symbols, social networks, and material goods and services – and to present a more compelling interpretation of 'social capital'. This framework sets the stage for detailed analysis of the social embeddedness of markets in Newar society and its articulation with macroeconomic processes.

In Chapter 2, 'Anthropologies and Geographies of Globalization', I consider contributions to the study of globalization from contemporary literatures in the anthropology of practice and the political economy of place-making. Geographers have illustrated how the local shape of global capitalism depends in part on *where* it develops, on the social and spatial structures already in place. Yet we still see remarkably few accounts in this field of how large-scale political-economic processes are experienced and interpreted by people in communities, or how local experiences and responses are socially differentiated. The distinctive contribution of anthropology has been to view large-scale systems from the ground level, understanding local people as 'active agents and subjects of their own history' (Ortner 1984). Too often, however, anthropologists pay microscopic attention to complex cultural and symbolic topographies at the expense of situating local 'maps of meaning' on the larger map of global change. This chapter draws on the strengths of both orientations to chart an approach to studying localities on the periphery of the capitalist global system as sites constituted by and constructed in the vortex of regional and global transformation, and as a site of 'practice anthropology' – where social and cultural filters interpret what is coming in from outside and local agency produces distinctively local social systems.[6]

Chapters 3–6 are historical and ethnographic in nature. Collectively they consider how local cultural economies in the merchant town of Sankhu articulate with macroeconomic processes operating at wider spatial scales – from the pan-Asian trade and cultural exchanges of the early Christian era, to the neoliberal economic restructuring governing national planning today. Chapter 3, 'Genealogy of Markets and Exchange', investigates the historical construction of markets in the Kathmandu Valley, focusing especially on the relationship of the history of Buddhist doctrine and the process of state-building to Sankhu's special position on the lucrative trans-Himalayan trade route. This discussion provides a foundation for elaborating in Chapter 4, 'Newar Representations of Finance', the details of Sankhu's cultural economy, including mechanisms within it for accumulating material and symbolic capital and for justifying private gain through social investments. Chapter 5, 'Caste and Gender Economics', introduces the perspectives of those in subordinate social positions on the regimes of value that organize financial and economic activity in Sankhu; the emphasis here is on how power operates through culture and the evidence for both acquiescence and critical consciousness on the part of women and low castes.

The extensive discussion of the cultural construction of markets in Chapters 3–5 allows me in Chapter 6, 'Global–Local Articulations in an Age of Neoliberalism', to consider how Sankhu's cultural economy articulates with the economic rationalities of neoliberalism and its associated economic policies. I devote special attention to the opportunities and constraints presented for low castes and women in the newly expanding urban labour markets and the increased availability of consumer commodities, especially foreign imports. On the basis of this understanding of the relationships among culture, markets, and global political-economic processes, I then draw some conclusions in Chapter 7, 'Planning and Development', about the nature of social change and the scope for development to provide the intended social protections. Here I return to the core theoretical tenets established in Chapters 1–2 to consider specifically the role of an activist state in providing social protections and the role of planners in facilitating social criticism. These considerations ultimately offer some guidelines for claiming a politically progressive agenda in planning theory and practice.

1 THE CULTURAL POLITICS OF MARKETS

This chapter addresses the major debates animating contemporary social sciences about the role of culture and social life in economic processes. It examines the origins of neoliberalism in the opus of Friedrich von Hayek and explores the implications of the current neoliberal hegemony for how scholars and policy makers conventionally view the practice of planning and economy–society relations today. A special note of caution is sounded about the idea of social capital, which has assumed a prominent position within development discourse in the past decade. The idea appears to promise that social factors of economic development – namely social networks expressing trust and reciprocity – have finally received due attention in the corridors of the World Bank. Here it is shown that incorporating the social in this way has not challenged economic orthodoxies; rather, 'social capital' is shown to sit comfortably with the epistemological foundations of neoliberalism. In reviewing these currents of development thought, the chapter rejects instrumental interpretations of culture as 'receptivity to change' or as a technical input to economic growth and good governance, and advocates instead revitalizing the efforts of Karl Polanyi in order both to understand how markets are embedded in socio-cultural frameworks and to defend a role for planning even in the hallowed realm of the market. Polanyi's cross-cultural and historical research spawned the sub-discipline of economic anthropology, which emerged in the 1960s to document the enormous variation in economic practices across cultures and over time, thereby challenging the role of economics in rendering capitalist ideology as natural law. The recent 'cultural turn' in geography, meanwhile, has inspired policy planners to consider cultural determinants of regional economic competitiveness and to understand the non-capitalist economic activities operative in their midst.

While acknowledging their role in specifying the limitations of econo-centric analysis, the chapter also questions the ways in which much of the anthropological and geographical literature in these traditions has imagined non-market societies. The impulse in both sub-fields to seek alternative, non-monetized economic arrangements suggests a nostalgic (and problematic) quest for an imaginary world structured by principles of reciprocity and cooperation. This quest is riddled with several problematic assumptions, each of which is rejected here. I argue that an understanding of the role of culture and social life in economic processes today can best be achieved with recourse to Pierre Bourdieu's notion of an 'economics of practice'. With this concept, Bourdieu provides a framework for exploring the cultural processes through which value is created in both material and symbolic domains and how competing regimes of value in turn structure socio-spatial organization and behaviour. Bourdieu offers an alternative – and more politically potent – interpretation of social capital (and of the related concept of symbolic capital), one that emphasizes its role in structuring differential access to resources and in reproducing social hierarchy and inequality. The approach developed here to studying the cultural politics of markets sets the stage for detailed analysis in the ethnographic chapters of the social embeddedness of economic life in Newar society and its articulation with state macroeconomic policies.

HAYEK AND NEOLIBERALISM: MARKETS AGAINST PLANNING

The origins of the idea that free-market capitalism is the only practical way to organize a modern society can be traced to economic philosopher and Nobel laureate Friedrich von Hayek. Writing his major treatise as the Second World War was drawing to a close, Hayek sustained an argument for the efficiency and justice of markets and gave a damning indictment of state planning. The times were not congenial for such arguments: socialism had been established as a viable alternative to capitalism; Keynesian economic philosophies tempered turn-of-the-century free-market rationality with unemployment benefits, social security and other welfare policies; and, in the realm of international development, cooperatives, development banking, subsidized credit, and other socialized forms of economic organization were widely promoted. 'Planning the economy' was the dominant practice, even in most advanced capitalist corners of the world.

Hayek's *Road to Serfdom* (1944), which has since been called 'the founding charter of Neo-liberalism' (Anderson 2000), set out to combat Keynesianism and prepare the theoretical foundations for a more 'liberated' kind of capitalism. It likened planning to a dictatorship of social ideals. For Hayek, planning (construed as state intervention in the economy) posed the tyranny of 'wanting to organize the whole of society and all its resources for [a] unitary end and ... refusing to recognize the autonomous sphere in which the ends of individuals are supreme'; in so doing planning presupposed 'the existence of a complete ethical code in which all the different human values are allotted their due place' (1944: 56, 57). But for Hayek, no such end or common goal existed, and the attempt by planners to establish one could only lead to totalitarianism: 'In the end somebody's views will have to decide whose interests are ... important; and these views must become part of the law of the land, a new distinction of rank [that] the coercive apparatus of government imposes upon the people' (Hayek 1944, quoted in Cassidy 2000: 49). Thus, 'planning leads to dictatorship because dictatorship is the most effective instrument of ... the enforcement of ideals and, as such, essential if ... planning on a large scale is to be possible' (Hayek 1944: 70). Hayek identified two further problems with planning, which he considered to generate fundamental inefficiencies. First, the principle of egalitarianism underlying planning undermines individual freedom and the 'vitality of abilities', both of which are necessary for the prosperity of all (Anderson 2000). Second, planning suffers from a fundamental 'division of knowledge' problem. John Cassidy (2000: 47) paraphrases Hayek's argument on this point:

In order to know where resources should be directed, the central planner needs to know both what goods people want to buy and how they can most cheaply be produced. But this knowledge is held in the minds of individual consumers and businessmen, not in the filing cabinets ... of a government planning agency, and the only practical way for customers and firms to relay this knowledge to each other, Hayek argued, is through a system of market-determined prices.

According to Hayek, then, the competitive market, rather than planning, was the superior and most democratic way of establishing what everyone wanted. Foremost, the market liberates society from the tyranny of the central plan based on information distorted by the individual will of the planner. Planning, as a form of arbitrary power, is anti-democratic; the market mechanism – and the capitalist system that sustains it – a necessary condition for democracy. Further, the price system offers an efficient medium for communicating information and allocating scarce resources, by allowing millions of decision-makers to respond individually to freely determined prices. It also tolerates, even values, inequality in social Darwinist fashion. As Susan George (1999) explains the neoliberal position on this issue, '[p]eople are unequal by nature, but this is good because the contributions of the well-born, the best-educated, the toughest, will eventually benefit everyone'.

Hayek peddled these extreme and unpopular views unrelentingly for decades, from the post-Depression heyday of Keynesianism to the election of Margaret Thatcher in 1979, when they finally took root as economic policy. Although Hayek himself remained a remarkably invisible public figure (and he is rarely mentioned in mainstream economics textbooks), it is fair to say that his central argument about the vitality of capitalism has been vindicated 'to such an extent that it is hardly an exaggeration to refer to the 20th century as the Hayek century' (Cassidy 2000: 45). Thatcher's election set in place the policies and practices that could breathe life into the key tenets of neoliberalism worked out by Hayek, namely: the downsizing of the public sector and its corollary, the privatization of public enterprises; the consequent gutting of unions, reduction in public sector jobs, and rise in unemployment; tax reforms that benefit the rich and burden the poor; the transfer of wealth from public to private sectors, from the poor and middle-class to the corporate sector and the rich; the deregulation of the finance sector and the consequent explosion of corporate mergers and acquisition as a source of wealth; and an increasing lack of democratic accountability in the economic sphere (see Anderson 2000 and George 1999).[1] With the election of Ronald Reagan in 1980, the United States – the world's largest economy – lent hegemonic force to neoliberal economic philosophies, which henceforth have come to dominate economies large and small on all six continents via the instruments of conditional lending (notwithstanding the US's own divergence from neoliberal orthodoxy, under Reagan and since, with its own brand of 'military Keynesianism' [Anderson 2000]).

In development the embrace of neoliberal principles was sparked off largely by Deepak Lal's formative *Poverty of Development Economics* (1983), which argued, following Hayek, that the developmental state is essentially 'predatory' and susceptible to 'capture', and should therefore be rolled back to enable markets to do their good work. The so-called 'Washington Consensus' – identified in 1990 by John Williamson and now widely understood to be comprised of the major development agencies located in Washington DC (especially the International Monetary Fund [IMF] and World Bank), their creditors and the US Treasury Department – emerged as a powerful ideological block setting the terms of the periphery's integration into the New World Order. It promoted the position that economic development and related problems that development planners sought to address would more or less take care of themselves if markets were freed from government intervention. World Bank structural

adjustment programmes and IMF stabilization loans were the mechanisms
by which development agencies could produce a regulatory environment
favourable to market-led growth in the Third World – by making credit
conditional on fiscal discipline, trade liberalization, strengthened bank
supervision, privatization, deregulation, tax reform and other neoliberal
'remedies'. In both the centres of neoliberal orthodoxy and on the Third
World periphery, the Washington Consensus represented a radical shift
from previous approaches to development rooted in Keynesianism,
modernization and welfarism ('the McNamara Era' at the World Bank;
Fine 2001), which posited a role for state intervention in bringing
about progressive structural changes to developing economies. As will
be discussed at greater length below, the irony is that neoliberals, too,
required state intervention in order to create the enabling environment
for 'free markets'.

On its own terms, the outcomes of two decades of neoliberal hegemony
are contradictory. Regarding the ultimate objective of achieving a stable
growth rate in the developed capitalist economies (such as existed before
the economic crisis of 1973) 'the failure is manifest, without any possible
doubt' (Anderson 2000). And in the Third World adjustment policies 'failed
to deliver significant differences in performance, let alone development'
(Fine 2001: 139). On several counts, neoliberalism has kept its promise:
in all countries of the OECD, neoliberal policies correlate with a decline
in the rate of inflation, revival of profits, defeat of the union movement
and increased levels of unemployment (Anderson 2000). The record of
the 'Asian Tigers' in the 1980s offered a contradictory theory, however
– that strong economic growth could be achieved by 'governing the
market', through state-led industrial policy backed by state-owned financial
institutions and controls on foreign investment (and all build on histories
of fundamental socio-economic redistribution through land reform).[2]
The East Asian experience is particularly instructive when viewed in
relation to another outcome most significant for our concern here with
planning and development: the growing extremes of social inequality
that have persisted even in the midst of formal political equalities we
call 'democracy'. The relevant statistics speak for themselves. Taking
the paradigmatic example of the USA, Mike Davis notes that:

In the late 1990s … America's 400 richest families increased their net worth by
almost a billion dollars apiece, while the pie slice of the bottom 40 percent of
the population plummeted 80 percent … . Globally, the Wealth Decade of the
1990s translated into negative income trends for 80 African and Latin American
countries, while 200 masters of the universe, led by Bill Gates … amassed personal

fortunes equivalent to the total income of the world's 2.5 billion poorest people. (Davis 2000, cited in Goonewardena 2002: 30; see also Philips 1990)

So severe were the social costs in places like Mexico where structural adjustment was most aggressively and hastily applied that the UNDP (United Nations Development Programme) called in 1995 for 'Adjustment with a Human Face' to account for the welfare needs of those unable to survive the 'shocks' of adjustment (see Cornia 1987).

How, we must ask, is this inequality politically sustainable, how could it be given a 'human face', especially in the context of the political freedoms that liberal democracy promises? Given the widespread social costs, why have electoral majorities not voted neoliberalism out of office? Marx answered this question over 150 years ago with respect to economic liberalism in his essay 'On the Jewish Question': socio-economic inequality has been able to survive only by means of a hegemonic separation of the 'economic' from 'political', 'social' and 'cultural' spheres within liberal capitalism. As political scientist Ellen Wood incisively notes 'It is, in fact, a specific feature of capitalism that a particular kind of universal equality is possible which does not extend to class relations – that is, precisely, a formal equality, having to do with political and legal principles and procedures rather than with the disposition of social or class power' (1995: 259; see also Buck-Morss 1995).

Thus the owners of private property can carry out surplus extraction (economic coercion) without wielding direct political power in the conventional liberal sense – sheltered as they are from lines of political accountability or any obligation to perform social functions. In so separating private appropriation from public duties, Wood continues, capitalism transforms certain essentially *political* issues – struggles over domination and exploitation – into merely technocratic-economic issues, making it difficult for the economically disenfranchised to organize beyond the point of production (say, for job security) to the scale of the nation-state (the locus of power on which capitalist property ultimately rests) for more powerful forms of accountability (1995: 45).

The separation of 'economic' and 'political' domains is a necessary condition for the global reach of neoliberalism today, although its origins lie deeper, within eighteenth-century classical economic liberalism, when economists discovered 'the economy' in the abstract and began emptying capitalism of its social and political content (Wood 1995: 19; see also Buck-Morss 1995). This discovery rested on a neat reification of the economy: the transformation of human attributes, relations and actions into an objective entity independent of subjective human experience. A brief look at any mainstream economics textbook reveals that such abstraction persists today; here, too, 'the economy' appears as a fully autonomous entity, governed by its own objective laws, impervious to politics and human agency.

At the heart of 'the economy' so abstracted is a vision of the market as a self-regulating sphere of human activity: individual, self-interested pursuits of consumers and producers 'naturally' regulate the market by keeping prices responsive to consumer preference and producer capacity. As Hayek once argued, the claim here is that rational, profit-maximizing individuals freely pursuing their own self-interest will produce the maximum public good. Money, as the medium of exchange, is taken to be a fungible, homogeneous instrument that can level social differences by conjoining rational economic actors in the neutral realm of the self-regulating market. And any behaviour interfering with the price mechanism is understood to contradict 'economic' behaviour – so that 'community', 'the collective', even 'the extended family' are conceived in antithesis to benign individual self-interest.

Within a purely neoliberal perspective, then, culture is relevant only to the extent that it may be identified as a barrier (or catalyst) to the expansion of markets. In this framework, culture, like state regulation, may introduce more or less 'friction' to the efficient and optimal functioning of markets. A World Bank publication addressing the scope for economic liberalization in small, low-income countries, for instance, construes culture in terms of 'receptivity to change':

Market-based adaptive economy requires a population willing to take action to maximize material benefits it may derive from changing conditions. This implies an individualistic ... welfare-maximizing approach, and mobility in pursuit of this objective. These attributes may clash with traditional values, which often place more stress on collective well-being and erect a number of obstacles to mobility. (Killick 1993)[3]

Culture 'may be at odds with the modernization of outlook that is necessary for the adaptive economy, and hence may dull responsiveness'; Killick compares Hinduism and Buddhism to Christianity and Judaism on the grounds that the former inculcate a 'passive fatalism that dulls responsiveness to economic challenges', while the latter 'emphasize responsibility for one's action and well-being' (Killick 1993: 53, 54; note that it is a short step from these 'observations' to more subtly orientalist notions of 'Asian Values' that likewise seek to distinguish the West from the Rest; see Corbridge 2002). The task of the planner/economist in developing contexts is thus to understand the specific obstacles and opportunities posed by culture to expanding the self-regulating market.

SOCIAL CAPITAL AND THE POST-WASHINGTON CONSENSUS

In spite of the power of these ideological mystifications, the Washington Consensus has ultimately been forced to modify the purely neoliberal position underlying conditional lending of the 1980s, to re-visit the role of the state and social institutions. For the contradictions between political freedom and economic inequality have come starkly into focus through the 'democratic deficits' economic liberalization has visited upon Third World countries, whose national economic policies have been so thoroughly determined outside the national polity. The contradiction has awakened critiques in the form of global justice movements, and even a thrust for reform from within the Washington Consensus, in the form of 'the new institutionalism' in economic theory. The World Bank has been at the centre of a new 'post-Washington Consensus' (Fine 2001), pushed as it has been to respond to critiques arising also from the brutal social costs of adjustment, the ambivalent record of economic performance in the aftermath of adjustment and the Asian example of state-led industrialization – and motivated, it must be said, by the search for a new rationale for its business of making loans.

Developments in economic theory have provided the necessary intellectual basis for the renewed interest in the role of the state and social institutions in economic development that underlies the post-Washington Consensus. In the 1990s a group of economists, most notably Nobel laureate Douglass North and then-World Bank Chief Economist Joseph Stiglitz, had been pursuing work on 'institutions' – construed as norms and values that guide practice in the context of real-life risks and knowledge imperfections – as significant 'players' in market economies. Economists were 'discovering', that is, that in the real world, markets are imperfect, fraught especially with 'information asymmetries' that result in 'non-optimising' behaviour, and that individuals attempt to manage such imbalances through non-market institutions. These then lay down 'path dependencies', social structures and customs, which influence the flow of information for generations to come: 'accidents of history matter', as the rather unspectacular saying introduced by Stiglitz goes (Stiglitz and Hoff 1999, cited in Fine 2001: 141). The rationale for 'bringing the state back in' lies in the quest to correct for information asymmetries so that actually existing markets will be able to function better. Writes Stiglitz (1998: 25, cited in Fine 2001: 139), 'we should not see the state and markets as substitutes ... the government should see itself as a complement to markets, undertaking those actions that make markets fulfil their functions better'. Thus there is a mandate for the World Bank to sponsor 'good governance', a key slogan of the post-Washington Consensus.

The 'new institutionalists' hold 'good governance' to mean 'government that is transparent and accountable, working with a clear legal framework, such as will provide the conditions for effective and efficient markets' (Harriss 2001: 78). The World Bank thus has a role to play in promoting the right kind of state, or, better yet (given ongoing anxieties about capture by powerful elites), in promoting scope for governing capacity outside the state and market, in the realm of civil society. This is where the idea of social capital – construed as local forms of association that express trust and norms of reciprocity – comes in. The idea, as it has been taken up by the World Bank, rests on another 'discovery', by Robert Putnam (1993) who is the term's most vociferous proponent, that dense associational networks within civil society correlate positively with indicators of political democracy and economic growth.[4] For a vibrant civil society – full of social networks and people participating in voluntary associations – helps those marginalized by mainstream economic processes forge links to the market and performs a vital check upon the activities of the state. If we take the World Bank (2002) as a reliable authority on the matter, the task of development has thus become one of identifying, using, creating an enabling environment for and investing in this particular form of capital.

Now, it is crucial to recognize how the new emphasis on 'getting the social relations right' (Woolcock 1999, cited in 2001: 76) sits very comfortably with neoliberalism, focused as it is on securing a proper environment for markets. The implicit assumption in the idea of social capital, moreover, that people can take care of themselves through their own social networks better than corrupt state programmes can, offers not only a convenient rationale, but also a populist appeal for cuts in public expenditure. Social capital, that is, can be expected to fill the vacuum left by the restructuring of the welfare state mandated by economic liberalization processes in countries around the world (see Harriss 2001; Rankin 2002). By focusing on the poor as agents of their own survival, moreover, the framework obscures the structural sources of inequality *produced* by such restructuring. The incursions of economic theory into the domain of the social represented in the idea of social capital (see Fine 2001), then, may appear to soften the political implications of neoliberalism, but they certainly do not constitute a fundamental rethinking of state–economy relations. And, while it is tempting to draw parallels to 1960s Keynesianism given all the talk these days of 'good governance' and 'bringing the state back in', a crucial distinction must be drawn. For the post-Washington Consensus depends on a notion of development in which socio-economic change is the outcome of the actions of *individuals* (whether or not they actually behave in an optimizing manner), while Keynesianism is concerned with 'broad structural features of the economy and the broad processes of development, and how the two interact with one another' (Fine 2001: 142).

The continuities with neoliberalism perhaps come most clearly into focus if we recognize how the idea of social capital serves to perpetuate the false separation of 'the economic' from 'the political', 'cultural' and 'social', in spite of its claims to encompass social factors in economic analysis. In the first instance, as Ben Fine (2001) has argued, the very name 'social capital' smacks of commodity fetishism; it perpetuates the myth that 'capital' itself has no 'social' dimension – thus obscuring the exploitative class relations that constitute capital socially. Second, it deftly avoids the contradiction between the claims to equality in political liberalism and the reality of inequality in capitalism, by suggesting that 'good governance' in fact transcends democracy. For social capital – as participation in voluntary organizations – holds out the prospect that it is possible to have effective democracy 'without the inconveniences of contestational politics and the conflicts of values and ideas which are a necessary part of democratic politics' (Harriss 2001: 8) – thus working to buffer the economy even further from electoral politics. And within the social capital framework, culture is still viewed as 'an exogenously given starting point laid down by history or accident or … an outcome of aggregation over optimizing individuals' (Fine 2001: 141–2). Market imperfection, that is to say, is held to *explain* non-market behaviour – institutions, customs, culture – as the rational response of optimizing individuals. Thus culture remains a technocratic, determinate concept, free of concerns with power and meaning. Given its uncritical acceptance of the false separation of economic from other spheres of social life, and the moral justification it provides for cuts in public expenditure, then, the idea of social capital can and must be seen as an extension of the Washington Consensus, rather than a radical rethinking of it.

POLANYI, PLANNING AND ANTHROPOLOGY

If the tenets of neoliberalism can be traced to Friedrich von Hayek (however much the current preoccupation with social capital may seek to disguise them), then its antidote – a counter-ideology providing moral justification for planning today – is perhaps best articulated by a contemporary of Hayek, equally forgotten in mainstream textbooks and equally significant for the fields of planning and development studies. Karl Polanyi conjoined comparative ethnographic research on economic organization among 'primitive and archaic societies' (Arensberg et al. 1957; Polanyi 1966) with a social history of market societies in Western Europe (Polanyi 1944) to offer a powerful illustration of the failures and contradictions of economic liberalism, as well as of the significance of socio-cultural factors in constituting the economy. Polanyi's collective works show how the self-regulating market, Hayek's locus of 'freedom', had become 'disembedded' from its social base by the mid-twentieth century. From its inception this utopic experiment produced not liberty, but 'counter-movements' for social protection.

The argument, elaborated in *The Great Transformation*, can perhaps best be captured with recourse to Figure 1.1.

MARKETS and PLANNING
KARL POLANYI on Markets [1944]

[a] The [dis]embedded economy:

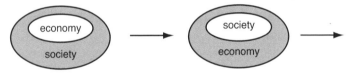

[b] The double movement:

[c] PLANNING: rescue 'freedom' from pure market rationality, reintegrate it with social considerations and democratic political processes!

Figure 1.1   Karl Polanyi on markets and planning (1944)

Throughout most of human history, the economy, defined broadly as livelihood, or the economic process of provisioning, has been embedded in social relations. Under these circumstances, social ties limit the destructive effects of individual self-interest. It was only with experiments instituting self-regulating markets in England (beginning with the enclosure movement in the sixteenth century) that individual gain could become the dominant organizing principle in the economy. Here, the economy could become autonomous from society (and politics) and operate according to its own law of supply and demand; society thus became *subordinate to*, in fact *embedded within*, the economy; or, in Polanyi's terms, the economy became 'disembedded from' society.[5] Polanyi thus demonstrated that this historical transition from an embedded to a disembedded economy (or from the integration to the separation of 'economy' and 'politics') did not reflect a natural, evolutionary process inherent to the logic of markets, as neoclassical economists of his day (prodded by economic philosophers like Hayek) would argue; the self-regulating market mechanism was rather *produced* by concrete state interventions and political practices. As he starkly put it, 'Laissez-faire was planned ...' (1944: 141).

For Polanyi, moreover, the condition of the disembedded economy posed a poignant ethico-political problem that reveals the contradictions – or the 'double movement' – of industrial capitalism. As the self-regulating market widens its influence geographically and deepens its autonomy from social relations, it also tears apart the social fabric and cultural bonds by which people once organized their way of life. 'To allow the market mechanisms to be sole director of the fate of human beings and their natural environment', Polanyi prophetically wrote, 'would result in the demolition of society' (1944: 73). In so disrupting social life, the self-regulating market would spark 'counter-movements' expressing popular demands for 'social protection'. Social costs generated by the expansion of the self-regulating market, that is, have historically provoked spontaneous, grassroots reactions – counter-movements – demanding social protection against the market's devastating effects. 'Laissez-faire was planned', Polanyi continued: 'planning was not' (1944: 141). Consolidated on a global scale by the turn of the century, the 'myth' of the self-regulating market, as he called it, thus generated the conditions for its own demise and, most catastrophically for Polanyi, for its resolution in fascism. The question for the optimist in Polanyi, and for us now in the current global economic conjuncture is: what kind of new economy–society configurations could emerge from this tension between economic liberalism and social protections today?

Polanyi's work has itself historically had two different kinds of implications, both of which bear significantly on the concern here with the cultural politics of markets. On the one hand, Polanyi's arguments have provided a firm normative foundation for the practice of planning in the metropolitan core as much as in the 'developing' periphery. The concepts of the double movement, the disembedded economy and social protection offer a compelling antidote to Hayek's assault on planning and his celebration of markets as a source of freedom. Viewed as a social construction unique to a specific historical and political conjuncture, self-regulating markets can be seen to be every bit as much penetrated by power as planning. The 'freedoms' it generates are thus illusory: the '[l]iberal economy gave a false direction to our ideals', wrote Polanyi, by degenerating 'the idea of freedom ... into a mere advocacy of free enterprise' (1944: 257).

Polanyi thus regarded it the burden of *planning* to rescue the idea of freedom from market rationality – and give it instead a social base and political means. Uncompromising in his commitment to an ethical code, he advocated a role for planning in guaranteeing freedom in what he called a 'moral', rather than 'institutional' sense: 'Freedom not as an appurtenance of privilege, tainted at the source, but as a prescriptive right extending far beyond the narrow confines of the political sphere into the intimate organization of society itself' (1944: 256). Although Polanyi had in mind planning functions at the scale of the central state, his ideas are equally relevant for other scales of state planning and indeed the field of city and regional planning emerged in North America as a discipline committed to tempering market rationality with social rationality and to embedding social science analysis within an explicit ethical code (e.g. Friedmann 1987). Too-frequent claims for 'comprehensive rationality' notwithstanding, university planning departments (which train not only urban planners for North American contexts, but also development planners with ambitions to work in the Third World) have a strong tradition, at least since the 1960s, of approaching questions of local economic development and urban design as *tools* for promoting the explicit *end* of social justice.[6]

Of course this progressive legacy in planning is currently threatened by the resurgence of a specifically Hayekian brand of liberalism, which purges a normative dimension from economics so that justice gets defined as whatever is delivered by the market. In a related development, many planning practitioners and scholars have themselves recently come under the spell of 'social capital' and 'civil society', enamoured with the prospect that citizen 'participation' could at once give new voice to the disadvantaged and alleviate allegations that left-leaning 'advocacy' and 'equity' planners are guilty of an oppressive sort of vanguardism (Douglass and Friedmann 1998). Their embrace of these now-mainstream concepts in the context of the contemporary economic orthodoxy suggests a surprising lack of awareness of how the idea of social capital could serve neoliberal objectives. Polanyi's poignant appeals for planning as a state function (not merely spontaneous citizens' activity), offers a far more compelling strategy for forging a progressive politics and asserting an oppositional role for planning and development vis-à-vis neoliberalism – and, I might add, moving development studies beyond the well-worn critiques of development as a 'governmental technology' of neoliberal rationality to claiming a normative agenda (Escobar 1995; Rankin 2001a).[7] Polanyi's ethical grounds for rejecting the 'market myth', that is, can help planning theory counter neoliberalism with its own theory of social justice – by arguing explicitly for embedding market rationality within an overriding concern for the role of the state (at local as much as central scale) in providing social protections.

The second implication of Polanyi's work relates to the imperative he instilled in a generation of anthropologists to describe the differences between 'tribal' economies and industrial capitalism. Much of Polanyi's opus is devoted to documenting alternative economic arrangements in non-capitalist contexts, and specifically the myriad ways in which the economy has been embedded in social institutions (Arensberg et al. 1957; Polanyi 1966; see also Dalton 1965, 1990; Wilk 1996). Polanyi searched the anthropological and historical record for economy–society configurations in which economic activity exercised a social function. These he catalogued as reciprocity (obligatory gift-giving among kin and friends), redistribution (obligatory payments to a central authority which provides community services) and householding (subsistence production). Within each of these alternative forms of economy, he claimed, individuals are motivated foremost by the requirements of social status, which foster responsibility to the collective and thus exercise a check on the destructive effects of individual self-interest.

These arguments spawned the 'Substantivist' school of economic anthropology and challenged the prevailing formalism in anthropology as much as economics itself, which confined its understanding of 'economic activity' to the 'economizing' of individuals negotiating scarce resources. Polanyi argued instead that while 'material provisioning' was universally practised in all economies, 'formal micro-economic theory designed to explain processes of economizing in market systems explained nothing about material provisioning in the Trobriands, Dahomey, or Inca Peru'

(Dalton 1990: 165). In these non-market contexts, an entirely different set of analytical concepts was required to explain the material process of making a living – or, as he calls it, the 'substantive' dimensions of the economy.[8] Here institutions governing livelihood have not been limited to markets (the domain of economic rationality), but have encompassed kinship relations, religious institutions and other socially embedded logics for organizing the economy. Polanyi's theory of embeddedness thus posed a challenge to recognize – and reject – the role of economics in rendering neoliberal ideology as natural law (Dalton 1965; Wilk 1996). In his formulation, the task of the researcher was to chart these varying forms of economic organization and the way they are embedded in social institutions. He hoped that such cross-cultural exploration could inspire a fresh imagining of alternative futures to the self-regulating market.

Notwithstanding this explicit mandate to engage ethnography for political ends, the Substantivist school (whose chief proponent was Polanyi's student, George Dalton) construed its mission in a rather narrow empirical sense, in terms of documenting livelihood processes and understanding their underlying principles. The resulting research produced a taxonomy of forms of exchange and distribution not conforming to neoclassical principles of economic rationality. Foremost among these has been a long-standing fascination with gifting – the phenomenon of giving wealth away rather than accumulating it, as formal economic theory would expect. Thus anthropologists have debated the cultural specificities surrounding the valuation of objects exchanged as gifts (Weiner 1992), the mechanisms by which the gift inspires a counter-gift (Mauss 1925), and the notions of identity informing gifting relationships (Munn 1986; Strathern 1988; see also Graeber 2001 for a refreshing discussion of this literature). The seminal work in this tradition was Mauss's *Essai sur le don*, published in 1925 (and translated into English in 1965) well before the substantivist–formalist debate even got under way. For Mauss the key to understanding 'the spirit of the gift' lay in the webs of sociality within which gifting is embedded and its fundamental distinction from the alienated social universe of capitalist market exchange. Mauss, like Polanyi, assembled his comparative data with an eye to the revolutionary potential in alternative logics of exchange. Although much of the ethnographic work in the Maussian tradition, like substantivist anthropology more generally, has confined itself to empirical description, several anthropologists have recently called for a revitalization of the normative thrust in Mauss's work to revive the spirit of the gift (Godbout 1998; Graeber 2001). The arguments here similarly present a case for reviving the connections first drawn by Polanyi between documenting the social embeddedness of markets and defending a role for planning in market societies.

GEOGRAPHIES OF ECONOMIES

The search for an antidote to neoliberal influences in planning and development must also certainly visit the important contributions of geographers who, through their emphasis on spatial determinants of economic growth, had been examining the relationship between economic, political and social spheres long before economists 'discovered' path dependency (e.g. Britton 1988; Isard 1956). Geography has produced an extensive literature re-interpreting the boundaries of the 'economic' in far more imaginative and diverse ways than the new institutional economics – rejecting both the positivist and empiricist legacy in economics and its focus on market principles (e.g. Lee and Wills 1997). This work has explored how socio-spatial factors underpin economic competitiveness (Amin and Thrift 1997), how market institutions are embedded in regulatory structures and networks of social relations at various spatial scales (Tickell and Peck 1995) and (at the more creative end of the spectrum) how economic discourse constitutes capitalist globalization as dominant and totalizing (Gibson-Graham 1996) or how metaphor shapes economic space (Barnes 1996). Economic geographers have, for example, chronicled the legacy of an 'artisanal culture' in shaping the economic success of Northern Italy, a 'social model of innovation' in Germany and the 'culture of cooperation' which distinguishes firms in California's Silicon Valley (see Gertler 1995; Piore and Sabel 1984; Saxenian 1994). Meanwhile, efforts to chronicle non-capitalist activities as a foundation for posing alternatives to market-led planning have most recently been spearheaded by J.K. Gibson-Graham's *The End of Capitalism (As We Knew It): A Feminist Critique of Political Economy* (1996) and their subsequent more action-oriented research on models of development planning that construct socially embedded economies (e.g. Gibson and Cameron 2001). Cumulatively, this work has reassessed 'what social and spatial portions of life count as economic, what portions (if any) are therefore non-economic, and how these designated spheres of the economic and non-economic interrelate' (Crang 1997: 2).

Much of the recent rethinking in geography about economy–society relations goes beyond a mere 'colonizing of the social by the economic' (Fine 2001) because it has been informed – whether self-consciously or not – by the earlier work of feminist geographers challenging conventional notions of work and the capacity of macroeconomic statistics to capture non-market modes of economic activity (see McDowell 2000 for a recent review of this literature). It also reflects a more general 'cultural turn' across the social sciences (which itself has been duly inspired by feminist scholarship): a shared interest in cultural practices of identity formation and meaning signification (Crang 1997). Strains of the old functionalist–substantivist debate in anthropology can be witnessed today in the way economic geographers have responded to their cultural turn. Some have attempted to apply existing notions of economic behaviour and analysis to cultural life, by exploring, for example, the ways in which culture is 'materialized in the economic' through the production, exchange and consumption of material goods (Crang 1997: 4; Harvey 1989; Lash and Urry 1994; Painter 1997; Willis 1991). Others have argued instead, in Polanyian substantivist fashion, that economic processes are embedded in and represented through cultural media – symbols, signs, discourses, practices and institutions (Barnes 1992; Gertler 1997; McDowell 1997). Both approaches can be taken to extreme policy and political positions, to suggest on the one hand that capitalism increasingly colonizes cultural life, or on the other hand that economic competitiveness can be explained by the presence or absence of a particular 'culture' – 'manufacturing culture', 'business culture', 'traditional Japanese culture'.

Although these discussions in geography have focused relatively little on 'peripheral' contexts beyond the 'core' of the capitalist world system, they have important implications for the epistemological frameworks within which 'development' is planned and implemented. For example, the recent interest in the socio-spatial construction of markets challenges a key assumption underlying the now dominant market-led approaches to development, namely that market access *in itself* (fostered, if necessary, by ample stocks of social capital) creates opportunity for the poor and disenfranchised. Within the field of gender and development in particular it challenges the expectation that economic opportunity – say, income or access to credit – can help women overcome their subordinate social position and ultimately transform hierarchical social relations (e.g. Dràze and Sen 1995). A social constructivist view of the economy points instead to the significance of cultural ideologies (that may persist or even intensify in the wake of economic change) in configuring structures of inequality, as well as the significance of cultural and spatial practices for both reproducing and resisting those structures. It also points, like Polanyian strains of anthropology and political theory, to a firm justification for state intervention in markets, in the name of social justice.

Both literatures – the earlier economic anthropology inspired by Polanyi and the more recent 'cultural turn' in economic geography – have thus been associated with practical applications, in justifying a role for planning in market societies and in considering the cultural determinants of regional economic competitiveness. These literatures also raise the possibility that non-capitalist economic activities in 'peripheral' contexts as much as in the 'core' can offer critical perspectives on capitalist economic arrangements and inspire the imagination of alternative futures. They thus pose a potent challenge to the reigning neoliberal orthodoxy, and in particular to Hayekian and/or information-theoretic arguments about efficiency of naturally occurring self-regulating markets; the separation of 'economic' from 'political', 'social' and 'cultural' spheres; the tyranny of planning; and the scope for social capital accumulating in civil society to foster economic growth and good governance.

At the same time, the anthropological and geographical literatures in this tradition, and especially their attendant applications in planning and development, have too often themselves suffered from problematic assumptions about the culture–economy nexus. The problem is three-fold. First, the search for cultural bases of economic competitiveness as much as for non-capitalist alternatives encourages a best-practice approach: we can best craft competitive and humane economies, the argument goes, by drawing on cultural practices informing economic alternatives at the periphery of the world capitalist system – or in its most economically successful regions. The tendency among scholars and policy planners to select 'best practices' for replication reifies culture as an explanatory variable in its own right (see also Gertler 1997 on this point).[9] Second, in the search for alternatives to capitalism, scholars too easily overlook the role of culture in producing inequality within 'non-capitalist' as much as capitalist contexts (see also Nagar et al. 2002). The haste to valorize 'other' forms of economic organization stems from a progressive impulse, but in practice often neglects to distinguish between progressive and regressive forms of gifting, reciprocity, householding and redistribution. Socially embedded economies, that is, are not necessarily socially progressive. In the absence of an evaluative capacity, nostalgic idealizations of gifting and other non-monetized modes of exchange can end up exacerbating already existing lines of hierarchy, coercion and exclusion. The practice is particularly dangerous in the context of the present neoliberal orthodoxy, which these days promotes 'social capital' and 'civil society' among the poor as resources for economic growth in the absence of a strong state welfare system. Third and finally, when scholars and practitioners debate the cultural foundations of regional competitiveness, they too often take economic value itself as given.

THE ECONOMICS OF PRACTICE

Each of the above-mentioned assumptions is rejected here. As elaborated at length in Chapter 2, culture is treated not as a given set of gender, ethnic, religious and other social relations that can either retard or facilitate economic growth, but as systems of meaning and signification that are produced, experienced and negotiated by human intention and action. As geographer Don Mitchell (2000: xvi) puts it:

> … no decent cultural analysis (geographic or otherwise) can draw on culture itself as a source of explanation; rather culture is always something to be explained as it is socially produced through myriad struggles over and in spaces, scales, and landscapes … 'culture' is always and everywhere inextricably related to social, political, and economic forces and practices.

Within anthropology, the tradition of 'practice theory' has been particularly committed to studying processes of cultural production, and is thus engaged here to explore the role of human agency in producing, maintaining and challenging the cultural norms and values within which economic practice occurs. I thus follow anthropologists Jean and John Comaroff (1991: 21) in viewing culture as:

> … the semantic ground on which human beings seek to construct and represent themselves and others – and hence society and history … . It has form as well as content; is born in action as well as thought; is a product of human creativity as well as mimesis; and, above all, is empowered.

Chapter 2 is devoted entirely to developing an approach to engaging this understanding of culture to study on-the-ground outcomes of macroeconomic processes and policies. The remainder of this chapter will consider how an ethnographic analysis of the interrelationships between economic strategies, socio-spatial practices and symbols of status can contribute to ongoing debates about the mutual embeddedness of economy and culture, so defined, and to a normative framework for planning and development.

The emphasis here on cultural production requires at the outset an understanding of economic value as culturally given, rather than as an inherent property of commodities or markets, as microeconomic theory would have it.[10] Arjun Appadurai has argued that objects circulate in different 'regimes of value', through which 'desire and demand, reciprocal sacrifice and power interact to create economic value in specific social situations' (1986: 4). By examining the *contexts* of exchange it is possible to think of capital not merely in the narrow (material) sense often reserved for money, machinery and other physical assets, but as any form of wealth intended for exchange or investment. Through a much-cited analysis of 'symbolic capital', for instance, Pierre Bourdieu extends economic analysis beyond material processes to encompass any form of symbolic value that may be in demand within specific social situations.

Bourdieu's 'economics of practice' thus accounts for the social and cultural dimensions of profit and exchange:

... the theory of strictly economic practice is simply a particular case of a general theory of the economics of practice. The only way to escape from the ethnocentric naiveties of economism, without falling into populist exaltation of the generous naivety of earlier forms of society, is to carry out in full what economism does only partially, and to extend economic calculation to all the goods, material and symbolic, without distinction, that present themselves as rare and worthy of being sought after in a particular social formation – which may be 'fair words' or smiles, handshakes or shrugs, compliments or attention, challenges or insults, honour or honours, powers or pleasures, gossip or scientific information, distinction or distinctions ... (Bourdieu 1977: 177–8)

Within an economics of practice, then, 'symbolic capital' refers to the 'sum of cultural recognition ... which an individual ... could acquire through skillful manipulation of the system of social symbols' (Honneth 1995: 187). Encompassed within Bourdieu's understanding of symbolic capital are the kinds of cultural recognition acquired through cultural knowledge ('cultural capital') and through social relations ('social capital'). Where honour is a central form of capital (in Sankhu as much as in most culturally South Asian societies), then much of social practice must be interpreted in terms of producing and exchanging, hoarding or squandering honour. Thus the 'markets' to which the title of this book and chapter refer encompass transactions not only in land, money, labour and commodities, but also in honour and other forms of 'social investment'. The focus is not so much on the mechanics of supply, demand and the flow of information – although these are also worthy and important areas of ethnographic investigation (see Harriss-White 1996) – but on the cultural meanings that surround markets as a form of social production, on the ways in which social institutions and economies of practice interact.[11]

The evaluative capacity in Bourdieu's approach lies in its commitment to tracking the ways in which power infuses these processes of 'social investment' – investments that generate non-material forms of wealth – every bit as much as the capitalist self-regulating market. In Bourdieu's

Marxist-leaning approach to economic embeddedness, that is, non-capitalist forms of exchange appear not as benign and harmonious alternatives to capitalism, but as themselves inherently conflictual and contradictory. Expanding an understanding of capital to encompass symbolic forms circulating within an 'economics of practice' thus facilitates an analysis of the exploitative dimensions of culture and social practice. It clarifies the *ideological* dimensions of economic practice (its role in maintaining social hierarchies) and the modes of domination inherent in some forms of reciprocity, redistribution and householding.

First, a theory of the economics of practice highlights the role not only of individual self-interest, but also of *class* interest in the logic (or ideology) of reciprocity. Among equals, gifting and acts of generosity provide an economic guarantee because they oblige a return. Among those of unequal status, however, gifting and other modes of reciprocity generate affective bonds that obfuscate – and cement – social hierarchy. In Nepal, the affection and kindness high-caste patrons may lavish on their low-caste inferiors, for instance, serve as a palliative for the abuses of caste distinctions.[12] Writes Bourdieu of gifting practices among the Kabyle of Algeria:

> Goods are for giving. The rich man is 'rich so as to be able to give to the poor,' say the Kabyles. This is an exemplary disclaimer: because giving is also a way of possessing (a gift which is not matched by a counter-gift creates a lasting bond, restricting the debtor's freedom and forcing him to adopt a peaceful, cooperative attitude); because in the absence of any juridical guarantee, or any coercive force, one of the few ways of 'holding' someone is to *keep up* a lasting asymmetrical relationship such as indebtedness, and because the only recognized, legitimate form of possession is that achieved by dispossessing oneself – i.e., obligation, gratitude, prestige, or personal loyalty. Wealth, the ultimate basis of power, can exert power, and exert it durably, only in the form of symbolic capital ... (1977: 195)

Bourdieu thus urges us to recognize a second ideological function of symbolic capital: gestures of giving and kindness through which honour is accrued can in fact function as a form of domination, a 'symbolic violence' with the pernicious effect of binding the oppressed to their oppressors through feelings of trust and obligation:

> ... the best way in which the master can serve his own interests is to work away, day in, day out, with constant care and attention, weaving the ethical and affective, as well as economic, bonds which durably tie his *khammes* [bonded labourer – or low-caste client in the Nepal context] ... to him ... . In a society in which overt violence ... meets with collective reprobation ... symbolic violence, the gentle, invisible form of violence, which is never recognized as such, and is not so much undergone as chosen, the violence of credit, confidence, obligation,

personal loyalty, hospitality, gratitude, piety – in short, all the virtues honoured by the code of honour – cannot fail to be seen as the *most economical mode of domination*. (1977: 190, 192; emphasis added)[13]

Third, to the extent that such forms of symbolic capital generate common values, a shared moral community, we may begin to question how such values operate as forms of power within culture. For Bourdieu, morality falls within the realm of 'doxa' – 'that which is accepted as a natural and self-evident part of the social order and is not open to questioning or contestation' (Agarwal 1994: 58). When social hierarchy assumes a moral force in society, ideological constructions and perceptions of the subordinate can converge, as revealed in the domain of practice Bourdieu calls 'habitus' (see Chapter 2 for further discussion of these terms). Thus when I use the expression '*cultural politics* of markets', I am signalling my intention to explore markets in material and symbolic goods as a locus for inequality maintained not just through uneven distribution but also through cultural ideologies that make the established order appear natural and immutable. A focus on the politics of culture suggests that social change requires material redistribution, to be sure, but also the awakening of 'political consciousness', through which subordinate groups recognize the established order as an arbitrary human construction and fashion alternative moralities. It is in the domain of facilitating such political consciousness that we can begin to detect some clear, if controversial, imperatives for the content and process of planning – to be explored in the final chapter of this book.

BOURDIEU AND THE POLITICS OF DEVELOPMENT

Bourdieu's perspectives on cultural economies, and especially symbolic capital, have recently come under considerable criticism for adhering to the same formalist principles that Polanyi once rejected as narrowly ethnocentric (e.g. Crang 1997; Graeber 2001; Ortner 1984; Sayer 1999). David Graeber (2001: 28) notes, for example, that in Bourdieu's understanding, 'economy', although encompassing symbolic forms of capital, is nonetheless reduced to:

... a matter of self-interested calculation, making rational decisions about the allocation of scarce resources with the aim of getting as much as possible for oneself. In real, 'objective' terms, [Bourdieu] argues, economizing – or something very much like it – is always going on. It's just that where there is no market, everyone goes to enormous lengths to disguise this fact. This endless labor of camouflage is such a burden ... that it tends to dissolve away immediately, as soon as a market economy is introduced, whereon the hidden reality of calculated self-interest is openly revealed.

Jacques Godbout argues similarly that theories such as Bourdieu's, in trying to explain the gift, 'boil it down to the point where it disappears, and give the impression that it is a mirage that never had any life other than in the realm of ideology' (1998: 103).

By viewing the participation of subordinate groups in systems of gifting that exercise 'symbolic violence' as a function of their 'habitus', moreover, some have argued that Bourdieu's analysis risks attributing 'false consciousness' to them, along with all the patronizing assumptions of ignorance of oppression associated with this concept (see Bourdieu and Eagleton 1992). Beyond the injuries of recognition to which feminists have long objected in such representations, the political implications here are remarkably bleak. If, in the most stark interpretation of Bourdieu, the oppressed are unable to recognize their own oppression, resistance to power could never arise from the experience of those in subordinate social locations, but must rather be 'sparked' by outside intervention (like the radical anthropologist asking probing questions). More fundamentally still, Bourdieu can leave one with a rather cynical view of humanity, one that precludes compassion, solidarity, disinterestedness or even subversion of power as motivations for participating in reciprocal exchanges, or in an economy more generally. As Graeber writes, Bourdieu makes 'power and domination so fundamental to the very nature of social reality that it [becomes] impossible to imagine a world without [them]' (2001: 30; see also Gibson-Graham 1996).

I certainly concur with the assertion implicit in these critiques (and made explicit by Crang 1997: 10) that 'there are some aspects of cultural practice that economic metaphors cannot grasp …'. To be fair, however, as his later publications (1990, 1993) have since clarified, Bourdieu did not argue simply that all cultural practice could be reduced to economizing in the neoliberal sense, but rather that cultural practice always has its own forms of economic rationality (of which there may be more than one). It is thus the anthropologist's task to analyse and understand these multiple, sometimes conflicting, logics. The point to emphasize here is that in studying the economic rationality of culture, Bourdieu's focus is not on the optimizing ambitions of *individuals*, but on the social structures that facilitate and constrain action. While there certainly may be other rationalities at work, it strikes me as a worthy *political* endeavour to study the role of symbolic capital in creating and reproducing those structures, not least because its appearance as honour, gifting, reciprocity and so on may disguise its role in social reproduction.

It must also be noted that Bourdieu's perspective on consciousness in relation to the economics of practice stems not only from ethnographic research in Algeria, but also from his personal experience growing up in a rural French peasant and working-class community. Bourdieu speaks poignantly (and uncharacteristically lucidly) about the disjunctures between those origins and his adult 'home' in metropolitan French academia, where resistance transpires through the medium of theory:

Even in Marxism, I think the capacity for resistance, as a capacity of consciousness, was overestimated. I fear that what I have to say is shocking for the self-confidence of intellectuals, especially for the more generous, left-wing intellectuals. But I think it is better to know the truth; and the fact is that when we see with our own eyes people living in poor conditions – such as existed when I was a young scholar, among the local proletariat, the workers in factories – it is clear that they are prepared to accept much more than we would have believed. That was a very strong experience for me: they put up with a great deal, and this is what I mean by doxa – that there are many things people accept without knowing … . Now that is a fact – in my view it is an appalling fact – one that intellectuals don't like to accept, but which they must accept. It doesn't mean that the dominated individuals tolerate everything; but they assent to much more than we believe and much more than they know. (Bourdieu and Eagleton 1992: 114)

I find these observations compelling, not least because, as illustrated in Chapters 5 and 6, they corroborate my findings from ethnographic research among women and low castes in Sankhu, Nepal. In *Masculine Domination* (2001), Bourdieu clarifies that notions of 'consciousness' are inadequate to understand the ways in which domination works at the level of 'cognitive structures' or 'frames of perception' (and is written on the body in the form of gestures and comportments that express submission or domination). Thus a liberatory awakening of consciousness may be a necessary condition to disrupt domination, but not always a sufficient one:

Although it is true that … recognition of domination always presupposes an act of knowledge, this does not imply that one is entitled to describe it in the language of consciousness, in an intellectualist and scholastic fallacy which, as in Marx (and above all, those who, from Lukács onwards, have spoken of 'false consciousness'), leads one to expect the liberation of women to come through the immediate effect of the 'rising of consciousness', forgetting – for lack of a dispositional theory of practices – the opacity and inertia that stem from the embedding of social structures in bodies. (2001: 40)

There are important implications here for a mode of planning that wishes to mobilize 'local knowledge' and 'participation' – but which must also recognize a role for social scientific research in helping to transform the 'instruments of knowledge' into 'objects of knowledge' (as will be elaborated further in Chapter 7).

There are other reasons to resurrect Bourdieu's economics of practice here, having to do with the extent to which mainstream notions of 'social capital' have captured the imagination of development planners today. As we have seen, in the past decade a (post-Washington-) Consensus has emerged among scholars and practitioners of development that 'social capital' – construed differently from Bourdieu's interpretation as local forms of association expressing trust and reciprocity – can contribute significantly to the alleviation of poverty and the promotion of good governance worldwide. A World Bank web page, now an international clearinghouse for the latest research and theories on the promises of social capital, announces at the outset that 'social capital is critical for poverty alleviation and sustainable human and economic development' (accessed 8/24/02: URL: http://www.worldbank.org/poverty/scapital/). Such claims rest largely on the idea promoted by Robert Putnam that dense associational networks within civil society build a strong foundation for political participation and help link the poor to the mainstream economy. Here, the notion of 'social capital' is developed in the tradition of political liberalism and methodological individualism, as a benign cultural property that enhances efficiency by facilitating cooperation. As John Harriss (2001) and Ben Fine (2001) note, Putnam's interpretations can be traced to the ideas of James Coleman, whose *Foundations of Social Theory* (1990) argues in formalist fashion that the reasoning of neo-classical economics, specifically its theory of rational choice, can be applied to social spheres. The emphasis in the World Bank version of social capital is thus on the collective good that can arise from individual membership in associations. Like neoliberalism itself, this theoretical orientation conflates development with economic growth and embraces the rational, utility-maximizing individual as the locus of progressive change.

We have seen that Bourdieu offers a radically different understanding of associational life. His analysis focuses squarely at the level of social structure (as opposed to individual preferences and behaviours).[14] Individuals do not generate social capital and are not the primary unit of analysis. Rather, social capital (linked as it is to symbolic capital), inheres in the social structure and must be conferred value by a society consenting to its cultural logic. It is contextual and socially constructed, and cannot be seen to function as an exogenous, independent variable of economic growth. One does not acquire or expend social capital on the basis of individual choice; rather, one accrues obligation and opportunity to participate in social networks by virtue of one's social position. Within this logic, moreover, the benefits and costs of participation are distributed unequally: some benefit at the expense of others. Social capital thus exists in a field of power and enters significantly into formation and reproduction of class. The task for development planners from this point of view is to foster forms of associational life specifically among the oppressed and specifically with the capacity to transform individual recognition of oppression into more collective, overt forms of consciousness and resistance (Agarwal 1994). Bourdieu's interpretation of associational life also sounds a note of caution against the uncritical celebration of social capital evident in mainstream development circles. For, when development programmes nourish local forms of association, they risk exacerbating already existing lines of hierarchy, coercion and exclusion.

For all his cautionary and pragmatic insights for planning practice, Bourdieu's views on social capital have gone largely unacknowledged at the centres of development planning, and it is for this reason that I advocate its due consideration in the evaluation of local cultural economies.[15] It is no wonder that liberal interpretations have found wide favour, for they enable the architects of neoliberal economic policy to cast the recent reconfiguration of state–society relations in progressive terms – local capacity-building, local self-reliance, net social benefits from reduced transaction costs and increased returns to human capital. Social capital, that is, can be expected to fill the vacuum left by the restructuring of the welfare state mandated by economic liberalization processes in countries around the world. It transmutes discourses of grassroots self-reliance into policies rooted in an expectation that the most disadvantaged can pull themselves up by their own bootstraps. Needless to say, representations of social capital as implicated in maintaining dominant social and political ideologies in different cultural contexts, as Bourdieu argues, could readily upset the governmental function of the term noted here.[16] And mainstream development discourse has too great a political investment in diverting attention from the ways in which political economy structures associational life, to admit into its analytical frame such Marxian perspectives on social capital.[17]

Bourdieu's Marxian perspective thus clarifies the potentially coercive and exploitative dimensions of social capital (as one among many goods in an 'economics of practice'), and its role in maintaining social hierarchies. It extends the Polanyian imperative to understand the social constitution of economies and to commit such analysis toward the political task of buffering markets with social protections (in antithesis to the Hayekian 'self-regulating' version of markets peddled so widely today). But it does so without succumbing to naïve optimism toward non-western societies as the locus for alternative economic arrangements free from the inequalities and injustices of neoliberalism. In the ethnographic analysis of a Nepalese merchant community that follows (in Chapters 3–6), I demonstrate the ways in which common moral frameworks generated by social norms and networks can be implicated in cultural ideologies that justify and perpetuate inequality. The evidence from the Nepal context suggests that promoting social capital through networks and norms of reciprocity may in fact leave people – even the oppressed – free to carry on oppressive relations. With the notions of 'symbolic capital', 'economics of practice', 'cultural economy', 'social investment', we have now set the stage for a detailed analysis of the social embeddedness of markets in Newar society, and of how socially embedded markets articulate with state macroeconomic policies. The next chapter offers further theoretical introduction to the approach I take specifically in relation to linking local cultural economic processes to wider political-economic currents. It considers contributions to the study of globalization from contemporary literatures in the 'anthropology of practice' and the political economy of place-making.

2 ANTHROPOLOGIES AND GEOGRAPHIES OF GLOBALIZATION

Local 'economics of practice' occur in particular places, but they reflect political-economic and cultural processes that extend beyond place, as much as those rooted within it. The concern here with neoliberalism and market-led approaches to development requires a focus on economic, political and cultural processes transpiring at regional and global scales, as capitalist processes of accumulation become increasingly integrated across geographically dispersed locations. The analytical focus of this chapter is, in a word, globalization, although the chapter has equal relevance for any historical inquiry of place-making that examines the articulation of local with macro scales of influence. We return here to the theme of cross-disciplinary travel noted in the introduction, for globalization is one of the few issues of our times that challenges the core identities of academic disciplines clear across the social, and indeed natural, sciences. Economists grapple with the growing contradictions between theories of economic 'liberalization' and mounting inequality and social unrest around the world; political scientists wonder whatever happened to the nation-state as a viable political actor in its own right; and anthropologists rush to abandon characteristic 'village studies' in favour of more trendy explorations of 'flows', 'border-crossings' and 'globalist projects'. The phenomenon of globalization, moreover, threatens to rupture established boundaries *between* academic disciplines, as well as render irrelevant old modes of inquiry *within* them.

The widespread unease that globalization provokes within academia can also be attributed to its prominence in public discourse. Located historically at the close of the Cold War and the dismantling of the Soviet Union, the idea of globalization has become, as Anna Tsing (2000) put it, 'the definitional characteristic of an era'; it is wielded in the media and advertising, in corporate management and policy circles, in social movements and campaigns for multiculturalism. Academics are called on to offer their expertise: Is globalization really anything new? Has it undermined the legitimacy of national governments? Will it destroy the planet? What is the best way to defend social justice against it? Yet in practice scholarship on globalization – at least outside the field of economics – has rarely played a significant role in directly shaping its course.

In this chapter I argue that anthropology and geography are two social science disciplines particularly well poised to grapple with these anxieties about globalization. While both fields have at times fallen prey to the allure of globalization, they have also produced some of its most trenchant critiques (e.g. Graeber 2001; D. Mitchell 2000). The critical capacity derives in large part from the fact that anthropology and geography stand out among the social sciences for avoiding the false separation of the 'economic' from the 'political', the 'social' and the 'cultural' that underpins the dominant (ultimately Hayekian) neoliberal version of the globalization story. Rather, anthropologists and geographers are more inclined to explore the mutual embeddedness of these spheres, the processes through which they are socially constructed and the scope for change. Both fields, as well, have been particularly open to disciplinary self-reflexivity in relation to changing global conditions. The openness stems in part from long internal histories of negotiation across the 'physical' and 'socio-cultural' divides that uniquely characterize both fields. It can also be attributed to solid traditions of critical self-reflection developed to cope with their mutual implication in histories of empire-building and colonization (e.g. Clifford 1988; Gregory 1994).

Given these similar trajectories, it is not surprising that anthropologists and geographers are increasingly turning to one another for tools to analyse the present conjuncture. The cross-fertilization can be witnessed in references to one another's publications in scholarly writing (e.g. Inda and Rosaldo 2002; Lawson 1995; K. Mitchell 2001; Tsing 2000), cross-disciplinary traffic at the major academic conferences, occasional publication by authors of one field in the major academic journals of the other (e.g. Escobar 2001), and a few attempts to institutionalize collaborations (e.g. Center for Place, Culture and Politics established by geographer Neil Smith at the City University of New York). Such practices notwithstanding, disciplinary insularity prevails at the most crucial junctures of social reproduction: in administration, hiring and promotion decisions, and norms guiding 'legitimate' research process, to name a few.

In light of these entrenched forms of institutional separation, this chapter offers a systematic accounting of the comparative advantages each field brings to studies of globalization – anthropology with its emphasis on the role of culture in anchoring (or resisting) globalizing processes within particular societies and geography with its more comparative emphasis on the politics of place and scale. It presents the strengths and deficiencies of both and seeks out complementarities, by noting how the strengths of each can respond to the deficiencies of the other. It argues that a constructive (and self-conscious) synthesis offers a more compelling framework for studying globalization and, indeed, resisting its deleterious effects, than can be found within narrowly defined disciplinary boundaries. As an exercise in distilling 'core essences' of each field as it relates to globalization studies, the argument here may strike some readers, especially those well-travelled across disciplinary divides, as overstating differences. The exercise is nonetheless important for specifying a rationale for extending cross-disciplinary fertilization beyond the domain of individual practice to the domain of institutional culture. To others, the chapter may appear to offer highly selective versions of anthropology and geography, born as it is out of my particular cross-disciplinary travel from undergraduate and graduate studies in an American anthropology department to a faculty appointment in a Canadian geography department (where I was hired to teach planning). Omitted in particular is the sub-field of 'applied anthropology', a post-Second World War development (aptly reviewed in Gardner and Lewis 1996), which has sought to link issues of indigenous rights and cultural difference to the practice and study of development, but which has also been sidelined in the dominant North American anthropology departments (rural sociology has been a more conventional institutional home for such endeavours). I could not possibly claim here to represent the totality of two disciplines so fraught with disagreement about what constitutes their core concerns. Rather, I have selected strains within each field that express its contribution to the study of globalization and that have the most to offer interdisciplinary engagement.

The chapter begins with a clarification of the political, cultural and economic dimensions of globalization. It then considers contributions to the study of globalization deriving from practice theories in anthropology on the one hand and the political economy of place and scale in geography on the other. In the Gramscian tradition of Raymond Williams and Pierre Bourdieu, anthropologists have argued that culture must be viewed not as a given set of relations and ideas structuring social life, but as something that is produced through human intention and action. The emphasis on agency offers several key analytical advantages to the study of local–global articulations which are duly explored here. In their attention to the fine-grained details of local agency, however, anthropological texts too often accord subordinate analytical status to the macro-regulatory contexts for human agency. Here insights from geography, which has pioneered in understanding place-making in relation to large-scale political-economic systems, prove useful. While it has had much to say about flows, spaces, states, even institutions, however, geography as a whole has devoted less attention to the everyday lives of the people producing on-the-ground cultural systems through which macro processes are always interpreted and shaped. The chapter concludes by arguing for a constructive synthesis geared toward understanding how 'local' cultural systems articulate with political-economic currents operating at wider spatial scales, as well as for a politically engaged role for globalization research.

GLOBALIZATION: ECONOMIC, POLITICAL, CULTURAL

Much of the anxiety surrounding the idea of globalization relates to the considerable ambiguity in the meanings and effects attributed to it. The economic dimension has received the widest airing, both within academia and beyond. There now exists widespread agreement that globalization entails 'a functional integration of internationally dispersed activities' that is qualitatively different from mere internationalization, involving 'the simple extension of economic activities across national boundaries' (Dicken 1998: 5). While the globalization 'boosters' represent global economic integration as a natural and benign outcome of market processes, geographers and anthropologists have been at the forefront of documenting how economic globalization is moored to particular places by political and cultural means and how it is mediated by the actions of individuals and institutions at different scales. As economic geographers have argued, the economic restructuring required within nation-states to accomplish economic globalization entails a political process – not 'deregulation' (as neoliberal discourse would have it) but *re*-regulation according to more strictly neoliberal principles (e.g. Amin and Thrift 1997). The emphasis here on market rules governing globalization offers a more critical stance. It has, for instance, paved the way for studies documenting an increasingly uneven distribution of goods and services where economic convergence has been most aggressively pursued (e.g. Christopherson 1993) and the erosion of local social investments as market relations become increasingly disembedded from social life in locations on the 'periphery' of the capitalist world system (e.g. Steedly 1993).

Focusing on the political, or regulatory, dimensions of globalization in this way highlights a fundamental difference between core and peripheral states. Among core, industrialized nations, the *agency* for economic restructuring lies primarily with the national state (powerfully lobbied though it may be by corporate interests). State capacity is evident in the considerable variation that persists in national regulatory systems, even amidst the expanding authority of the World Trade Organization (WTO). The participation of peripheral nations in economic globalization has typically required a more stark political restructuring, as the scale of regulatory authority transcends the national state to reside at higher spatial scales. Re-regulation has largely been coordinated through the regulatory apparatus of Structural Adjustment Programs (SAPs) and other debt regimes. These undoubtedly require a national political constituency to advocate and enact the currency devaluations, trade liberalization and austerity measures. Yet the real locus of decision-making lies with the IMF and World Bank, their creditors and dominant member states. The more distant scale of regulation in the periphery means that the 'democratic deficits' of economic globalization (McMichael 1995; Mittleman 1996) are felt here with particular force. Thus when peripheral states enact global regulatory regimes the lines of accountability run not to the citizens they govern, but to the transnational market forces intended to be 'liberated'; meanwhile, the architects of economic globalization are non-elected officials with no mandate for political accountability. In Nepal, for example, the economic policies of the United Marxist-Leninist (UML) government elected to power in 1995 clearly reveal how global regulatory regimes have undermined national electoral processes: during its brief nine-month tenure, the UML government proposed to institute a Value Added Tax, privatize public enterprises, liberalize trade to encourage foreign investment and promote exports, reform the finance sector, and cut subsidies. Such stark contradiction between the political ideology of a governing party and the neoliberal economic policies it promulgates suggests a 'recolonization' of the periphery as global forms of regulation replace national development projects (McMichael and Myhre 1991).

Regulatory structures thus create an enabling political environment for global economic integration. But in order to understand how ordinary people around the world come to adopt the production and consumption practices necessary to sustain economic globalization, a cultural analysis is required. How, for example, do Malay gender ideologies accommodate and resist a shift of women's productive labour from subsistence family farms to the shop floor of transnational garment corporations (Ong 1987)? How do microfinance programmes in Nepal cultivate the subjectivity of 'rational economic woman' to ensure high repayment rates (Rankin 2001a)? How could Canadian immigration policies favouring wealthy East Asian entrepreneurs ultimately generate the cultural reworkings in Vancouver, British Columbia necessary to support cuts in social services (K. Mitchell 2001)? Here again the discursive regime of globalization as economic liberalization belies important areas of complexity. In the cultural domain, on-the-ground, local experiences and interpretations play a crucial role in sustaining – or challenging – large-scale political economic processes. It follows that globalization can only be accomplished within particular political and cultural parameters – and that it is incumbent on academic scholarship to elucidate the interconnections between these economic, political and cultural dimensions. The remainder of this chapter is devoted to exploring the analytical insights offered by anthropology and geography respectively about these interconnections, and how these insights might be joined to forge a nuanced and politically potent analysis of globalization so construed.

ANTHROPOLOGY: THE PRACTICE OF CULTURE

Among these dimensions, anthropology contributes foremost a perspective on the local, cultural contexts for economic globalization. Within anthropology, 'culture' itself has been construed in many different ways, and this chapter draws particularly on an approach derived from theories of practice. In the age-old structure–agency debate, practice theory puts the emphasis on how the structure is produced, reproduced and transformed through human agency. An 'anthropology of practice' thus approaches culture through what people *do*, not, as with more structural approaches, through symbolic or economic calculations assigned to them.[1] Before proceeding to elaborate how this approach to culture can contribute to studying globalization, let me first note that I am imposing a unity here upon a range of anthropological scholarship that converged in the 1970s and 1980s around a common interest in exploring the *processes* through which cultural systems are produced and how they change. At that time words like 'practice', 'experience', 'performance' and 'action', as well as 'agents', 'actors', 'individuals', 'subjects' began to dominate the anthropological lexicon – although considerable disagreement developed about which kinds of actions to privilege and how to view the agency–structure dialectic. Today the significance of practice is all but taken for granted within most anthropological scholarship, but it is important to recapture the moment of its emergence for the synthetic task at hand.

The term 'practice anthropology' was first invoked by Sherry Ortner in a widely cited 1984 article on 'Theory in Anthropology since the Sixties'. The article claims that new experiments with practice theory in the 1980s offered a unifying force to an otherwise contested and heterogeneous discipline, and in particular she cites Pierre Bourdieu (1977) and Marshall Sahlins (1981) for early attempts to demonstrate how practice constitutes cultural systems. The article acknowledges the Marxian legacy in practice theory – namely the emphasis on domination, asymmetry and inequality as core features of cultural systems – but also establishes distance from it, in particular with an injunction for anthropologists to attend to practices of sharing, reciprocity and cooperation as much as domination and resistance. Here I wish to recuperate the explicitly critical dimensions of practice theory, drawing on Bourdieu and Gramsci (who is scarcely mentioned in Ortner's 1984 article, or – perhaps even more mysteriously – in Bourdieu's *Outline of a Theory of Practice* [1977]), but also on Raymond Williams, whose *Marxism and Literature* (1977) offers a highly influential interpretation of Gramsci for understanding the role of cultural practices in reproducing and transforming social systems. The strong materialist thrust in Williams (and implicit in Gramsci) finds expression in the cultural materialist tradition of anthropologist William Roseberry (and his students and colleagues like Gavin Smith and Susana Narotzky), who sought to establish anthropology as an eminently political and historical project that emphasizes the material as well as semiological dimensions of culture. These latter strands of practice anthropology are brought together by anthropologists Jean Comaroff and John Comaroff, who in *Of Revelation and Revolution* (1991) work out what Gramscian cultural politics might look like in the practice of ethnographic research, with due reference to Bourdieu and Williams.

To begin, then, it is worth returning to Comaroff and Comaroff's interpretation of culture as:

… the semantic ground on which human beings seek to construct and represent themselves and others – and hence society and history. As this suggests, it is not merely a pot of messages, a repertoire of signs to be flashed across a neutral mental screen. It has form as well as content; is born in action as well as thought; is a product of human creativity as well as mimesis; and, above all, is empowered. (1991: 21–2)

While culture has symbolic content deriving from the meanings people assign to the world and their actions in it, it is also dynamic – never fixed or given. Culture is not a pre-constituted object, but must be created through human intention and action. As a form of production culture has material as well as semantic dimensions. And cultural practices can work to reproduce or transform existing social structures. As Susana Narotzky puts it,

> ... 'a culture' is never an homogeneous superstructure or essence, evenly distributed among a local people. Rather cultures are real, lived experiences turned into reason, engendering reason for action and thus embodied in material life and material goods. (1997: 222)

The Gramscian legacy in this interpretation of culture is apparent through the focus it gives to politics and history. An anthropology of practice takes individuals' actions as its object of analysis, but only in relation to the material circumstances and dynamics of power within which they live. It strives, as did Gramsci from prison in Mussolini's Italy, to understand why people consent to oppressive rule and under what circumstances they resist. In exploring the relationship between consent and coercion, Gramsci recognized the role of culture in manufacturing consent – in permitting the exercise of control in the absence of overt violence. He discovered that it is in the domain of culture that economic and political 'persuasions' become inserted into the moral universe and get taken up by individuals as common sense (G. Smith 1999: 241). People consent to rule when they accept as given (or at least desirable relative to perceived alternatives) the values, norms and versions of justice supporting the existing distribution of goods and identifying the permissible range of dissent (D. Mitchell 2000). They resist when they recognize the arbitrary foundations of rule and when that 'rule' ceases to serve their interests. Individual practice thus expresses a tenuous relationship among consent, domination and resistance. And the anthropologist's task is to understand the historical specificity of these relationships, to 'look at the combination of people's situated daily practices and their material history to see how agency and structure come together in specific cultural expressions' (G. Smith 1999: 223).

Let me be clear that by contrasting 'structural' and 'practice' anthropology here I am not suggesting an exclusive either/or emphasis on structure versus practice. What are structures after all other than repetitive patterns of practice? The point is that an approach rooted in practice seeks to understand the process by which structures are created, while structuralists view their task as one of discerning structures from the flux of individual practices. Structural approaches to culture have certainly fallen out of fashion within anthropology today, but their remnants can be found within a resurgent interest in 'culture' within theories of economic development, including some strains of economic geography. Thus it is worth noting here that the emphasis on agency and cultural production in practice anthropology offers three analytical benefits to the study of globalization: (1) it points to social differentiation even within apparently uniform cultures; (2) it emphasizes the role of consciousness and ideology in conditioning agency; (3) and it enables anthropologists to view political-economic systems from the ground level. Let us take each of these points in turn.

Social Differentiation

The emphasis in practice anthropology on how culture is produced through human intention and action raises questions foremost about *who* is doing the producing. In any given society, that is, some people have the capacity to assert (or at least derive advantage from) the dominant values, norms and beliefs guiding social practice. For others, security of livelihood depends on accommodating (consciously or not) the ideologies, rituals, divisions of labour and forms of socialization through which those values seep into daily life. While acknowledging that all social actors seek to exercise control over their conditions of livelihood, practice theory begins with the premise that power is unevenly distributed (and that the symbols and meanings produced through practice are themselves empowered). As material conditions change people alter their practices, resulting (however unintentionally) in new meanings of existing relationships and a reorganization of power (Roseberry 1989; Sahlins 1981).

Two points follow from this discussion of social differentiation. First, practice theory rejects an interpretation of social identity as pre-configured by culture. Rather, it considers how social categories – women, low castes, priests, landlords – are themselves produced, reproduced and transformed within particular historical conjunctures. In so doing it highlights the dialectical relationship between the material circumstances and shared meanings animating individual practice and constituting social categories. For example, as explored in Chapter 6, a person may be 'low caste' in the context of traditional patronage relations, but upon earning a cash income and accumulating 'modern' consumer goods, the same person may identify and ultimately become identified as 'middle class'. As they enter into wage relations outside their neighbourhoods, that is, low castes loosen the patronage bonds assigned at birth, thus transforming the meaning of their caste identity and the local landscape of power (Rankin 2003). Second, practice theorists also reject the functionalist notion that the *objective* of a society as expressed in cultural traditions is to reproduce itself, in favour of an analysis of how social differentiation introduces the possibility of dissent and conflict between groups – the outcome of which may be radical change or the construction of alternative epistemological frames within an existing repertoire of symbols and meanings (Narotzky 1997: 177). The emphasis on social differentiation, that is, foregrounds the social struggle in culture and introduces the possibility of rupture.

It is important to note that practice anthropologists have generally relied on theories of interest that are distinctly different from those underpinning economic liberalism. The latter begins resolutely with the individual as the unit of analysis. It builds a theory of markets as the benign arbiter of justice, rooted in the idea that rational profit-maximizing individuals freely pursuing their own self-interest will generate the maximum public good. This position conveniently removes structure from the picture altogether (and erases politics and history from the domain of 'the economy'). While it is tempting to read a narrow interpretation of practice as individual economizing activity into Bourdieu (Crang 1997; Fine 2001; Sayer 1999) – this conflation should be resisted. For the focus in Bourdieu is rather on the collective efforts of socially differentiated individual practice in constituting social class. For a clear understanding of the relationship between practice and class interest, it is necessary now to turn to the concepts of hegemony, ideology and consciousness.

Hegemony, Ideology and Consciousness

The Gramscian concepts of hegemony, ideology and consciousness have furnished anthropologists with important – though admittedly contested – tools for understanding how power operates through culture. When power is hegemonic, Gramsci argued, those in subordinate positions experience the order that oppresses them as self-evident and natural.[2] In such cases:

> … power … hides itself in forms of everyday life. Sometimes ascribed to transcendental, suprahistorical forces (gods or ancestors, nature or physics, biological instinct or probability), these forms are not easily questioned. Being 'natural' or 'ineffable', they seem to be beyond human agency, notwithstanding the fact that the interests they serve may be all too human. (Comaroff and Comaroff 1991: 22)

Thus hegemony is a form of power, which, though never entirely homologous with culture, reflects that part of the dominant world view that has come to be taken for granted as the established way of things (Williams 1977: 110). Neoliberalism can thus be said to be hegemonic to the extent that it not only expresses dominant capitalist interests, but also is accepted as normal reality, or common sense, even by those who are hardest hit by 'deregulation', fiscal austerity and workfare. Hegemony thus has a special relationship with ideas of justice. When hegemony prevails, people can believe, at least some of the time, that they live in a just and moral world, even if they inhabit a subordinate place within it (see also Parish 1997).

If Gramsci recognized culture as a domain of coercion – and indeed of revolution – then Bourdieu contributed analytical tools that could yield empirically detailed accounts of how hegemonic power gets enacted in minute ways through the mundane routines of everyday life (see also Eagleton 1991: 156–8). The condition in which there is a correspondence between objective order and subjective experience, Bourdieu calls 'doxa' – a realm of social life within which 'what is essential *goes without saying because it comes without saying … tradition is silent, not least about itself as a tradition' (1977: 167). For Bourdieu, doxa presents a paradox that must be documented carefully through scientific ethnographic research – and that must ultimately become the domain of resistance. In *Masculine Domination* (2001: 1–2) he writes:

I have always been astonished by what might be called the *paradox of doxa* … that the established order, with its relations of domination, its rights and prerogatives, privileges and injustices, ultimately perpetuates itself so easily, apart from a few historical accidents, and that the most intolerable conditions of existence can so often be perceived as acceptable and even natural. And I have also seen masculine domination, and the way it is imposed and suffered, as the prime example of this paradoxical submission, an effect of what I call symbolic violence, a gentle violence, imperceptible and invisible to its victims, exerted for the most part through the purely symbolic channels of communication and cognition (more precisely, misrecognition), recognition, or even feeling.

For that part of culture in which hegemony prevails, individuals assume dispositions and orientations beyond their own horizon of meaning – 'habitus' in Bourdieu's lexicon – and thus collude, often unwittingly, in the production of a system that may oppress them. In these circumstances, the practices of individuals, right down to their bodily comportment, can acquire a unity and consistency without being the result of conscious obedience to rules. Thus anthropologists have documented the processes by which abstract ideologies circulating at a global scale – neoliberalism, political democracy, development, modernization – assume historically and culturally specific textures and become rooted as common sense in particular societies (Li 1999; Pigg 1992, 2001; Tsing 1993). For Bourdieu, the documentation always entailed a civic mission – to expose the cognitive structures underlying the wide-ranging (though always related) forms of oppression, from neoliberal globalization to male domination.

Of course, the possibility for culture to bind people to political programmes is limited. There is always the possibility that people will begin to see the arbitrary foundations of the established order, to recognize it as a human construction. When this happens, as Comaroff and Comaroff (1991: 8) put it, 'the contradictions between the world as represented and the world as experienced [will] become ever more palpable, ever more insupportable' – a dissonance which Gramsci identified as 'contradictory consciousness' (a fecund state for critical consciousness) and Bourdieu as 'political consciousness'. Thus, as Steven Parish points out in the context of caste societies of South Asia, people are not merely *Homo Hierarchicus* – to use the gloss of French structuralist Louis Dumont – though they are certainly influenced by the values of hierarchy; they 'are not solely constituted by hierarchical premises', but also have 'moments of insight into the social order as a constructed political order' (Parish 1997: 8). Feminist anthropologists have long documented the complex relationships among 'doxa', 'habitus' and 'political consciousness' – rejecting the linear formulations in Bourdieu and Gramsci and revealing a far more complex and self-conscious politics of consent (see Kabeer 1994; Moore 1988 for summaries; see also Kandyoti 1991; Ong 1987; and Chapter 5 this volume for examples). The key point for our purpose here is to acknowledge the potential for contradictory forms of consciousness to catalyse politically more potent and collective forms of reflection on structural patterns of oppression.

Once hegemony is recognized, 'once its internal contradictions [have been] revealed, when what seemed natural comes to be negotiable, when the ineffable is put into words, then hegemony becomes something other than itself. It turns into ideology…' (Comaroff and Comaroff 1991: 23–4). Within the domain of ideology, domination requires self-conscious cultural work, the assertion of control over the various modes of cultural production.[3] Thus while:

> … [h]egemony consists of constructs and conventional practices that have come to permeate a political community[,] ideology originates in the assertion of a particular social group. Hegemony is beyond argument; ideology is more likely to be perceived as a matter of inimical opinion and interest and hence is more open to contestation. Hegemony, at its most effective, is mute; ideology invites argument. (Comaroff and Comaroff 1992: 29; cited in G. Smith 1999: 242)

The dominant ideology of any historical moment or spatial location – Bourdieu's 'orthodoxy' – will of course reflect the orientations of the dominant social group(s), 'although it may be widely peddled beyond' (Comaroff and Comaroff 1991: 24). To the extent that subordinate populations view their interests collectively and attempt to assert themselves against a dominant order, they may also have ideologies – their own explicit and *articulated* world view – through which they critique the established orthodoxy and attempt to control the cultural terms in which the world is ordered.

Gramscian interpretations of culture are not, of course, the exclusive domain of anthropologists. Cultural geographers, too, have recently taken an interest in the politics of culture in an effort to shed light on the politically regressive context of geographic scholarship since the rise of the Thatcher–Reagan neoliberal hegemony (e.g. Lee and Wills 1997). In so doing, they have rejected their own functionalist roots as a subdiscipline concerned with chronicling the uniqueness of peoples and places through artifacts, landscapes and other material dimensions of culture.[4] The 'new cultural geography' turned not to anthropology, but to cultural studies – also steeped in various appropriations of Gramsci – for an analysis of power, and specifically for understanding how such regressive ideologies could become the common sense of electoral majorities in advanced industrialized countries (P. Jackson 1989; D. Mitchell 2000). To studies in the politics of culture, geographers have contributed an understanding of how culture is spatially constituted; as Don Mitchell puts it, 'arguments over "culture" are arguments over real spaces, over landscapes, over the social relations that define the places in which we and others live' (2000: 5–6).

This contribution notwithstanding, the 'new cultural geographers' have resembled their cultural studies counterparts in three significant respects which diminish their effectiveness for understanding culturally variable experiences of globalization. First, they commonly take as the subject of their analysis the media, fashion, the education system and other components of the 'critical infrastructure' performing the cultural work of making and marking distinction (Dwyer and Crang 2002; D. Mitchell 2000; Zukin 1991, 1995). In so doing, they generate data that, if not specifically textual, entails at least some form of public discourse – a screenplay, messages about beauty embedded in the spring catwalk fashions, the high school curriculum. These discourses certainly travel the globe, but in themselves they do not tell us anything about how they are experienced by people in different social locations. Second, cultural geography, like cultural studies, has tended to concentrate on the macro scales of cultural production – such as how suburban landscapes codify gender beliefs (Mackenzie and Rose 1983; McDowell 1983), or how apartheid and racism operate as geographical systems (P. Jackson 1992; D. Mitchell 2000). With some notable exceptions (e.g. Peake and Trotz 1999; Ruddick 1996; Stiell and England 1997), cultural geographers have less experience with reading narratives and practices of individuals 'on the ground' within communities as themselves providing 'texts' with messages to impart. Finally, both cultural geography and cultural studies tend to concentrate on the North American and European contexts for globalization.

Ground-level View of Political-economic Systems

Anthropologists, by contrast, generally examine the dialectics of ideology and consciousness at a finer grain, concentrating as they do on how culture is produced and resisted within civil society. Their data often consists in the minutiae of what people say and do in their everyday lives, notwithstanding the interventions of a 'reflexive turn' promoted by postmodern social theory and concerned foremost with the politics of representation (Clifford 1988; Visweswaran 1994). Methodologically, that is, anthropologists generally rely on ethnography, entailing not just interviewing, mapping and other conventional qualitative research methods, but also, characteristically, participant observation – long-term residence in the research community during which the ethnographer observes people in their own time and space and as far as possible participates in community events and daily life activities. As Michael Burawoy et al. (1991) have argued, participant observation makes possible a hermeneutic dimension of social science research; it enables the investigator to juxtapose claims against practice, assess how people interpret events that are observed, and account for how the presence of the researcher influences the research context. It also enables the investigator to build rapport with people in the community, which can facilitate and deepen the interview process beyond the conventional isolated one-to-two-hour interview transpiring between strangers (see also Clifford 1988; Hammersley and Atkinson 1989; B. Jackson 1987).

Anthropologists, moreover, characteristically have concentrated their research on peripheral areas, or (increasingly) the participation of formerly 'peripheral' peoples and cultures in border-crossings and flows. The commitment to cross-cultural research, of course, has significant regressive origins in the colonial enterprise ('knowing' the natives as a necessary condition to subjugating them), and has come under assault as a form of neocolonialism (Escobar 1995; Visweswaran 1994; prompting, it must be added, calls to 'exoticize the West' and deconstruct the classic ethnographic texts).[5] But it also has a politically progressive legacy. Particularly in the American tradition established by Franz Boas and taken up most explicitly by his students Ruth Benedict and Margaret Mead in the 1930s and 1940s, anthropology construed itself as offering a critique of scientific racism, economic rationalism and other dimensions of 'western culture'. The idea was to expand knowledge (specifically institutionalized knowledge in the West) about the possible ways of organizing economic and social life, in order to challenge American middle-class socio-cultural assumptions (much as Polanyi was to argue in establishing the Substantivist School). In the wake of the two world wars, the comparative efforts of anthropologists were framed specifically in terms of understanding difference for the sake of diffusing what Mike Davis (2000) has called 'the ecology of fear' on a global scale; anthropology could play a role in making the world safe for difference, by encouraging people to suspend judgement of cultural 'others' until their differences could be made sense of.[6]

In a practice-theory framework, then, these methods and scalar priorities generate empirically detailed accounts of ideology as part of everyday life – accounts of the cultural work entailed in enforcing and legitimating established norms and values, in routine daily experience as much as in public rituals like marriages or independence day celebrations. An anthropology of practice considers how these forms of cultural production can assume hegemonic proportions and achieve a strong grip on people's common sense by detailing their 'habitus' – their practical modes of consent and collusion. Most significantly, it explores the contradictions of prevailing ideologies, how those contradictions touch the consciousness of social actors, and under what circumstances individuals collectively articulate a critique of culture and attempt to transform it. Within this kind of ethnography, learning to read the modes of representation that convey contradictory consciousness – the personal testimonies, ambivalent expressions, utopian narratives – becomes the primary methodological act (Comaroff and Comaroff 1991: 30).

The emphasis in 'practice anthropology' on fine-grained ethnographic accounts of everyday life highlights how wider-scale political–economic relations are experienced in local contexts. This commitment is important within scholarship on globalization, which typically operates at more macro scales of analysis. With respect to the periphery in particular, practice theory offers the analytical tools for understanding *how* change transpires, without falling prey to simplistic models of 'global culture' encompassing 'local places' within a single ideological system (Tsing 2000). Global justice movements have mobilized such discourses of cultural imperialism to protest the imposition of western culture around the world (Tomlinson 1999), and the understanding of culture upon which such accounts are based continues to inform academic critiques of globalization, even if stark theories of cultural homogenization have fallen out of favour (see Kelly 1999 for a review of this literature). The emphasis on agency, on the contrary, highlights how local social and cultural filters interpret and in turn give shape to what is coming in from the outside. Without losing sight of the broader macroeconomic currents of power, that is, practice theory opens up analytical space not just to explore how local societies change as they are increasingly integrated into the global capitalist system, but also to view global processes *as* local processes, as embedded within communities, neighbourhoods, and households. The question then becomes, how do globalizing processes facilitate or hinder counter-hegemonic social change in particular locations? To the extent that old hegemonic forms of power unravel, how do cultural claims – to history, tradition, justice – get fought out in the domain of ideology, and what are the material conditions of that struggle?

Several possibilities arise from this disciplinary stance. 'Taking local perspectives' can offer novel interpretations of universal phenomena, as Anna Tsing (1993) demonstrates in an ethnography exploring 'primitive' (Dayak) perspectives on urban civilization and Indonesia's place in the global political-economic system. It also allows for ethnography to reveal different kinds of globalizing processes – globalization not just as a transnational force dismantling state authority (Rouse 1995 cited in Tsing 2000), but also as networking among feminist activists to secure lines of state–society accountability (Riles 1998 cited in Tsing 2000; see also Burawoy et al 1991 on the advantages of multi-sited ethnography). Descriptions of subtle changes in one place can provide a new window on globalizing processes, which, as Stacy Pigg's work has pioneered in exploring, may not only refute conventional formulations that the global system universally determines local processes, but also uncover grounded, contextualized interpretations of justice as a foundation for progressive social change (2001).

The Limits to Practice

For the most part, however, cultural anthropologists do not explicitly develop the normative dimension in practice theory to engage directly with policy, or even the epistemological frameworks for policy making. With some notable exceptions (e.g. Burawoy et al. 1991; Roseberry 1989; G. Smith 1989), still less do they venture to articulate explicit critiques of the cultures they visit – a reticence which is particularly inconsistent with theories of practice designed to facilitate social critique. Rather, anthropological writing generally confines itself to the domain of description – to 'reduc[ing] the puzzlement' and 'clarify[ing] what goes on' in another place (Geertz 1973: 16). To the extent that anthropologists have engaged practice theory in a critique of culture, the effort has concentrated on the intransigencies of colonialism and on generating critical questions from ethnographic research to probe the ethnographer's own culture (e.g. Comaroff and Comaroff 1991; Dirks 2001; Marcus and Fisher 1999) – rather than on subjecting the cultural politics of 'the other' to critical scrutiny.

The motivation for these textual and substantive priorities resides, as we have seen, at least in part with a progressive sentiment, namely the wish to assert the equality of cultures and root out discrimination stemming from ignorance. The penchant for political neutrality vis-à-vis other cultures also no doubt derives from the positivist standards of objectivity that have historically infused even the most humanist branches of the social sciences with prescriptions to detach morality and political interest from properly scholarly research. There is also a personal politics that must be noted here. For ethnographic research hinges crucially on the generosity, assistance and friendship of the anthropologist's hosts. Explicit social critique of the cultures in which those hosts are embedded could cause offence, if not personal harm – especially given the power differentials that typically characterize anthropologists' relationships with their hosts.

Thus most anthropological writing has not taken the 'practice' in practice theory to its logical conclusion – to the domain of 'praxis' encompassing research itself as a form of practice. Here there is firmer ground for political engagement. First comes the recognition that in the absence of guiding standards of justice against which to judge culture (others' as much as one's own), much of anthropology in fact suffers from a kind of relativism that could contribute to perpetuating the hegemonic and ideological forms of power it is so well-poised to describe. 'If all cultures are in principle equally valuable ...', as Perry Anderson (1992: 54–5) famously asked, 'why fight for a better one?' A second layer of engaging research as praxis, then, could involve using the tools of practice theory not merely to document the dialectics of domination and resistance, but also to empower those participating as informants in ethnographic research to view their world critically and to mobilize those critical capacities as resources for progressive social change.

Another pitfall of anthropological approaches to globalization follows: in its own practice, anthropology often gives subordinate status to the macro-regulatory contexts for human agency. The 'long-term, mainly qualitative, highly participative, and almost obsessively fine-combed field-study' (Geertz 1973: 23), that is, pays microscopic attention to local cultural topographies at the expense of situating local maps of meaning on larger maps of global changes. The strength of recent transcultural studies focusing on cultural flows and border crossings lies in documenting the diversity of globalization through the specific 'conjunctures' of movement and travel (Clifford 1988; Gupta and Ferguson 2002; Inda and Rosaldo 2002). As Tsing (2000: 10) argues, however, 'the possibility that capitalisms and governmentalities are themselves situated, contradictory, effervescent or culturally circumscribed is much less explored'. Simply posing the local–global dichotomy obscures the multiple scales through which economic, political and cultural forms of globalization are mediated.

GEOGRAPHIES OF GLOBALIZATION

Geography offers some remedies to these limitations in the study of globalization, while at the same time suffering from its own weaknesses, which require anthropological perspectives for their redress. Geographers share the fundamental premise that all life is 'placed'; in 'situating' social and economic processes, geographers approach space not as a neutral or fixed container of human activity, but rather as playing a structuring role in those processes. The emphasis on space lends geography a comparative tendency, useful for placing local processes in macroeconomic perspective. Geography can thus offer a spatial dimension to Gramscian interpretations of cultural politics; it offers a much-needed 'geometry of power', to borrow Doreen Massey's (1992) now widely cited interpretation of space as an arena through which social relations of empowerment and disempowerment, domination and subordination, participation and exclusion, operate and continually transform social and physical nature.

Much of the work on globalization in geography takes place within the subfield of economic geography, which views its task primarily in terms of documenting the spatial factors of capitalist accumulation and economic growth. Increasingly, however, the lines between economic and cultural geography have blurred as economic geographers have explored the social and institutional dimensions of production, consumption, value and exchange (e.g. Lee and Wills 1997), and economic geographers have considered the economies of cultures (e.g. P. Jackson 2002a). As Richa Nagar et al. (2002) have recently pointed out, feminist geographers have pioneered in analysing macro-scale political economic processes in relation to the social identities of women and others in subordinate social positions. The objective here in exploring geographical contributions to and limitations of the study of globalization is thus to review approaches in economic, cultural and feminist geography. I note three spheres of comparative advantage: the insights offered by making (a) 'place' and (b) 'scale' a central category of analysis, and (c) the explicit normative position vis-à-vis neoliberalism and economic governance.

Everything in its Place

Anthropologists have meticulously studied in diverse and faraway places, yet until very recently they have largely overlooked the significance of place itself in the production and reproduction of social life (see Low 2001; Pigg 1992; Rodman 1992 for some notable exceptions). For all its explorations of cultural difference, that is, the tendency in anthropology, remarkably, has been to assume an isomorphism between place and culture (Gupta and Ferguson 2002; Inda and Rosaldo 2002). It has rather been the task of geographers to document 'the difference that space makes' (Sayer 1985): to argue that cultures and economies are not bounded entities occupying specific territories, but are themselves constituted through spatial structures and that 'there are spatial as well as social divisions of labour' (P. Jackson 2002c). Accordingly, in geography, 'place' moves from a derivative position to playing a formative role in social and economic processes; as geographer Michael Watts argues, 'how things develop depends on *where* they develop, on what has been historically sedimented there, on the social and spatial structures that are already in place' (Pred and Watts 1992: 11).

Feminist geographers have been particularly persuasive in documenting that space, as a constitutive element of culture, is socially constructed, filled with power, struggled over (e.g. Jones et al. 1997; Massey 1999). Their work shows how gender ideology entails spatial practices and how the social construction of space produces and maintains power relations. Take, for example, the design of many a public lectern on the stage of a university auditorium. How often do women speakers alight the podium to confront a structure that nearly obscures them from the view of the audience (or a microphone placed to suit the stature of a generic 6-foot professor)? Such spatial configurations carry unequivocal messages about the gendering of authority in professional settings. Feminist geographers have thus examined the physical construction of the built environment (Robson 2000); the social and economic paths women trace in places (Massey 1994); the dialectical relationship between space and identity (Peake and Trotz 1999); and how women in different localities combine different forms of work, as well as the implications of work for women's location in space (McDowell 2000). Implicit in these studies of how gendered power relations are produced through, and in turn transform, space is a tactical understanding of the role of space in challenging and transforming dominant cultural ideologies.

Economic geographers, especially those driving the 'cultural turn' in the subdiscipline, have focused more on the institutional dimensions of place – firms, markets, intermediary organizations like universities, civil society organizations and the institutions like national states that provide the regulatory framework for formal-sector economic activity. Their research on regions has, for example, paid increasing attention to the social factors underpinning competitiveness – to the 'enduring significance of place-bound institutional and cultural assets' (Amin and Thrift 1997: 155). Thus Michael Storper (1995) has introduced the notion of regions as loci for 'untraded interdependencies' – unpriced technological spillovers such as common labour markets and 'conventions' for learning and interpreting knowledge – that flow in the form of technological skills from one activity to another in the spatial context of the region. These interdependencies are place-specific and serve as the basis for regional differentiation (Maskell and Malmberg 1999; Storper 1995). Ash Amin and Nigel Thrift (e.g. 1997) have similarly argued that regional competitiveness depends on adequate degrees of 'institutional thickness' – a combination of dense and diverse institutional activity, high levels of institutional interaction, shared cultural norms and values, and common industrial purpose – that enhances learning, innovation and profitability by embedding institutions in their regional social context. Here again, socio-spatial practices and social relations rooted in particular places assume central importance in assessing regional economic competitiveness (see also K. Cox 1997; Gertler 1995; Saxenian 1994).

Two points follow from this discussion about the significance of place in the specific context of economic globalization: (a) global economic integration notwithstanding, place still plays a determining role in economic and social life; (b) place must always, however, be viewed in dialectical relationship with global economic and cultural processes. With regard to the first point, some geographers have taken their cue from globalization boosters declaring the 'end of history' and the 'dawn of a borderless world' (Fukuyama 1992; Ohmae 1990) to argue that the rise of information technology and global financial integration has signalled the 'end of geography', the 'demise of the state' (O'Brian 1992) and rendered industries 'footloose', no longer bound to place (Storper and Walker 1989). A more subtle version of the globalization thesis argues that the national state remains politically significant as a site of struggle and arbiter of democratic accountability, but its capacity to wield power within its own national borders has been 'hollowed out' in the shift to internationalized production systems (Jessop 1994). Thus a 'space of flows' – global networks of production processes within and between firms – is said to be replacing a 'space of places' – territorially based national economies (Castells 1996; Dicken 1998). On the cultural side, too, a new subset of geographic research has similarly subordinated the conventional focus on place contained within the boundaries of physical contiguity to privilege 'transnational cultural flows' as a determining force in local social life (Crang 1997; K. Mitchell 1998).

Feminist and institutionalist perspectives discussed above contest the 'false' dualism of mobility versus fixity in boosterist theories of globalization and argue that 'place still matters' even in the flux of global economic and cultural flows. Institutionalists have emphasized how divergent national regulatory structures (Boyer 1996; Jessop 1990, 1994; Peck and Tickell 1994), market rules (Christopherson 1993), national systems of innovation (Lundvall 1992), regional institutional configurations (Saxenian 1994; Storper 1995) and the territorial embeddedness of firms (K. Cox 1997) continue to construct geographically unique forms of capitalism. They suggest that even with opportunities for 'footloose' organization of production on a global scale, practices of agglomeration, networking, knowledge-sharing and social learning within place reveal that socio-spatial embeddedness remains important for firms' profitability (Amin and Thrift 1997; Gertler 1995). Feminist geographers have concentrated at more micro scales to assert the enduring significance of place. They have argued that globalization theories overlook the economic, political and cultural practices taking place within households and communities:

… in daily activities of caring, consumption, and religion, and networks of alternative politics where women's contribution to globalization are often located. We see these informal sites for understanding globalization processes in their own right because … *it is precisely these spheres and activities that underwrite and actively constitute the public spheres of globalization.* (Nagar et al. 2002: 4, emphasis in original)

Thus, feminist geographers have shown how economic globalization has been constituted (and subsidized) locally – through gendered labour practices within households and communities (e.g. Lawson 1999), through relations between formal and informal economies and between high-skill and low-skill work (Sassen 1998), and through gendered politics of inequality, difference and resistance in specific communities (Nagar 2000).

The second contribution of feminist and institutionalist economic geographers in relation to the study of globalization has to do with their relational approach to (local) fixities and (global) flows. In their emphasis on the institutional and regulatory specificities of capitalist development, economic geographers favour an understanding of the local in dialectical relationship with wider fields of influence and action (Amin and Thrift 1997). Thus, for example, Erik Swyngedouw offers the 1995 collapse of the Barings Bank in the wake of the speculative activities of a Singapore-based trader, as an instance in which 'local actions shape global money flows, while global processes, in turn, affect local actions' (1997: 137). Michael Watts engages the notion of 'dialectical tacking' to examine core–periphery relations (in Pred and Watts 1992). He illustrates how in West Africa agro-industrialization associated with macroeconomic restructuring transforms peasant production systems, resulting in a reworking of modernity itself, as a changing culture of work intensifies struggles within households and communities. Such case studies suggest that:

> ... a sensitive analysis does not argue for [global] against [local] but focuses on the relations. Local communities may be buffeted by global forces but they are not helpless victims with no coping strategies. However, neither can they be autonomous of the world they inhabit, so that their strategies will invariably involve consequences beyond their direct control. In this case, geographers deal with a local–global dialectic, where local events constitute global structures which then impinge on local events in an iterative continuum. (Taylor et al. 1995: 9)

Pred and Watts (1992), Katz (2001) and Nagar et al. (2002) describe this kind of geographic research as 'topographical' insofar as it approaches 'place' not as a unique or self-contained space, but rather as an entry point for developing a relational approach to globalization that situates places in their broader context and in relation to other geographic scales.

The Politics of Scale

The latter notion of scale was 'discovered' by geographers seeking to add a finer-grained analysis to a relational understanding of space in the context of economic globalization. These days no doctoral comprehensive exam or dissertation proposal in human geography passes muster without ample reference to the 'politics of scale', now viewed as a disciplinary trademark (to the point that its meaning sometimes becomes diluted beyond recognition). In my view the novelty and analytical force of scale has been overstated, since geographers treat scale much as they do place and space – as a relational and socially constructed dimension of human life that bears on the distribution of resources and opportunity. In spite of the dizzying rate (and occasional cross-purpose) at which 'scale' is summoned in the contemporary geographic literature, it is nonetheless useful to distil here its contribution for a 'topographical' approach to globalization that wishes to trace how places become interconnected through processes of globalization.

'Scale' first acquired its broad currency through the promotional efforts of Erik Swyngedouw, who (building on the tradition of 'locality studies', see Massey 1994) argues that conventional bipolar perspectives relating 'the local' to 'the global' are too narrow and overlook the multiple, intersecting scales through which everyday life is constituted (for a summary of this argument see Kelly 1999; Swyngedouw 1997). The conventional view of scale consigns certain activities to particular levels of hierarchically embedded physical spaces – social networks to the local level, for example, or surfing the web to the global level. By this logic, the anthropologist studying social networks would focus her gaze exclusively at the local scale. Swyngedouw argued that this formulation of scale as a container for action is too simple and that activities transpiring at one scale must be viewed in relation to other scales of influence: '[t]he scaling of everyday life', for example, 'is expressed in bodily, community, urban, regional, national, supranational and global configurations' (1997: 144).

Feminist geographers have thus identified the body as a key site for understanding the gender politics of globalization insofar as it serves as a 'cultural battleground' (NACLA 2001: 12 cited in Nagar et al. 2002) on which such issues as reproductive rights, the commodification of sexuality and the gendered construction of workers are negotiated and struggled over (Nagar 2000; Nagar et al. 2002). At the local scale they have traced how men's and women's engagement with global capitalisms, mediated by state economic restructuring, transforms or entrenches gender relations and identities within the household and community (e.g. Peake and Trotz 1999). Institutionalists have explored how other forms of economic and social foundations of global competitiveness – untraded interdependencies, social learning, institutional thickness

– operate at regional as much as national scales. And urban geographers have argued that the distribution of resources and processes of change can only be understood if cities are recognized as nodes within 'dense inter-scalar networks' (Brenner 2000).

Not only must scale (like place) be viewed relationally, but it must also be recognized as a socially produced and politically contested category of analysis. In other words, scale is not ontologically given or a politically neutral discursive strategy; rather it embodies and expresses relations of power (Swyngedouw 1997: 140). Thus Swyngedouw (1997) notes how analysts might evoke competing 'scalar narratives' when representing particular public events. The Barings Bank collapse, for example, could be attributed to an individual male body (rogue trader), inadequate national regulatory regimes (Singapore and England), the global derivatives market or the absence of supra-national financial oversight (by an EU central bank) – depending on the positionality and political agenda of the analyst. A constructivist approach to scale becomes increasingly apposite as the globe becomes ever more interconnected and 'dynamics at one scale are increasingly implicated at other scales' (Kelly 1999: 381). Such an approach allows geographers to recognize that in the context of neoliberal capitalism, the scale of regulation has shifted from the conventional, democratically accountable scale of the nation-state, upwards to the undemocratic supranational scale and downwards to the (relatively) politically impotent scale of community and neighbourhood. As regulation 'jumps scale' in this way (N. Smith 1993), the political point for geographers is to assess who gains and who loses, as well as to identify key 'scalar strategies' for resistance.

Accountability and Normative Position

When compared to anthropology, the tendency in geography has been toward more explicit discussion about the normative implications of research. Having established that place and scale are socially constructed, for example, it becomes possible, indeed imperative, to take issue with the easy conflation of neoliberalism and globalization (Kelly 1999: 380). Geographers (along with global justice movements) have thus sought to claim the global scale as a site for politically progressive projects – systems of global governance and new social movements that constitute a global civil society within which are forged collective strategies out of enduring local particularisms (e.g. Herod 1997; Peck and Tickell 1994). 'To ignore the global scale in progressive practice', writes Kelly (1999:

386), 'would be to defer to the orthodox ways in which it is represented and the neoliberal policy conclusions that are drawn.'

In addition to arguing that reconfiguration of scale can either challenge or reproduce existing power relations, so too geographers have noted that 'scale capabilities' – abilities to exercise power and influence across particular spatial scales – vary by social position along class, gender, ethnic and other lines (Swyngedouw 1997: 142). Since strategies for social change must always have a spatial dimension (see Peake and Trotz 1999), politically, the task is to enhance the scale capabilities of those in subordinate social locations. Feminist geographers have argued that the injustices of globalization are not limited to the hegemony of neoliberalism, but also include imperialist, racist and sexist dimensions that must be confronted in a 'geography-crossing and scale-jumping political response' (Katz 2001: 1216). Their work has shown how neocolonial power relations and political economic structures combine with religious and other cultural ideologies to produce new racialized and class-based sexual and labour practices (Katz 2001; Pratt 1999; Nagar 2000). Within a feminist cultural politics, then, recognizing place and identity 'as embedded and intimately related through globalization processes can lay the grounds for building a gendered oppositional politics that moves across space and scale' (Nagar et al. 2002: 16).

Within geography different strategies have thus emerged to counter the deleterious effects of globalization. Notwithstanding these differences, much of human geography shares a fundamental normative thrust in the oppositional politics it wishes to construct vis-à-vis neoliberal forms of globalization. The normative commitment is related to the direct commentary on economic development policy that geographers – even those with explicitly oppositional politics – are occasionally called upon to offer, through professional consultancies for governments and regulatory bodies at supranational, national, regional and local scales. Thus, geographers have advised national governments about global patterns of technological development (e.g. Britton 1978; Steed 1982) and about the significance of cities for regional systems of innovation (e.g. Wolfe and Gertler 1998), and municipal governments about the relationship between economic stability and a positive environment of diversity (e.g. Florida 2002; Gibson et al. 1999). Danny Dorling and Mary Shaw (2002) have recently argued that geographers do not contribute *enough* to public policy. The point to emphasize here, however, is that the responsibility for policy engagement implicit in the study of spatial and scalar dimensions of globalization holds geographers accountable to the constituencies they claim to represent in a way that is less apparent for ethnographic studies of isolated, out-of-the-way places. Relative to anthropology, the comparative perspectives offered through a relational view of place and scale provide a foundation for taking a firm normative stand – not only documenting the socio-spatial costs of economic globalization, but also taking a stand about what is to be done.

The Limits to Geography

The relational view of place and scale represents an important theoretical contribution, but it is more difficult to reflect this commitment in the *practice* of conducting empirical research. Qualitative research in particular must transpire *in* a place and, as Nagar et al. have argued, the contingencies (and politics) of the research process have tended to favour a focus on certain places, scales, sectors and actors in the global economy. The feminist contribution notwithstanding, geographers have tended to concentrate their analysis at more macro scales, to focus on the formal sector (governments, markets and formal institutions), and to consider primarily certain kinds of networks – regulated international trade, investment flows, economic integration. The emphasis has generally been on the political economy of globalization, rather than socially differentiated experiences and responses, or the role of households, communities, individual subjectivities and the informal sector in rooting economic globalization at the local scale (see also Pred and Watts 1992).[7] To the extent that geographers have considered the local scale, they have largely concentrated on exploring how the phenomena in question – firm behaviour, labour markets, cultural economies and so on – have been 'touched' or 'influenced' by economic globalization (see also Gibson-Graham 1996; Roberts 2003); framing the local–global relation in terms of impacts tends to 'reinscribe the centrality of corporations, markets, financial and development institutions even as these are critiqued' for their deleterious effects (Nagar et al. 2002: 4).

   Economic geographers have deepened the conventional analysis of formal-sector institutions by exploring the role of social networks and trust in fostering 'social learning' and 'systems of innovation'. Yet we miss a clear understanding of how people in informal sectors, households and communities, as well as in economies of the periphery, have subsidized economic globalization – absorbing the social costs of privatized public services, deregulated markets and social welfare cuts. Nor do we get a sense of who pays and who benefits when 'social learning' and 'institutional thickness' are achieved; what, for example, are the gendered, racialized and class dimensions of these indicators of economic success? And some economic geographers embarking on the 'cultural turn' have tended to reify culture in seeking isolable, even replicable, cultural determinants of economic growth (e.g. Piore and Sabel 1984).

Taking important cues from feminist theories of identity, cultural geography has been the subfield making the most concerted attempts to represent local agency, especially vis-à-vis processes of commodification (e.g. Dwyer and Crang 2002; Jackson 2002b). The commitment here has been to capturing the pleasure, desire and creativity in the production and consumption of commodities, rather than merely mapping the impacts of social exclusion. Cultural geographers, moreover, have been sceptical of tendencies towards the reification of culture in other subdisciplines, to the extent even of debating whether culture can be assigned an ontological status at all. The debate has been fuelled by the provocations of Don Mitchell, who argues that in fact culture is politics by another name:

… cultural geographers should be engaged in the task of determining not what culture is – since it is nothing – but rather how the *idea* of culture works in society. To call culture a level or domain makes little sense. Culture is instead a powerful name – powerful because it obscures what it is meant to identify. If 'culture' is politics by another name (as it is), then it is so by dint of its function as *ideology*. (2000: 77, emphasis in original)

The proposal here is to attend instead to how the 'idea of culture' (like the idea of scale) gets deployed as a means of defining what and who is legitimate in society, in the service of 'culture wars' like the ethno-religious nationalisms raging in parts of Asia and the Middle East. The problem is that in so conflating culture with ideology, this approach overlooks other forms of cultural production and the potential for critical resistance they pose.

We thus return again to the contingencies of the research process. Even when geographers have given priority to neglected scales, spaces and actors of globalization, they have tended to favour relatively short-term fieldwork involving formal interviews and content analysis of textual and visual media – falling short of ethnographic methods geared toward documenting the *practice* of cultural production. In general, geography departments lack an institutional culture that values, even tolerates, long-term ethnographic research through which it is possible to explore how 'households', 'markets', 'gender' and other often taken-for-granted institutions and ideologies are themselves culturally constructed. This kind of insight is crucial for understanding how globalization processes become embedded *culturally* and are in turn shaped by local cultural economies.

ARTICULATION: SYNTHESIS

I argue here for an approach to the study of globalization that synthesizes the strengths of anthropology and geography in a manner that also remedies the deficiencies of each. In particular I advocate joining an ethnographic approach to exploring the politics of culture in peripheral places, with the multi-scalar and normative commitments developed within geography. To be sure, the very fact of increased economic and cultural integration entailed in globalization has prompted considerable erosion of disciplinary boundaries, as anthropologists recognize the spatiality of culture and geographers explore the social embeddedness of markets, institutions and governments. Yet within the institutional cultures of academia itself, segregation prevails at the most crucial junctures of disciplinary reproduction – in hiring and promotion decisions, for example, or in the norms surrounding what constitutes good research method. To the extent that there has been cross-fertilization in the individual practices of anthropologists and geographers, there has not been adequate accounting of where the opportunities and pitfalls lie. Thus the objective here in clarifying the benefits of interdisciplinary exchange is not to identify the 'essential core' of two extraordinarily diverse and contested fields, but rather to encourage a synthesis that moves beyond (not replicates) the limitations of each and to justify disciplinary integration at the scale of academic institutions (not just the publishing practices of individual scholars).

The first point of convergence could build on the injunction from anthropology to understand how globalizing processes exist in the context of the realities of particular societies – with their historically specific cultures and ways of life (Inda and Rosaldo 2002). Globalization studies must encompass an understanding of how macroeconomic processes and transnational cultural flows articulate with historically specific cultures and ways of life at the local scale. For however much more powerful other scales of influence and action may be, it is at the local scale that globalization is anchored, subsidized, transformed in the individual consumption and production practices necessary for its sustenance. Viewing the 'local' and the 'global' relationally in this way highlights how global capitalism and the international state system have been decisively shaped at the local scale – through the diverse ways people have interpreted what was happening to them, as well as through the ways so-called peripheral peoples in particular constitute the centre by demarcating a zone of marginality. Thus, for example, Tanya Li (1999) illustrates how national development planners mobilize the category of 'primitive people' to define the centre as 'ordinary'. Sidney Mintz shows how the meaning of sugar for the lives of English people and its meaning for the British imperial economy converged in the nineteenth century as a critical conjuncture in the development of global capitalism: English people began to see sugar as essential for living and supplying them with it became as much a political as an economic obligation (1986: 157). Mintz's study of cultural meanings corroborates other anthropological evidence that demand, fashion and taste are central to a cultural account of the origins of capitalism (e.g. Appadurai 1986; Mukerji 1983). It also poses a challenge to study the spread and intensification of global capitalism in terms of everyday practices and interpretations in local communities.

Second, globalization studies should explicitly consider the role and position of the periphery in globalizing processes. Too often theories of globalization are developed with exclusive reference to western experiences of state building and colonial expansion. For example, as Philip Kelly argues, the idea that globalization has entailed a 'hollowing out' of the nation-state, an idea that circulates widely within geography, is built on ethnocentric assumptions about the 'common experience of the emergence of the state in the nineteenth century and its zenith in the postwar Fordist regime of accumulation' (1999: 390). It ignores ongoing processes of postcolonial state building in the East and South. Were the latter to become part of the equation, a more nuanced understanding of the relationship between the state and economic globalization might emerge, one that recognized that '[w]hile some State functions … might be rendered more difficult to implement under globalization, others are in fact more effectively conducted' (Kelly 1999: 390).

Cultural geographers and, increasingly, cultural anthropologists have argued that it is no longer necessary to conduct research in peripheral areas in order to see and understand difference (Gupta and Ferguson 2002; Inda and Rosaldo 2002). Indeed, the metropolitan centres of the West, which are also the centres of academic production, have themselves become sites of rich cross-cultural exchange, as important destinations in the diasporas of cultures and peoples. The possibilities for conducting cross-cultural research in the metropolitan centres of academia, notwithstanding, I believe anthropology still offers an important rationale for travel away from metropolitan centres; for it is only by conducting research in peripheral areas that we can understand the implications of globalization for places that have less influence in the imperial balance of power. Sherry Ortner's comments about the limitations of narrowly

political-economic approaches in anthropology are relevant to illustrate
this latter point:

> History is often treated as something that arrives, like a ship, from outside the
> society in question. Political economists ... tend to situate themselves more on
> the ship of (capitalist) history than on the shore. They say in effect that we can
> never know what the other system ... really looked like anyway ... . To such a
> position we can only respond: Try. The effort is as important as the results ... .
> It is our [anthropologists'] capacity, largely developed in fieldwork, to take the
> perspective of the folks on the shore, that allows us to learn anything at all ...
> beyond what we already know. Further, it is our location 'on the ground' that puts
> us in a position to see people not simply as passive reactors to ... some 'system,'
> but as active agents and subjects of their own history. (1984: 143)

With its emphasis on local agency, in other words, anthropology pushes
globalization studies to recognize the dialectical relationship between
local and global scales of practice. While the articulation of local culture
with macroeconomic processes is always ordered by asymmetrical power
relations, it cannot be reduced merely to the exercise of power by the
latter over the former; rather the joining of local and global produces an
interplay of systems that reorders both, creating new social formations.
As Jean Comaroff argues, 'the relationship of a global system to a
local formation must be viewed as a historical problem – inherently
contradictory and unequal, and not universally determining' (1985 cited
in Pigg 1990: 22).

Third, globalization studies can turn to geography for tools to analyse
the significance of place and scale in understanding the cultures and
economies of globalization. Clearly, the context of globalization has
made it impossible, at least unreasonable, to assume (as anthropologists
are wont to do) an isomorphism between culture and place. Transnational
patterns of migration, the circulation of certain commodities to the far
corners of the globe, the ease with which television and the Internet
now transmit images around the world – all these forms of cultural
flow weaken ties between culture and place. Drawing especially on the
work of David Harvey, anthropologists have begun to recognize the
importance of a 'spatial consciousness' for grappling with the contemporary
movement of peoples, ideas and images. Thus Inda and Rosaldo (2002)
and Gupta and Ferguson (2002) talk about the 'deterritorialization of
culture' associated with the 'dislodging of cultural subjects and objects
from particular or fixed locations in space and time' (Inda and Rodaldo
2002: 11). At the same time, they have emphasized how culture has
been 'reterritorialized' – how cultural forms and products, images and
ideas, as well as human diasporas are always reinscribed in specific

cultural environments, however much they may travel the world. Thus culture continues to have a 'territorialized existence', but the placing of culture has grown increasingly unstable. Place still matters, but only in articulation with other scales of cultural and economic production – regional and national, as much as global.

Crucially, an emphasis on place and scale also challenges conventional models of articulation that rely on the notion of 'traditional', 'pre-capitalist', 'primitive' cultures that once existed autonomously but have now been violated by global capitalism. Traditional articulation models, however much they leave analytical space to explore the unintended consequences of inter-scalar connections, are analogous to discourses of cultural imperialism and homogenization in their treatment of culture as a fixed system of symbols and meanings that structure social life. The geographic intervention calls for historical explorations of the processes that go into place-making in the first instance; as Gupta and Ferguson put it (and as illustrated in Chapter 3), 'instead of assuming the autonomy of the primeval community, we need to examine how it was formed *as a community* out of the interconnected space that always already existed' (2002: 67). A historical approach to the construction of place foregrounds changes in the spatial distribution of hierarchical relations over time. It thus offers an antidote to the tendency in much of the critical literature on neoliberalism to essentialize, romanticize and indeed imagine the lingering existence of autonomous 'remote', 'non-capitalist' cultures that might offer guidelines for constructing an alternative to capitalism.

In so doing, it guards against uncritical celebrations of 'local culture' by documenting systems of domination that operate within the periphery as much as across the core–periphery divide.

Finally, a synthesis of the contributions of anthropology and geography in the study of globalization could draw out the normative thrust implicit in anthropological theories of practice, to reflect the more explicit normative stance characteristic of geography. Practice theory has provided anthropologists with the tools to highlight social differentiation and analyse how power operates through culture. It has offered a framework for distinguishing acquiescence from critical consciousness and for recognizing the political possibilities opened up in the present political–economic conjuncture for those in subordinate social locations. Yet anthropologists have not conventionally taken practice theory to its logical (and intended) conclusion as a foundation for cultural critique and action. Here there is considerable scope to draw on the normative commitments expressed by geographers – for example in the recent attempts to claim the global scale as a site not just for neoliberal hegemony but also for accountability to a global civil society. The call here for synthesis thus presents an opportunity to extend the concern with 'practice' into the more activist domain of 'praxis'. In the domain of praxis, research itself becomes a form of practice with the injunction to make judgements, advocate change and empower informants to view their world critically.

To this end, the remaining chapters of this book conjoin an ethnographic approach to exploring the politics of culture with the multi-scalar and normative commitments developed within geography. Approaches deriving from practice theory within anthropology highlight social differentiation within any given social system; they emphasize how power operates through culture and provide the tools to detect both acquiescence and critical consciousness on the part of those in subordinate social positions. I investigate specifically caste and gender ideologies that underpin the Newar cultural economy in Sankhu, stressing the disadvantages faced by (and strategically mobilized by) low castes and women in the accumulation of symbolic and material capital. The geographic concern with multiple scales of influence raises the question of how local cultural economies articulate with political-economic processes operating at wider spatial scales. The book devotes two chapters to pursuing this question: Chapter 3 examines the historical constitution of Sankhu in relation to the evolution of Buddhism in India and the development of the trans-Himalayan overland trade in the early centuries of the Christian era. It also traces how the town's historical position as a trading entrepôt interfaced in the nineteenth and twentieth centuries with the consolidation of a national Hindu polity in Nepal – itself formed in relation to British colonial ambitions on the subcontinent. Chapter 6 examines the contemporary context of economic liberalization and concentrates particularly on how ideologies of caste and gender in Sankhu filter macroeconomic currents, setting new parameters for individual practice and mediating experiences of globalization. The emphasis throughout on culture as political practice highlights the critical resources within culture, should planners learn how to recognize them.

3 GENEALOGY OF MARKETS AND EXCHANGE

The synthesis of anthropological and geographical approaches offered in Chapter 2 and the notion of an 'economics of practice' introduced in Chapter 1 provide a theoretical foundation for turning now to the ethnographic content of the book – in Chapters 3 to 6 – which detail the intricacies of social production at the local scale and their articulation with wider-scale macroeconomic processes. We begin with a 'genealogy of markets and exchange' that locates the Newar merchant town of Sankhu in relation to cultural, political and economic currents on the Indian subcontinent and illustrates the significance of place-making for understanding processes of social production. The goal here is to illustrate the Polanyian notion of social embeddedness by showing how Sankhu constitutes a site where religion and trade historically interacted (and reinforced each other), and where trade likewise played an important role in processes of state-building. This historical inquiry provides a foundation for interpreting, in the following ethnographic chapters, the cultural economy of Sankhu today and how it articulates with the economic rationalities of neoliberalism.

The Kathmandu Valley, within which Sankhu lies, has been engaged in monetary exchanges and market integration on a continental scale from as far back as the fifth century BCE. This chapter thus views the Valley as a society constructing its cultures and economies in interaction with the populations of the trans-Himalayan, South Asian and Central Asian region (see Map 3.1). It traces how markets developed first in articulation with the evolution of Buddhist doctrine and later with the consolidation of a Hindu polity and the construction of the Nepalese nation-state in the vortex of British imperialist expansion on the Indian subcontinent. The chapter views this history from the perspective of the culturally, commercially and politically significant town of Sankhu. Through its strategic location in the northeast corner of the Kathmandu Valley, Sankhu occupied an important position in trans-Himalayan

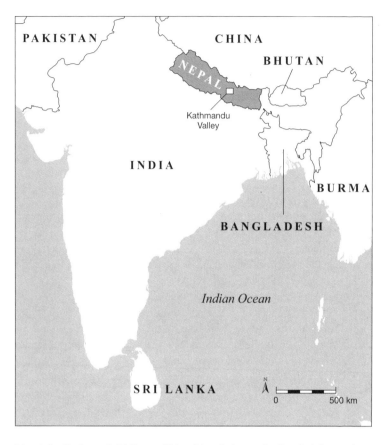

Map 3.1   Kathmandu Valley and Nepal in relation to the South Asian region

trade networks, which were bound up with the emergence of Vajrayana
Buddhism, and, as the site of the popular Vajrayogini temple, Sankhu
still enjoys distinction in these important cultural developments. From
the mid-eighteenth century, Sankhu played a role in the military conquest
that consolidated the territorial origins of present-day Nepal. Within the
national polity, Sankhu was the seat of administration of the Tibet trade,
and its lands contributed to a regressive system of rewarding political
patronage of the ruling elite.

The account here of Nepal's relationship with political-economic and
cultural forces stirring on the subcontinent and beyond is intended to
disrupt two dominant narratives that have typically shaped ideas about
how to develop peripheral economies. First, as discussed in Chapter 1,

is the view that markets, and the economy in general, could be separate from the spheres of politics and culture. I argue that the political and cultural embeddedness of markets in Sankhu today can only be understood with recourse to the complex webs of their historical articulation with regional cultural and political processes. The second narrative relates specifically to Newars (who inhabit Sankhu and other major urbanized areas of the Kathmandu Valley), but has been applied with equal force, as noted in Chapter 2, to other societies with strong traditions of gifting, ritual practice and religious devotion. Popular representations (especially those for tourist consumption) and even some ethnographic writings portray Newar communities as frozen in the medieval past, isolated in a 'timeless ritual dance' (Levy 1990), available for viewing from a twenty-first-century lens (e.g. Haaland 1988; Sekelj 1959 cited in Liechty 1997). The viewing is made all the more compelling by the fact that much of the existing architecture and town planning, most notably the spectacular pagoda temples, hails from the sixteenth to nineteenth centuries. It is thus no accident that much of the development work that transpires in Newar towns of the Kathmandu Valley concentrates on historic preservation – on Newars' material culture as opposed to their health, education or income generation – as if to freeze their societies in time and space as living relics of the distant past.

Like all historical accounts, the representation offered in this chapter is partial and interpretive, and it is also 'genealogical' in the Foucauldian sense, to the extent that it is constructed in opposition to these dominant narratives (Foucault 1977). In exploring the genealogy of markets and exchange, it considers a 'heterogeneity of origins' and a 'multiplicity of factors' that might shed critical light on the cultural economy of Sankhu today. And it draws on both conventional historical sources, such as archival documents and inscriptions, and more 'subjugated' forms of knowledge, such as oral chronicles, legend and myth, in order to reflect the complex relationships among local forms of knowledge. Today Sankhu occupies a relatively marginal position in the Valley's political economy – as a satellite town beyond the reach of Kathmandu's sprawling development and cut off from the Valley's main arteries of development and transportation. Viewing the Valley's economic history from Sankhu, however, reveals just how misleading it can be to discard isolated places as 'peripheral' to modern developments.

NEWAR ETHNICITY IN THE NATION-STATE OF NEPAL

It must first be noted that the Newars indigenous to Sankhu and the other towns and cities of the Kathmandu Valley present some anomalies for those who wish to classify them. The first classificatory anomaly relates to the disjuncture between Newars' minority status and their indisputable significance in the history of Nepal. Newars are represented in national accounting statistics and in official discourses as one of the country's 47 designated ethnic groups. As such, according to the Central Bureau of Statistics (HMG 2001), they comprise only 5.5 per cent of Nepal's total population of 23.1 million.[1] Likewise, the Kathmandu Valley occupies a very small area of the national terrain – 25 km from east to west and about 19 km at its maximum width, relative to the roughly 150,000 square km that constitutes Nepal. Yet Newars of the Kathmandu Valley historically achieved a cultural and commercial significance entirely disproportionate to their relatively marginal demographic and territorial position. The high, fertile valley – located between the hazardous Himalayan passes to Tibet in the north and the malarial Gangetic plains to the south – has supported complex, urbanized, monarchical societies with sophisticated and distinct traditions in art, architecture and literature since at least the fourth century CE. Newar culture and society evolved and flourished in the Valley, largely impervious to threats of outside conquest, from the early centuries of the Christian era to the mid-eighteenth century. The rich Newar cultural legacy can be traced today as much in religious and social institutions governing contemporary social life as seen in the physical relics – temples and shrines, sacred sites and ancestral monuments – that are still scattered across the Valley's landscape and animate Newar ritual practice.

Newar cultural efflorescence developed in direct articulation with the Valley's important role in the trans-Himalayan trade. Of some two dozen passes into Tibet, the lowest lie directly northwest and northeast of the Valley, proximate to the Tibetan entrepôts, Kyirong and Kuti respectively (see Map 3.2). The routes through the Kathmandu Valley were also the shortest link between the cities of the Gangetic lowlands and China until an alternative route was opened through Sikkim in the late nineteenth century. This strategic geographic location, combined with the Valley's isolation from neighbouring Indian, Tibetan and Chinese civilizations, enabled its rulers to control these valuable trade routes between India and China for over a millennium. The wealth deriving from the trans-Himalayan trade endowed the impressive cultural institutions of the Kathmandu Valley (the monasteries, temples, religious associations and so on), as well as extraordinary traditions in art, architecture and literature necessary to sustain them. But it also eventually attracted the attention of neighbouring rulers. Most notable among these was Prithvi

Narayan Shah, king of the tiny, impoverished hill state of Gorkha, who conquered the Valley in 1768; from there he launched a spectacular campaign to unify the other warring principalities of the Himalayan region, constituting the origins of the present-day Hindu state of Nepal as a major regional power on the Indian subcontinent.

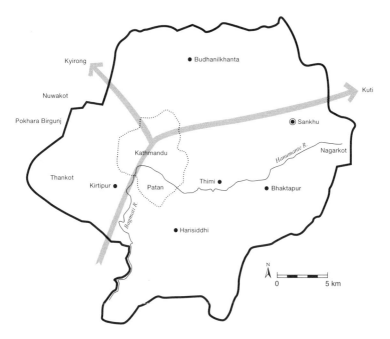

Map 3.2   Two overland trade routes through the Kathmandu Valley

Second, Newars are commonly classified, along with other ethnic groups residing in the middle hills, as 'Tibeto-Burman', on the basis of their mother-tongue, Newari, and their strong Buddhist traditions. Yet they can be distinguished from other Tibeto-Burman groups by their complex urban civilizations and well-articulated processes of Indian acculturation – beginning with Buddhism, but increasingly consolidating institutions and practices associated with Hinduism. By historian Mary Slusser's (1982: 38) reckoning, the proto-Newar society of the ancient Licchivi period (fourth to ninth centuries CE) 'was regulated in accordance with the norms of contemporary Indian society' – with an absolute monarch, a hierarchically stratified and occupationally determining caste system, the

Indian *gosthi* (common interest group; precursor to the Newar *guthi* to be discussed at length in Chapters 4 and 5), polygyny as the rule, 'divorce possible, and *sati* (widow immolation) a fact'.[2] Licchivi kings (the first known dynasty of the Kathmandu Valley) are known to have encouraged the practice of many faiths, but a second documented dynasty, that of the Malla kings, increasingly codified Hindu scriptures and institutions (most notably caste) beginning in the thirteenth century and eroded the status of Buddhism in Newar society. The prevalence of caste as a system ordering social and ritual life is particularly noteworthy given that its hierarchical premises contradict the fundamental Buddhist belief in the equal worth of all human beings. But it is not sufficient to understand Newar society solely in terms of the Brahmanical idiom of purity and pollution underpinning the caste system and the seclusion of women. In fact, Hindu and Buddhist deities continue to occupy an important place in Newar ritual life today and the Buddhist priest caste, the Varjaracharyas, are on an equal footing with Brahman priests in a caste structure that Gellner (1992) has described as 'double headed'. Despite the popular 'Tibeto-Burman' designation associated with their linguistic roots, then, Newar cultures are most aptly characterized as an accretion of influences, many of which derive from the Indian subcontinent.[3]

Third, Newar 'high' culture – its art, architecture and literature – climaxed during the medieval period of the Malla kings (1200–1769 CE), at a time when Newar society also experienced tremendous fragmentation. Following a period of relative stability – and associated prosperity and cultural efflorescence (1382–1482) – competing fraternal heirs to the Malla throne began competing for control over the three urban centres of the Kathmandu Valley. Competition between the Malla monarchs was manifested not merely in military rivalries over the city-states of Kathmandu, Patan and Bhaktapur, but also in cultural pursuits. Each sought to outdo the others in the beauty and magnificence of his own capital. As Slusser (1982: 74) describes, the Malla rulers 'built temples and *vihāras* [monasteries], commissioned diverse images, Buddhist and Hindu, and in accordance with *dharma*, donated water tanks, fountains, and rest houses, together with lavish endowments for their maintenance'. They also liberally patronized the arts – the bronze casting, stone carving, and architecture with its associated decorative wood carving and metal repoussé for which the Newars are renowned (as well as dance, music, literature and painting). The Mallas' characteristic pagoda temples still contour the skyline of Newar towns and cities today and the ornately carved wooden lattice windows hailing from the period of intense Malla patronage still distinguish their main thoroughfares. Such remnants of Malla patronage are the focus of contemporary efforts at historic preservation throughout the Kathmandu Valley. In the end, however, the long-standing feuds that had sparked the Mallas' cultural investments prevented them from standing up to incursions by outside rulers. Prithvi Narayan Shah, king of Gorkha, in particular, strategically played the competing Malla kings off against one another, ultimately to claim their impressive cultural institutions (and the Himalayan trade sustaining them) as his own.

The fourth classificatory problem relates to the fact that Newar identity evolved in relation to – indeed in opposition to – Parbatiya cultural domination, rather than as an expression of a single, primordial Newar culture.[4] In fact, each of the three Newar city-states (and to a lesser extent, the Newar towns of the Kathmandu Valley) developed its own distinctive dialect and cultural traditions. The use of the name 'Newar' to signify collectively the indigenous people of the Kathmandu Valley emerged only in the seventeeth century CE, about the time the Gorkhalis (themselves ethnically Parbatiya) made their first incursions into the Kathmandu Valley. According to Slusser (1982: 9) '[t]he word Newar is generally assumed to be interchangeable with and derived from Nepal and to signify simply the people of the Nepal [Kathmandu] Valley, specifically the indigenes'. British missionaries and Gorkhali rulers distinguished the designations 'Newar' and 'Nepal' – using the former for the indigenous peoples of the Kathmandu Valley and the latter for the national state comprised of the territories newly consolidated by Prithvi Narayan Shah and his successors.[5] The politics of classification (of Newars by Parbatiya rulers) extends as well to the matter of caste identity. For the purposes of administering a diffuse state and constructing a unifying national (Hindu) ideology, the early Shah rulers assimilated Newars, along with other non-Parbatiya groups, into the Parbatiya caste structure – assigning them a position below Chetris and, as 'clean castes', above Untouchables.[6] Except for Newar Brahmans and Newar Untouchables, Newars were designated as a single 'caste', in spite of the fact that Newar society itself has its own caste hierarchy, more ritually and occupationally elaborate than that of the Parbatiyas. Thus an early pan-Newar identity emerged only in the process of the Newars' collective subjugation to Parbatiya rulers through tactics of cultural assimilation.

Newar ethnic consciousness flourished into a strong *cultural-nationalist* movement precisely at the historical moment when the Newars faced the greatest cultural persecution within the national polity – during the century of oppressive rule by the Rana (warrior-caste Parbatiya) family, who reduced the line of Shah kings to the position of figureheads and ruled as a dynasty of hereditary prime ministers from 1850 to 1951. Elite Newars in particular turned to Newari literature and art as a means to resist Rana power, even as the Ranas banned the Newari language from official discourses and the press. Anthropologist Bal Gopal Shrestha (1999) calls the period from 1900 to 1940 the 'Newari literary renaissance', since this period witnessed the emergence of several prolific Newari authors (including several from the town of Sankhu) and hundreds of (underground) Newari publications. Newar Buddhist monks and scholars exiled to India convened the first Newari literary organization in 1926, but it was not until the late 1970s and early 1980s that formal (registered) Newar organizations and publications could operate in Nepal and begin to build a more popular sense of Newar consciousness. By this time the Ranas had been overthrown by a coalition of underground political parties and the Shah king. Under the succeeding Panchayat system of 'partyless democracy' and the more recent 'parliamentary democracy' (in which the king retains many absolute powers), Newars and other ethnic groups have been accorded still more freedom to organize along cultural nationalist lines.[7] Yet place-based differences continue to impede possibilities for a truly pan-Newar identity. Caste, too, presents another intractable fracture; in fact among Newars the term 'Newar' is commonly used to denote only the economically and ritually dominant Shrestha Merchant caste.[8]

SANKHU: SOCIO-ECONOMIC CONTEXT

The town of Sankhu illustrates well the cultural and commercial significance of Newars, the accretion of Tibeto-Burman and Indian influences, and the relational nature of Newar identity. It has been selected for this study specifically for its prominent position in the ancient trans-Himalayan trade route linking Central Asia with the Indian subcontinent and beyond to the Middle East, Europe and the New World. Sankhu is located in the northeast corner of the Kathmandu Valley, 17 km from Kathmandu City itself and is almost entirely populated by Newars, predominantly by Merchant-caste Shresthas (see Map 3.2). The town falls within Kathmandu District, but is administered politically by three different Village Development Committees.[9] Especially since the institution of a multi-party system in 1990, administrative fragmentation has spawned considerable political factionalism in Sankhu (see B.G. Shrestha 2002 for details). The factionalism in political matters starkly contradicts the socio-cultural and ritual unity deriving from webs of sociality among

Sankhu Newars and the characteristic occasions for feast and festival described in Chapter 4. The town has five government schools (three primary and two secondary) and seven private 'boarding schools' (code for 'English-medium' in Nepal). According to a survey conducted in 1997 by B.G. Shrestha (2002), primary education is nearly universal among children, but only 23 per cent of the population has completed a secondary education (up to grade 10), of which less than one-quarter have gone on to complete the 'intermediate' level (grades 11–12). Less than 1 per cent of the population of 5,340 (as estimated by Shrestha) has pursued studies beyond the BA level. And over one-fifth of the population (917 women, compared to 313 men) is illiterate. As there are no hospitals and only one rarely attended health post in the town, most residents rely on traditional healers (*vaidya*) engaging secret mantras and tantric methods. Most households do not have indoor plumbing; they draw their water from public wells and taps, and use open outdoor latrines or private indoor manual-flush toilets (located on the ground floor where they will not compromise the ritual purity of the house).

Like all Newar towns of the Valley, Sankhu can be described as an 'agritown' – characterized by dense residential settlements surrounded by agricultural lands which form an important source of livelihood for all but approximately one-sixth of the estimated 790 households (Shrestha 2002). The town's two main north–south thoroughfares abut four gates (*dhvākā*) marking the formal points of entry and exit still observed on various ritual occasions (see Map 3.3).[10] The thoroughfares are linked at regular intervals by several east–west running roads, forming a basic grid pattern within which winds a maze of congested laneways (*galli*) amidst the compact brick row-houses. The major roads are good enough for motor vehicles and are traversed by the occasional taxi or lorry. As the town's bus and truck depot is located outside the southwestern gate (*Bhaudvākā*), however, the brick, cobble and dirt roads within the town are travelled primarily by foot or, less frequently, motorcycle. (Shrestha's survey revealed that only 39 households in Sankhu own a motorcycle.)

At eight major intersections the roadways open into large, bricked public squares that form neighborhood centres (*tvaḥ*). These squares are populated by assemblages of temples, shrines, god-images, resting places, water taps and open stages and they are the site of much social, economic and ritual activity. Ponds and private gardens also break up the dense residential fabric. Roads, laneways and open squares are hemmed by the characteristic Newar two-to-four-storey brick row-houses (with tiled or thatched roofs and open wood-framed windows). Well-off households

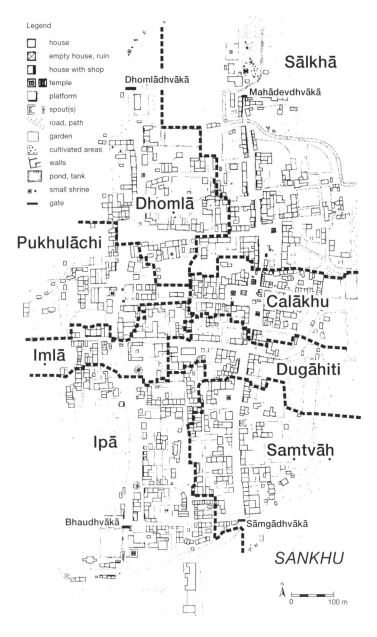

Map 3.3   Map of Sankhu showing significant thoroughfares and structures

Source: Shrestha (2002)

bordering the major roads often boast the intricately carved, latticed windows for which Newars are renowned (or, recently, they build cement houses with glassed windows and tin roofs). Some households must be entered via interior courtyards, accessible only by low, narrow passageways, and centred around a *caitya*, or small domed shrine. Shops and businesses, typically incorporated into the ground floor of houses and of which there are over 200 in Sankhu, line the major roads and are concentrated in the bazaar at the northern end of the eastern north–south thoroughfare.

Agricultural lands surrounding the town are terraced as necessary to maximize flat terrain suitable for wet rice cultivation. Newars farm the land intensively by hand (two rice crops per year with potato or wheat as the winter crop), on landholdings that range from 1 to 30 *ropāni* (Shrestha 2002; 8 *ropāni* equals 1 hectare), and (according to my randomly sampled 150-household survey conducted in 1995), average 5 *ropāni*. Though rarely producing rice in quantities sufficient for household consumption, most households (85 per cent) are engaged in agriculture to supplement other sources of livelihood.[11] There has been a steady decline in dependence on agriculture, as productivity decreases (due to long-term use of chemical fertilizers) and as landholdings are increasingly fragmented through inheritance distributions.[12] Nonetheless, the fields around Sankhu remain as agricultural land. They have not succumbed to high-end new home construction or the slow, steady spread of brick factories that are common in other agricultural areas of the Kathmandu Valley. Sankhu is thus relatively free from the air pollution choking the wider Valley, and is known for its fresh air, lush fields, and surrounding wooded hillsides.

CULTURAL FOUNDATIONS OF TRADE

Monastic Origins

Among the roughly 35 Newar towns that dot the Kathmandu Valley, Sankhu's notoriety derives from its historical prosperity as an important entrepôt on the trans-Himalayan trade route and from the temple of its patron goddess, Vajrayogini (as well as the less-known adjacent *Gum Vihāra*, forest monastery), located on the adjacent forested hillside to the north. These two key dimensions of the town's cohesion and identity are in fact closely linked, and it is impossible to understand one without recourse to the other. Sankhu's prominence as a trading entrepôt emerged in close relation to its status as a centre of Buddhist teachings and specifically as an important site for the articulation of Vajrayana Buddhism.

The specific 'path dependency' or historical trajectory of social embeddedness described here is significant for understanding how markets operate in Sankhu today – the role of social investments in religious and social institutions, for instance, or the distribution of wealth rooted in caste-based occupations. In order to emphasize these connections, the following sections offer considerable anthropological and historical detail about the cultural, religious and political contexts within which commerce evolved in Sankhu and the wider Kathmandu Valley.

Like all ritually significant Newar towns, Sankhu has its own oral tradition that details the town's mythic formation by its patron goddess. It is said that the goddess Vajrayogini formed the Sankhu Valley by cleaving the ridge on its southwestern edge with her sword.[13] According to the chronicles (*vaṃsāvalī*), the goddess Vajrayogini emanated as a bright light from a jewel stone at the centre of the mountain, Manicuda, which lies just north of Sankhu.[14] Many years later she sowed a seed below a tree in the forest of Manicuda mountain and the tree gave birth to a child whom Varjayogini named Samkhadeva (and from whom some believed Sankhu derived its name). Once he grew up, Vajroyogini instructed her *bodhisattva* priest to create a kingdom in the shape of a conch shell and make Samkhadeva its king.[15] The kingdom of Samkhapur was to be formed through the union of seven villages and it was to encompass eight quarters (*tvaḥ*), four gates, nine monasteries (*bahā*), eight shrines of the mother goddess (*pīṭha*), roads in all four directions and a palace at the centre. Some years later, Vajrayogini instructed the priest to initiate an eight-day festival in her honour, involving all the people of the kingdom. For this a statue was created in her image, which was to be carried down annually from the forested realm of the gods into the civilized realm of humankind, where her procession could map out the territory of Samkhapur and recall its divine creation.

Historical evidence does not corroborate the chronicles' claims for an independent kingdom, although the ordered system of quarters, roads, shrines and gates exist as prescribed in the chronicles and continue to hold ritual significance for the residents of Sankhu (the former palace no longer stands and monastic complexes serve today primarily as residences of Vajracharya priests). The oldest inscriptional evidence, discovered by anthropologist Bal Gopal Shrestha, is dated 538 CE and records a land donation to a socio-religious association (*guthi,* believed to have derived from the Indian Licchivi *goṣṭhī*).[16] Inscriptions dated through the Malla period do not offer details on the history of the town so it can only be speculated, based on Shrestha's discovery, that the town dates from at least the sixth century CE. Daniel Wright's (1958) edited chronicles attribute the founding of Sankhu to a King Sankaradeva in the eleventh century (1069–83), although there is no historical evidence to corroborate this claim. More likely, as Shrestha (2002: 54) suggests, Sankhu was 'like a princely state or a fort under control of Kantipur (Kathmandu) or Bhaktapur, but not a separate kingdom as the chronicles testify'. Meanwhile, Wright's chronicles attribute the initiation of the Vajrayogini festival to Surya Malla, King of Kathmandu (1520–30), who 'took ... Sankhapur from the Bhatgaon [Bhaktapur] Raja. He went to live at Sankhapur [Sankhu], and in order to please the goddess Bajra Jogini, he instituted her *ratha jātrā* [chariot festival]' (Wright 1958 [1877]: 125).[17]

The Vajrayogini festival continues to be staged annually, as a much-anticipated visit by the patron deity to the town and a ritual reminder of the town's mythical creation. An entourage of deities, their life-sized images cast in bronze, is hauled down from the temple to the town on huge wooden chariots, processed around the town, and rigorously bathed, dined and worshipped for the duration of the festival. The festival traces the spatial structure of the town, demarcating ritual borders between the human realm and the wilderness where Vajrayogini resides, and establishing the town's ritually significant physical features – the quarters, monastic complexes, procession routes and the central palace (among others). For the eight days of the festival, the streets of Sankhu swell with devotees and revellers, and the commercial activities of the town come to a virtual halt. Conventional economic and social relationships are suspended – money-lenders are prohibited from collecting debts and caste distinctions are relaxed, in order to emphasize the equality of humanity before the goddess. Households and local governments incur enormous expenses (estimated cumulatively by Shrestha [2002: 392] at NRs 3 million [US $55,000] in 1997) in order to orchestrate the public festival as well as carry out obligations of feasting, hospitality and gifting within the home.[18] For these eight days, then, an ancient ritual encompasses the socio-economic infrastructure of the town, constitutes the town ceremonially and imposes a cosmic order on the mundane trappings of human life – all of which demand enormous social investments.

Of greater significance for the immediate purpose of tracing the town's commercial history is a monastery called *Gum Vihāra* (Forest Monastery) located just above the Vajrayogini temple itself, and which may in fact significantly pre-date it. The earliest inscriptional evidence places the monastery in the fifth century CE, although historian Dhanavajra Vajracharya speculates that it actually dates from the pre-Licchivi period (before the fourth century CE), based on the nomenclature used in the

Licchivi inscriptions at the temple.[19] Vajracharya also suggests that *Gum Vihāra* housed a group of dissident *Mahāsāngik* monks by the early centuries of the Christian era, based on an undated Licchivi inscription found in Sankhu (Vajracharya 1973: 320–35, 382–3, 508–10, quoted in Slusser 1982: 273; see also Shrestha 2002). Following a series of disagreements over Buddha's doctrine, *Mahāsāngik* dissidents in India formed a sect in the first century BCE rejecting the strict interpretation of Buddha by Theravaada, in favour of adapting the Buddha's doctrine to the needs of the time. Vajracharya argues that the inscription in Sankhu marking a donation to a *Mahāsāngik* monk places the residence of sect members at *Gum Vihāra* in the pre-Licchivi period, because it refers to the monk as '*Mahāsāngik*' rather than '*Mahāyāna*', the name later applied to this sect.

The monastic complexes of the *Mahāsāngik* monks were centred on the northwestern Indian coast, from where they travelled overland with merchants between India and China (Kosambi 1965: 182–4) and it is through these markets that they must have taken up residence at *Gum Vihāra*. The monks are known to have provided both capital for the merchants' trading missions and a market for the luxury goods they obtained in China (through expenditures on their ornate monasteries). Such dissident sects gave rise to a new Vehicle in Buddhism, Vajrayana, characterized by its tantric practices and a priesthood that embraces the secular responsibilities of householding. When Indian Vajrayana Buddhism emerged in the third century CE within the Mahayana tradition, it 'challenged the superiority of monastic renunciation' and introduced Tantricism, the most essential feature of which is 'a belief in the efficacy of ritual and hence in the miraculous powers of those who possess the most effective rites' (Allen 1973: 2; see also Gellner 1992: 108–14; Leve 2000). By the mid-seventh century CE Vajrayana had become firmly established in Nepal; according to Zanen (1986: 126), 'The goddess Vajrayogini became one of its principle deities and in Nepal her cult was centred on the hill above Sankhu.'

The earliest records of the related flows of trade and Buddhist doctrine to and from Nepal refer more generally to the Kathmandu Valley. Monks from the early Buddhist centre of Sravasti left accounts dating from the fifth and sixth centuries BCE of their travels through the Valley with Indian wool merchants (Kosambi 1965). Sravasti, where the Buddha is known to have delivered most of his sermons, also lay at the intersection of the major Indian trade routes, *Uttarāpatha* (which linked the Gangetic plains with the Near East) and *Dakṣiṇāpatha* (which traversed south to the Deccan plain; see Map 3.4). It was via these routes that the teachings

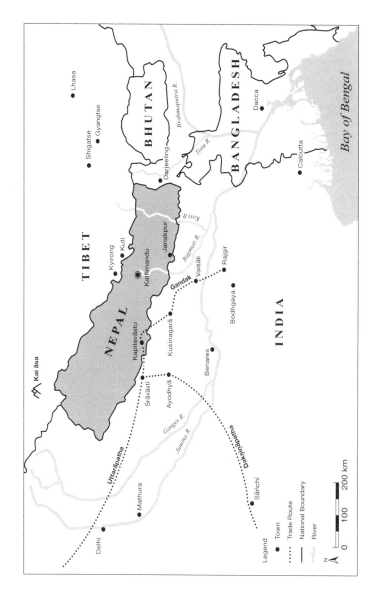

Map 3.4 Ancient overland trade routes in relation to contemporary political boundaries on the Indian subcontinent

of Buddha himself spread throughout India in the sixth century BCE. Buddhist doctrine travelled with trade to the Kathmandu Valley along the route that branched north at Sravasti.[20] By the time of the Licchivi period (fourth century CE), both commerce and Buddhism flourished in the Valley, where the temperate climate and fertile soil offered a preferred transfer point between the Buddhist centres and trading emporiums of South and Central Asia. Travellers were often detained for months at a time waiting for a suitable season to pass north through the Himalayas or south through the malarial jungles. There thus gathered an eclectic and cosmopolitan mix of characters – 'pilgrim and scholar, mendicant and monk, artisan and ambassadorial entourage' – among whom 'exchanges took place between hands and minds that profoundly affected Nepalese history' (Slusser 1982: 6).

The opening of the Kuti pass and the consolidation of Tibet in the seventh century CE greatly facilitated the transit of merchants and Buddhist teachers between India and China (D.R. Regmi 1960: 181–2). Legend has it that in his negotiations with the Licchivi king over the hand of a princess, Tibetan Emperor Srong-brstan-sgam-po promised to adopt the Buddhist doctrine for Tibet, and thus commenced the tradition of monastic Mahāyāna Buddhism in Tibet. Until the beginning of the Malla dynasty in the early thirteenth century, the Kathmandu Valley itself flourished as a centre of Buddhist scholarship in its own right. During this period, monks and pilgrims from India, China and Tibet travelled to study in Nepal's monastic complexes, some of which Slusser (1982: 281) likens to the Buddhist university centres of Bengal and Bihar. One of these was, of course, *Gum Vihāra*, and, given the historic relation between Buddhism and trade, it should be no surprise that a fully serviced trading entrepôt would also develop in this location. Residents of Sankhu today claim that the town's name derives from the Newari *Sakva*, which translates as 'below Tibet', and refers to the town's favourable location as the last market outpost within the Kathmandu Valley on the northeastern trade route to Lhasa through the Kuti pass.[21]

The Valley's prominence as a trading emporium long outlasted its role as a source of dynamism within Buddhism. The Muslim conquests, while sending a final wave of refugees to the Valley in the twelfth century, ultimately severed the revitalizing religious ties to India (Allen 1973: 4; see also Slusser 1982: 68, 288). A strong tradition of monastic Mahayana Buddhism soon developed within Tibet, thus attenuating its steady flow of monks and scholars travelling south for study. Within Nepal the Malla kings began aggressively to impose a Hindu theology, most notably with Sthiti Malla's codification of the caste system in the late fourteenth century. Partly in response to the loss of royal patronage, the Vajrayana Buddhism that had emerged within Nepal drifted from its original monastic to a more secular orientation grounded more deeply in the responsibilities of householding. Although this transition accorded Buddhist priests high status within secular contexts – basically as 'Buddhist Brahmans' (Slusser, 1982: 288) – it also irreversibly weakened the clerical institutions of Buddhism in the Valley.

Anthropologist Michael Allen (1973: 13–14) argues that the emergence of a 'folk' dimension to Vajrayana Buddhism – including its householder tradition; its high valuation of sexuality, meat, alcohol and other sensory pleasures; and its development of popular cults such as the Vajrayogini festival in Sankhu – enabled Buddhism in Nepal to survive the ascendance of a dominant Hindu polity. In Sankhu, the continued practice of Vajrayana Buddhism in the context of a national Hindu polity is often explained with recourse to a legend that describes how Vajracharya Priests subdued and accommodated a legendary Hindu reformer. Sankaracharya is said to have roamed the Indian subcontinent in the ninth century, burning Buddhist books, toppling Buddhist temples, and doing battle with Buddhist priests. In Sankhu Vajracharya priests used their tantric powers to immobilize Sankaracharya while he attempted to mount the steps to the Vajrayogini temple. In return, Sankaracharya worked his own powers of magic to overturn a Buddhist *stupa*, which can still be seen in its inverted position just below the entrance to the temple compound (Slusser 1982: 337).[22] Thus impressing one another with their magical powers, Sankaracharya and the Vajracharya priests agreed to allow both Hindus and Buddhists access to the goddess Vajrayogini.[23] The cohabitation of a Buddhist *caitya* and a Shiva *lignum* within the temple building next to the Vajrayogini temple is likewise said to illustrate the compatibility of Hinduism and Buddhism in the domain of Sankhu.[24]

Although politically and culturally marginal relative to the contemporary Hindu orthodoxy, Vajrayana is still practised by Newar Buddhists. Residents of Sankhu still refer to the Vajrayogini temple area as *Gum Vihāra* and to its deities as *Gubhādyo,* the 'deities of the Forest Monastery', though there are no longer any monks in residence there. Its buildings still stand and, as a tribute to the monastery's prominent past, the Vajracharya priest resident at the Vajrayogini temple daily circles the old monastic complex while ringing a bell, a common practice in all Buddhist monasteries. These practices are significant because they organize a range of important social investments, such as the Vajrayogini festival, and offer an organizing logic for caste occupations that still contour market relations in Sankhu today. They also reflect long histories

of the Valley's outward connection north and south – connections that
forged a South-Central Asian regionalism within which trade and religious
pursuits flourished and reinforced one another.

Zenith of Trans-Himalayan Trade

As for trade, it was under the auspices of the Malla rulers that commercial
relations with India and Tibet were most strenuously pursued. King
Pratapa Malla of Kathmandu (1641–74) in particular brokered the first
extensive treaty with Tibet in 1650, on terms extraordinarily favourable
to Nepal: Newars were permitted to live permanently in Kuti and to
establish duty-free trade marts in Lhasa; Tibet agreed to conduct all of
its trade with South Asia, including Sikkim and Bhutan, through the
Kathmandu Valley; and an unreciprocated customs duty was instituted
on Tibetans visiting the Kathmandu Valley.[25] In addition, Pratapa Malla's
commercial envoy to Tibet – the legendary Bhima Malla – orchestrated
another, most lucrative dimension of the 1650 treaty, Nepal's contract for
minting Tibetan coins. The coinage was supplied to Tibet against gold.
According to Ludwig F. Stiller (1975: 103–4), an easy profit derived from
minting coins for Lhasa when the Kathmandu mints debased the silver
bullion delivered from Lhasa with an alloy.[26] It was also Bhima Malla who
established numerous state trading firms in Lhasa, initiated the famous
'32 shops' in Kathmandu to ensure a market for the Tibetan enterprises,
and encouraged Newar merchants to participate in the Tibet trade.

Beyond the minting contract, benefits from the trans-Himalayan trade
for Nepal were limited primarily to Nepal's function as a transit route
for traded goods. Little of what was exported from Nepal was actually
produced there (exceptions include brassware, copper, herbs, hides, timber,
wool, cotton and rice) and imports did not generally spawn new spheres
of local production. From Tibet came salt, silver and gold, yak tails,
borax, musk, silk and wool, while India's exports to the north included
spices, silk, embroidery, pearls and amber, jewellery, sugar, cotton and
cotton fabrics, and (once the British East India Company arrived on the
scene) English glassware and cutlery. With the exception of salt, most of
these products were not consumed by the masses in Nepal, who (even in
urban areas) relied predominantly on agriculture for their livelihood well
into the twentieth century; some (especially European goods beginning
in the nineteenth century) were absorbed by the ruling elite, but most
simply passed en route to other markets.

Sankhu figured particularly prominently in the trans-Himalayan trade because of its location in the northeastern corner of the Valley where it controlled the exit of the Kuti route at the point where that route was thus most vulnerable to outside siege. For the Malla kings of the Kathmandu Valley – each desirous of the revenue generated from the Tibet trade – possession of Sankhu became a critical point of rivalry. The alternative northwestern route through Nuwakot and Trisuli to the Tibetan border town of Kyirong risked attack by the newly consolidated, rival kingdom of Gorkha, 145 km to the west. But between Sankhu and the Tibetan border town of Kuti – some six-days' journey for the unencumbered traveller – no other kingdoms posed threats to the Malla trade missions. Thus whoever controlled Sankhu could be sure to control this entire route to Tibet.[27] As the preferred route out of the valley, Sankhu became the 'apple of discord among the kings of the Valley' (Landon 1993 [1928]), and the chronicles indicate that representatives of the courts of Kathmandu and Bhaktapur alternately set up in residence there to defend their acquisition.

In addition to its ideal location for trade, Sankhu offered other unique benefits to the competing Malla kings. As the object of centuries of generous royal patronage the Vajrayogini temple had accumulated a considerable fortune in its upper vaults, second only to that of nearby Changu Narayan and Pashupati temples.[28] Sankhu was also coveted by the rival Malla kings as a centre of tantric practice. Although doctrinal Buddhist study had subsided during the Malla period, according to Slusser (1982: 290), Tantrism (which emphasizes the occult powers of an initiated leadership) 'had become the all-pervasive force that colored Buddhist and Hindu belief and practice'; its practitioners were believed to be able to 'fly, to appear and disappear, to foretell the future, animate the inanimate, and, especially, through their special skills, coerce the gods'. The realm of Sankhu was particularly renowned in this regard. For example, King Mahendra Malla of Kathmandu is said to have appealed to the Vajracharya attendant of Vajrayogini during a campaign to wrest Sankhu from Bhaktapur in 1568; the goddess answered his appeal by lifting a thick fog and thus paving the way to victory (Bledsoe 1998). Legends also abound of tantric competitions waged in Tibet between Newar and Tibetan specialists.[29] According to local sources, Vajracharya priests from Sankhu who participated in the trade missions did not commonly engage their tantric powers for commercial purposes as such secular ends were not considered worthy occasions for the 'high' ritual of tantra. But, as one Merchant-caste informant explained, 'They [Vajracharya priests] did not *have* to go by walking. Just like we [the uninitiated] turn the pages of a book, they could condense the road as they went.'

While Newars were Tibet's dominant trading partner at this time, Tibet itself had become the holy land of Mahayana Buddhism. The Tibet trade brought Newars into heightened contact with Buddhism *in* Tibet and it was Newars who now received Buddhist teachings from Tibetans. As Slusser (1982: 289) writes:

On their return to their homes … [Newar merchants] brought not only trade goods, but a revitalized doctrine and almost forgotten ideas respecting casteless social organization and the Buddhist's respected role in society. This operated as a powerful brake and deterrent to the Buddhist drift into Hinduism (cf. Allen 1973).

The ties to Tibetan Buddhist monks forged through Newars' commercial activities also brought Tibetan monks and scholars to the Kathmandu Valley during this period, several of whom are known to have patronized and invested in the restoration of important Buddhist landmarks in Nepal, including the Vajrayogini temple. Though the Mallas' institutionalization of Hinduism had directly contributed to the decline of Buddhism in Nepal, the Mallas nonetheless facilitated (with permissive regulations) this role for Tibetans in preserving Buddhist temples and shrines. A lingering official connection between the Nepalese state and Buddhist institutions in Tibet is evidenced in government regulations obliging the functionaries of Sankhu to assist in the transit of Tibetan monks through the territory under their jurisdiction.[30] Newar commercial interests, meanwhile, contributed to the commodification of Buddhist material culture.[31] Thus, the articulation of Buddhism with trade continued from at least the early centuries of the Christian era to the late eighteenth century.

STATE FORMATION AND COMMERCE (1768–1950)[32]

The crucial articulation between Buddhism and commerce in the early development of the trans-Himalayan trade gave way, after unification, to a nationalist campaign linking protectionist economic policies to the consolidation of a modern Hindu state and resisting the exploits of British capital (while also harnessing the benefits of European commodities) – a campaign which severely diminished the pan-Asian regionalism that had evolved through religious and commercial exchanges over the preceding centuries. The lucrative trans-Himalayan trade had ultimately threatened the Valley's prominence as a commercial entrepôt through the envy it inspired in neighbouring principalities. Gorkha King Prithvi Narayan

Shah launched his protracted conquest of the Kathmandu Valley in 1744 with an economic blockade, starting with the key outposts on the two trade routes running north to Tibet. Not surprisingly, Sankhu played a pivotal role.[33] Having sealed off the northwest pass out of the Valley on the Kyirong trade route, Prithvi Narayan took advantage of the rivalries among the Malla kings to entreat the assistance of the Bhaktapur king in capturing (from Kathmandu) Sankhu and its northern outposts.[34] For his services Ranjit Malla was awarded control over Sankhu. Though Sankhu shortly fell again to Kathmandu, Prithvi Narayan had succeeded both in sealing off the northern trade routes and in distracting the Malla rulers from recognizing a common enemy in him. By 1768, Prithvi Narayan had backed the Malla kings into their respective capitals, which he then broke through one by one to consolidate the territorial origins of present-day Nepal.

While the Shah king's 15-year siege of the Valley no doubt severely disturbed trans-Himalayan commerce, more compromising still were the trade policies he and his successors promulgated in the post-unification period. In the early years minting coins was the most lucrative enterprise (see D.R. Regmi 1966: 192–214; Uprety 1980: 21). Nepal's favourable relationship with Tibet suffered when the new monarch determined to stop debasing Tibet's silver bullion with an alloy in order to honour the original treaty negotiated by Bhima Malla. The king's initiative in this regard agitated the Tibetans, who, according to historian Ludwig Stiller (1975: 101–4), in fact preferred the alloyed coins.[35] Following failed negotiations with the Tibetan and Chinese governments on the coin issue, Prithvi Narayan Shah interrupted his expansionist conquests to the west and declared war on Tibet. An early and decisive victory for Nepal (culminating in a treaty meeting all of Nepal's conditions concerning the coin issue) incited the Chinese to retaliate with a prolonged siege of Nepalese territory that reached as far south as Nuwakot, within a day's walk of the Kathmandu Valley. Though the Chinese were finally defeated at Nuwakot, the treaty of 1792 dealt a final blow to Nepal's profitable contract for minting Tibetan coins and required Nepal to send periodic tribute to the Chinese court.

Trade was also the arena for Nepal's confrontations with the British empire and its expanding commercial exploits on the Indian subcontinent. The British East India Company had been present in India since the early seventeenth century and initiated its strategy of annexing Indian principalities.[36] The first contact with Nepal came in 1768 when the besieged Malla kings called upon the British for help in resisting the conquest of Prithvi Narayan Shah. The British complied by sending the ill-fated Kinloch expedition. Their motive was to open up new markets for European products at a time when the East India Company was experiencing a severe currency drain resulting from the costs of administration in India. With the American Revolution reaching a conclusion, the British anticipated a renewed supply of manufactured goods and viewed the regions north of the Gangetic plain, especially the overland trade with Tibet and China, as an unexplored market. The failure of the Kinloch expedition, turned back after the Malla capitals had already fallen to the Gorkhalis, was a spectacular 'monument to British naiveté concerning mountain warfare and the strength of the Gorkha army' and it established the Gorkhalis as one of the most powerful fighting forces on the subcontinent (Liechty 1995a: 497).[37]

Once Prithvi Narayan Shah completed his conquest of the principalities west and east of the Kathmandu Valley, he controlled all the existing routes to Tibet. These he guarded with fiercely protectionist economic policies, lest Nepal meet the same fate as the independent states of India routinely falling under British rule. He expelled Indian and British merchants, forbade Nepali merchants to deal independently with the British, and developed border towns in the Tarai (southern plains) to disrupt British trading relationships (M.C. Regmi 1971). He allowed only one route into the Kathmandu Valley and this he left in a constant state of disrepair, impassable to any beast of burden except human porters (the penalty for opening alternative routes was capital punishment (Liechty 1997: 32–3).[38] And he sought to prevent the drain of Nepali currency by banning imports of certain European and Indian goods. Instead he advocated local production, in a short-lived policy environment favouring local capital formation, and made arrangements for training local artisans in the fabrication of goods, such as cloth, commonly imported from India (M.C. Regmi 1971). In his nationalist treatise, *Dibya Upadesh* (1774), Shah linked these protectionist monetary policies directly to his state-building ambitions:

Our money will not go abroad. Send our herbs to India and bring back money. When you acquire money, keep it. If the citizens are wealthy, the country is strong. The King's storehouse is his people. (Cited in Liechty 1997: 3)

Economic protectionism was one leg of an anti-foreign ideology promoted by the Gorkhali king to construct a specifically Hindu polity in opposition to British colonial expansion. *Dibya Upadesh*, and indeed the rule of Prithvi Narayan Shah as a whole, sought to establish the Nepalese state as a sacred realm (*desa*), a zone of Hindu orthodoxy uncontaminated by the profanity of Christians and Muslims. Shah thus cast the expulsion of merchants and their wares in terms of moral disdain for foreigners as ritually defiling, as eaters of cows or otherwise worthy of untouchable status. For their part, Nepali merchants travelling to Tibet or India (even Buddhist-leaning Newars) were required to perform complicated and time-consuming rites of purification, *pāni patia*, upon return to the sacred Hindu realm of Nepal *desa*.

Given their interest in preserving a stake in the trans-Himalayan trade (if only from south of the Nepalese border) and the formidable showing of the Gorkhali army against the Kinloch expedition, the British were willing for a time to accept the mercantilist policies emanating from Kathmandu. During this period the small mountain kingdom even enjoyed a short-lived favourable balance of trade with colonial India. Good relations soured by the early nineteenth century, however, when tensions arose over the southern Nepalese border. Prithvi Narayan Shah had initiated a practice of sending Nepali troops (the British title 'Gurkhas' has held to this day) to help the East India Company suppress organized resistance within its territories, but the gesture of friendship came with the price of increasingly substantial exactions of Tarai lands in the southern border region. Tensions escalated into disputes (no doubt fuelled in part by the ongoing obstacles to exploiting the full commercial potential of the trans-Himalayan trade) and the British initiated hostilities with Nepal in 1814. This time Nepal's treacherous geography offered inadequate defence against the British army, now better prepared for mountain warfare; the treaty brokered upon Nepal's defeat in 1816 returned large portions of British territory and set out the terms for stationing a permanent British resident in Kathmandu. Because the treaty did not extend a role for the British resident in governing Nepal (as had been the practice with the colonized Indian principalities), the Gorkhali government could continue to circumscribe the movements of the British, both merchants and diplomatic representatives, and to rebuff the British effort to establish a secure trade route between China and India. In the short run, the trade account with India remained positive, but in the long run, Nepal's ongoing isolationist policies vis-à-vis British interests dealt a final blow to Nepal's mastery over the trans-Himalayan trade (M.C. Regmi 1971: 151).

The war of 1814, along with the East India Company's ongoing exploits in India, established the British as the strongest power on the subcontinent. By the time Jung Bahadur Rana wrested power from the Shah government (reducing the kingship to the status of figurehead), British predominance required a far more conciliatory posture on the part of Nepal's rulers. Nepali sovereignty now rested on the Nepali government's willingness and capacity to support the British Raj. This the Ranas (the ruling dynasty of hereditary prime ministers from 1850 to 1951) accomplished in two significant respects. First, they offered Gurkha regiments to quell Indian uprisings on an ongoing basis; most notable among these was the sepoy uprising of 1857, against which Jung Bahadur Rana himself led a regiment and as a result of which the British returned some of the Tarai lands seized in the war of 1814. Second, as Mark Liechty (1997) has argued, the cautious stance toward admitting foreigners into Nepal (initiated by the Shah kings but perpetuated by the Ranas) contrasted with an insatiable appetite the Ranas developed for European goods – creating a market for imports that turned the balance of trade securely in favour of the British.

Having fallen within the sphere of British colonial political economy and unable to wield economic and military might, Ranas sought their warrant to rule through a strategy of distinction based on flagrant consumption and display of European goods. They built immense white stucco palaces in the European neoclassical style (without a hint of the vernacular) and outfitted them with imported European and American goods – glass windows, mirrors, chandeliers, paintings, carpets, Venetian marble tiles, Victorian furniture and (by the early 1900s) luxury cars – all carried into the Kathmandu Valley on foot. One of the few extant palaces, Singha Durbar, was modelled in scale and design on Versailles and, along with its crystal staircase and hall of mirrors, distinguished itself as the largest structure in all of South and Southeast Asia (Liechty 1997: 51). Meanwhile the Ranas instituted sumptuary laws forbidding commoners from adopting European styles of clothing, house design or transportation – ensuring an enormous material and symbolic divide between ruler and ruled (Hodgson 1971 [1874]; Liechty 1997: 41; M.C. Regmi 1971: 209, 186). Thus the British granted Nepal sovereignty in exchange for a steady supply of human capital to wage its colonialist military campaigns in India; by engaging material manifestations of foreignness as a source of political legitimacy within Nepal, meanwhile, the power of the Ranas derived not from divine Hindu authority (rule of the king as an incarnation of Vishnu), but from secular and material sources of authority.

Within Nepal British commercial interests in the trans-Himalayan trade continued to be frustrated by unpredictable confiscations and deportations, arbitrary commercial regulation, and the lack of a legal framework for commerce (especially compared to the commercial laws the British had developed in the annexed principalities of northern India). The advent of railroads in the late 1800s in the end gave the British easy leverage over

Nepal through the control it afforded them over transport costs and transit rights. By 1877, the British had opened a railroad between Darjeeling and Calcutta; the route was soon extended as a track for horse-drawn carts in conjunction with a British military campaign on the Tibet border; and it ultimately penetrated Central Tibet on the occasion of an 1890 treaty between Great Britain and China, in which Peking granted the British rights to establish trade marts in Tibet. Lhasa could be reached from Calcutta on the Darjeeling route in three weeks, which was less than half the time required to make the journey through Kathmandu. By 1900, then, almost all of the British trans-Himalayan trade was conducted through Sikkim, circumventing Nepal entirely (M.C. Regmi 1971: 24, 1988: 189–90; Uprety 1980: 166–7).

As revenues from the Tibet trade dwindled, the Ranas turned increasingly to policies of internal economic colonization to sustain their practices of conspicuous consumption. Prithvi Narayan Shah had consolidated numerous principalities (including the three Malla kingdoms) to form the modern state of Nepal, but granted them considerable autonomy in economic and political affairs (largely for lack of capacity). The Ranas on the other hand viewed 'the entire state as a private feudal fiefdom' to be mined for the profit of the ruling elite (Liechty 1997: 59). By forming state timber monopolies to supply the expanding British rail network, for example, they enabled the Nepalese state to profit from the development of India while neglecting the development of Nepal. They mobilized *domestic* resources by taxing the peasantry. Taxes did not finance services. Rather they were used to create personal expense accounts for the Rana elite, to reward political patronage and to remunerate local functionaries for administering far-flung regions of a mountainous nation lacking in transportation and telecommunications infrastructure (for the details of the Rana taxation system and its relation to land tenure, see M.C. Regmi's encyclopaedic *Land Tenure and Taxation in Nepal,* 1978). The responsibility for extracting a meagre surplus from the peasantry fell to local functionaries who were granted large tracts of land in exchange for levying taxes and rents, some of which could be retained for personal income and some of which were delivered to national coffers. Administration and taxation of trade were subject to the same logic, ensuring that the dwindling benefits from trade fell exclusively to the Rana elite, local functionaries and Newar merchant middlemen. Revenues were taxed heavily and similarly financed a system of extremely regressive political administration over customs and trade. The *hulāki* or postal service associated with the Tibet trade was conducted through a *jhārā*, a system of *corvée*-like compulsory labour. Each household

not serving state functions in other capacities was required to make
one man available for this service, which required transporting goods,
including coins, for a distance of two *kos* (approximately 6.5 km) on
the Tibet route from Sankhu.[39] In addition, both the Shah and Rana
regimes maintained state export monopolies for the few goods produced
domestically (such as indigo, wax and cardamom) and they controlled
the retail trade marts in Lhasa established by their Malla predecessors,
even as they relied on the skills of Newar merchants to conduct trade
(D.R. Regmi 1966: 528).

  The strategy of rule by surplus extraction and symbolic distinction could
not be sustained. The steady flow of Gurkha soldiers eventually thwarted
Rana strategies of distancing foreign people and ideas while embracing
foreign commodities. The feudalistic rulers simply could not isolate their
people from the independence movements fomenting in India, while the
impoverishment of the Nepali peasantry at the hands of the Ranas spurred
widespread grassroots resentment, as well as some outright resistance,
within Nepal. The increasing exposure of common Nepalis to foreign
goods and ideas *outside Nepal* produced ever-diminishing returns to the
strategy of elite distinction through conspicuous consumption, at a time
when a significant component of the country's economic base – the Tibet
trade – disappeared virtually overnight with the opening of the alternative
trade route through Sikkim. Thus it is no coincidence the Rana regime,
whose very legitimacy rose in relation to the consolidation of British
colonial rule in India, would fall once again – when the British finally
pulled out of the subcontinent in the mid-1900s – to the hereditary line
of Shah kings now willing to experiment with more democratic forms
of governance (Liechty 1997: 53).

Role of Sankhu and Newar Merchants in the Tibet Trade of Post-unification Nepal

From Malla times, Sankhu was the seat of an administrative division called
pramāṇa, through which an appointed official, the *duāre*, was responsible
for collecting taxes in exchange for a large land grant and considerable
autonomy to exact compulsory labour. With unification, the Shah rulers
established a customs office in Sankhu, giving it an important administrative, as well as locational, role in the trans-Himalayan trade. In some
cases levies raised through customs duties were allocated as *jāgir* grants,
assigned by the state in lieu of a cash income as salary for its employees and
functionaries. Hamilton (1986 [1819] cited in B.G. Shrestha 2002) writes

that lands in the Sankhu region comprised the *jāgir* of the Maharani, Queen Regent, worth a staggering NRs 4,000 annually. Archival documents of the Records Section of the Department of Land Revenue in the Ministry of Finance indicate that Sankhu was the site of a large *jāgir* land grant covering the fertile Sankhu and Gokarna Valleys; this *jāgir* remunerated the state official overseeing the *hulāki*, or postal system, through which communication with Tibet, including the transport of silver bullion and minted coins, was organized.[40] Whenever possible the state preferred to administer customs duties more directly, by delegating authority to local agents who in turn paid a stipulated sum of money to the government. One such *ijāra* grant in Sankhu awarded the collection of customs duties to a contractor for an annual 'rent' of NRs 901.[41]

While these forms of profit generally accrued to central authorities in Kathmandu (or to their appointed local functionaries and favoured patrons), Newar merchants fared among the best of Nepal's subjugated peoples during the Shah and Rana periods. Those engaged in the transit trade *within* Nepal enjoyed preferential treatment to conduct trade through relatively low customs rates (Stiller 1975: 26–8). Newars also retained retail businesses in Lhasa established during the Malla period (and Sankhu merchants are known to have been among the original trading families with permanent residences there; Jest 1993: 160). Here, too, Newars received favourable treatment relative to other foreign merchants. The treaty between China and Nepal in 1792 had kept intact the trading rights for Newar merchants first brokered by Bhima Malla. In the mid-1800s hostilities again broke out between Nepal and Tibet following harassment of a Nepalese mission en route to Peking with a tribute payment. Though the Nepalese army failed to capture Tibetan territory, the treaty brokered in 1856 re-established favourable treatment for Newar merchants operating in Tibet: the merchants were given liberty to conduct their trade free from customs duties and Nepal was permitted to station an official in Lhasa to protect their interests.[42] Once the British opened the alternative trade route through Darjeeling, many Newar merchants returned permanently to Nepal, although those who remained in Tibet were quick to utilize this route to conduct their own commerce between Bengal and China (Bista 1978: 194). Uprety (1980: 167) estimates that the number of Newar merchants in Lhasa declined from about 2,000 in 1888, to about 500 in 1907, and again to only 42 in 1923. The Chinese occupation of Tibet in 1950, however, drove nearly all of the remaining merchants, including the last family from Sankhu, back to Nepal.

According to Sankhu merchants who had engaged in retail businesses in Tibet, Newar merchants were typically organized into groups of approximately 40 under the leadership of a *thakāli* (a position acquired through social standing and wealth and not officially recognized by the government). Groups were organized by the merchants' place of origin; thus, merchants in Sankhu are said to have operated under the auspices of a single *thakāli*. The *thakāli* were business leaders who set prices, kept stores of goods, arbitrated disputes between Tibetans and Newars, and operated a foreign exchange service (*hundi*) through which merchants could receive Tibetan currency in Tibet upon depositing Nepali currency with the *thakāli*'s family in Nepal. The *thakāli* also orchestrated ritual occasions within Newar communities residing in Tibet, such as Dasain (harvest festival, the biggest national holiday in Nepal) and Bhimsen Jatra (procession of the god Bhimsen, protector of the fortunes of businessmen), and functioned as social centres within residential communities of merchants.

By the early 1900s, when the Newar retail marts were already in decline, there were reportedly 25 to 30 merchants and one *thakāli* participating from Sankhu in particular. Most of the Newar traders operating in Lhasa were members of the lay Buddhist castes – Uray and Shakya. Low castes did not generally participate, partly because trade falls outside their vocational ambit, but also because of the requirements of commensality within a Newar diasporic community (high, or pure, castes cannot accept water or cooked rice from low, or impure, castes) and the demands of *pāni patia*, the mandatory ritual purification upon re-entry into the Nepal *desa* for which low castes were not eligible. From Sankhu it was primarily the numerically and politically dominant Shrestha Merchant caste who participated in the Tibet trade. Referred to locally by their most common vocation, *sāu* (shopkeeper), or simply as Newar, Shresthas include descendants of the Malla kings, their advisers, administrators and suppliers.[43] Most Shresthas in Sankhu today patronize a Newar Brahman (Hindu) priest. As any of the marginalized Vajracharya (Buddhist) priests in Sankhu will bitterly note, Shrestha patronage of Brahman priests is a relatively recent phenomenon. Most made the conversion from Buddhist priests for reasons of political expedience during the Rana and Panchayat periods, when upward mobility was accomplished through the adoption of Hindu practices.[44] In addition to trading, Shresthas were thus able to maintain relationships to a predominantly Parbatiya nobility by serving as their government functionaries.

Although the Darjeeling route to Tibet had obvious implications for the flow of transnational commerce, Sankhu remained an important regional bazaar supplying its northern hinterlands until the 1967 expansion of a motorable road from Kathmandu through Banepa to Kuti on the Tibetan border. In the late 1980s a branch road was built north from Banepa to Malemchi Gau in the heart of Sindhupalchowk District – thus robbing Sankhu of its commercial significance for even the most proximate segments of the former Tibet trade route. These developments almost entirely cut Sankhu off not only from the long-distance trade networks through which it came to prominence in the Kathmandu Valley, but also from the main artery of development within the Kathmandu Valley, running west from Kathmandu, through Bhaktapur, to Banepa and ultimately Dhulikhel on the eastern edge of the Valley.[45]

HISTORY OF THE PRESENT

From this history of market patterns in the Kathmandu Valley two crucial themes emerge, which will also inform the later discussion of the articulation of Sankhu's cultural economy with contemporary macroeconomic restructuring. First, we find that the conventional separation between economies, cultures and polities set up by economists obscures the processes by which these spheres are mutually constituted. Second, following Eric Wolf (1982: 23), we can view history in terms of 'the development of material relations, moving simultaneously on the level of the encompassing system and on the micro-level'. Such a processual, dialectical approach to history allows us to consider the populations of 'peripheral' places like Sankhu not merely as subjugated to regional political-economic developments (such as Hinduization on the Indian subcontinent, conquest by a Gorkhali king or British colonial expansion), but also as contouring and setting the parameters for those developments through people's interested actions at the local scale.

We have seen that the evolution of markets in Kathmandu Valley was also the evolution of Buddhism; we cannot understand the history of commerce without taking into account the trans-regional relationships that Newars developed with Buddhist monks and scholars first from India and then, via the Valley's own interventions, from Tibet. Narratives that emphasize the antiquity and isolation of a primordial Newar 'culture' must thus be viewed critically in relation to such histories of dynamic interaction between Newar towns, and the cultures and economies of the trans-Himalayan region. The Valley's economic history also provides a trace on the consolidation in the eighteenth and nineteenth centuries of a national Hindu polity. While this process led to Nepal's gradual isolation from regional commerce, it also enabled a notable resistance to the political reach of British capital. Yet, as the British gained stronger foothold on the subcontinent and Nepali sovereignty rested increasingly on British consent, Nepali rulers were forced to amend their isolationist strategies. They sought political legitimacy from a strategy of rule by distinction, through the display and consumption of foreign goods, while continuing to resist the dangers of foreign political occupation by strictly regulating the presence of Europeans in the Nepali realm (and often excluding them outright; Liechty 1997). As their expense accounts expanded to finance increasingly conspicuous consumption and as revenues from the Tibet trade dwindled, the Ranas could carry out this contradictory strategy only through subnational processes of colonization no less exploitative than those of the East by the West. Within a system that taxed the peasantry to impoverishment, neglected the development of Nepal, and established an enormous class divide between Rana-appointed local functionaries and resident populations throughout the country, high-caste Newars in the Kathmandu Valley carved out a relatively privileged position for themselves through recourse to their commercial and artistic talents.

This chapter has traced the specific roles Sankhu occupied in relation to the expansion and decline of Buddhism, national consolidation and internal colonial rule. These roles developed in articulation with the town's important location on the trans-Himalayan overland route from Central and South Asia. When viewed genealogically in this way, the town's economic history weaves webs of connection with cultural and political-economic developments across Asia, Europe and North America. It also provides a 'history of the present', by shedding light on an ethic of private gain that prevails in Sankhu today, even within a society renowned for practices of gifting, hospitality and other forms of social investment.[46] The next chapter considers how these two seemingly contradictory dimensions of Sankhu's cultural economy can also be viewed as relational and mutually determining.

4 NEWAR REPRESENTATIONS OF FINANCE: TOWARD AN ANTHROPOLOGY OF PROFIT

Sankhu's role in the economic history of the Kathmandu Valley has direct consequences for the kind of market system and wider cultural economy that have emerged in the town today. This chapter considers the legacy of this history in an ethic of private gain expressed through practices of money-lending, land tenure, commerce, corporate household structure, and a host of Newar proverbs and sayings sanctioning the acquisition of private wealth. In spite of the reputation for 'killing the poor' and 'eating the land' described below, however, Sankhu merchants impress even their Parbatiya and Tamang neighbours with their propensity to engage in feasts, carnivals, festivals and generous civil and religious charities – an observation echoed in the Nepali proverb that taunts *'Newar bigriyo bhojle'* (Feasting has ruined the Newars).[1] The Newar feast, *bhvay*, expresses a strong ethic throughout Newar society that profit earned through business acumen and treachery must be warranted by the generosity with which it is dispersed. Thus while money markets, land and household enterprise are key sources for the generation of material wealth, it is through feasting and other forms of social investment that one can expect to uphold the good reputation necessary for citizenship in Newar society. As other ethnographies of the role of prestige in regulating social and economic life in South Asian communities have also revealed, social investments in the 'honour economy' preclude extreme concentrations of wealth, but also, I would add, provide moral justification for acquisitive behaviour and a social order maintaining uneven accumulation.[2]

By viewing practices of self-interested acquisition and profit alongside the sphere of social investment in Newar society (as simultaneous dimensions of the Newar cultural economy), this chapter challenges assumptions about gifting and money that are grounded in experiences with the social costs of capitalism and a nostalgic longing for alternative economic arrangements. Literatures in the traditions of Simmel and Mauss in particular have conventionally posed gifting as an oppositional practice to monetary profit: building versus destroying communal bonds, reciprocal versus self-interested behaviour, creative expression versus rational calculation, traditional versus modern culture.[3] In this chapter I demonstrate not only how an ethic of financial profit finds moral sanction and thrives in a context where social and religious obligations demand a parallel set of investments in non-material forms of wealth, but also how these two 'transactional orders' (to borrow an expression from Bloch and Parry 1989) are mutually dependent. Rather than posing the Newar cultural economy in opposition to that of 'advanced, capitalist societies', I consider an analogous relationship between social reproduction and profit-making in the two systems. In this respect my interpretation diverges from that of Jonathan Parry (1989), James Laidlaw (1995), Gloria Raheja (1988) and other South Asianists who have emphasized South Asian exceptionalism in ethnographies of gift exchange.

The discussions here of self-interest and greed may provoke defensive reactions among those who have been touched by Newar generosity (as I also have). The point is neither to pass judgement on any quintessential 'Newar character' nor to expose individual acts of bad faith – for, as Bourdieu notes, 'symbolic violence' does not operate at the level of conscious intentions (2001). Rather, the objective is to show that representations emphasizing Newar practices of gifting and generosity (or indeed gifting practices in other societies perceived as 'pre-capitalist') as benign forms of 'social capital' are not sufficient to illustrate the Newar cultural economy in its full complexity. When social investments are viewed in relation to acquisitive activity, it becomes possible to foreground the role of the Newar 'honour economy' in maintaining social hierarchies, a subject which is developed in Chapter 5. Here it will be demonstrated how gifting and generosity function as modes of 'symbolic violence' that insinuate hierarchy and domination in the social institutions of Nepal as much as welfare functions of the state do in North America. The Newar cultural economies discussed here certainly express a different moral valuation of money and exchange from the Anglo-North American capitalist context I know best, but it is no less tolerant of inequality and it, too, must grapple with the fundamental contradiction between social regeneration and individual profit.

AN ETHIC OF PRIVATE GAIN

Tibet Trade Legacies

The fortunes earned by local merchants in Tibet are still legendary in Sankhu today. Narratives that celebrate their vast accumulations of wealth circulate and are recounted with pride among rich and poor, high and low castes alike. One legend tells the story of the handsome son of a wealthy Lhasa trader from Sankhu who offended the King of Bhaktapur by preceding him through the city on horseback on the day of a *sawāri*, or royal procession. Incensed that residents of Bhaktapur had confused the handsome and arrogant boy for the king himself, the king summoned and jailed the merchant's son, and fined the merchant an amount of 10,000 rupees for his son's indiscretion. In retaliation, the merchant determined to pay the fine – a small fraction of his fortune from the Tibet trade – in 1-*dām* coins.[4] When the king saw the line of porters bearing the coins, which stretched the entire distance from Bhaktapur to Sankhu, he repented for having insulted such a great merchant and ordered that the coins be returned. Because of taboos preventing householders from taking items viewed by the king into their own homes, the merchant used the coins to finance construction of the many *pāti,* or resting shelters that still line the roads in Sankhu. Other landmarks – shrines, water taps and so on – likewise boast tales of the wealth and magnanimity of the town's merchants.

Descendants of the big traders, most of whom comprise the oldest element of the elite class in Sankhu today, continue to draw on material wealth from the era of prosperous retailing in Tibet. Those who are heirs to the greatest fortunes generated through the trade have generally established primary residences in Kathmandu, multiplied their fortunes by investing in other lucrative enterprises and have even occupied influential political positions. One Sankhu merchant whose family is said to have held the *thakāli* position (leader of Newar merchants) in the Tibetan entrepôt of Kuti for 13 generations has continued to profit from importing consumer goods from China (through merchant contacts in Lhasa and Calcutta forged in the years of direct trading through Sankhu) – and also holds a monopoly contract for the sale of Japanese automobiles in Nepal. Some of the merchants remaining in Sankhu have maintained large landholdings, money-lending services, and shops in the Helambu region of Sindhupalchowk District north of Sankhu, which were established generations ago when Sankhu served as a gateway from the hinterlands to the Kathmandu Valley.

In most cases, smaller initial profits and division of wealth from the Tibet trade among generations of family heirs have precluded upward mobility into the class of Kathmandu elite. But as land becomes increasingly fragmented through inheritance patterns and as opportunities for retail diminish with the changing geography of transportation, 'economically active' adults have increasingly migrated from Sankhu to Kathmandu in search of wage employment or new retail markets.[5] Within Sankhu, according to the survey conducted by Bal Gopal Shrestha, only 40.5 per cent of able-bodied residents is in fact economically active, and of this only 10 per cent derive their primary income from business and industry (although there are over 200 shops, representing nearly one-third of the households in Sankhu). Nearly 50 per cent of the households in my survey had members working outside Sankhu, mostly in Kathmandu and most of whom sent remittances to Sankhu. While the changing political-economic context has in practice reduced the scope for commercial profit, moral valuations surrounding money, wealth and profit have been slower to change. The legacy of Sankhu's strategic location on the Kuti road to Lhasa is not limited to material wealth, but also includes ideas about business that prevail today.

These ideas derive in part from a moral sanctioning of wealth in Hindu ideology and Newari cultural teachings generally. Within Hindu ideology wealth is viewed as the provenance of certain caste-based professions; as Jonathan Parry (1989: 78) notes, 'the whole thrust of the … [Hindu] solution to the problem of theodicy – the doctrine of karma – is that the rich deserve and have earned their good fortune'. A Newari book of proverbs used as primary text for children's education before the institution of the modern public school system (*cānakya*) celebrates the accumulation of wealth as a matter of principle: 'wealth is the most important *dharma*; wealth can take care of everything; one who has wealth can be said to be living; one who has no wealth can be said to have died'; and 'wealth in the hands of others is not really wealth at all'.[6] To enlist celestial support for the accumulation of wealth specifically through commerce, Newars worship Bhimsen, Newar god of commerce, who is beloved for his qualities of deceitfulness and deviousness that earned him the title of 'unfair fighter' in the epic Mahabharata.[7] In most Newar towns a festival is staged annually in Bhimsen's honour, and most households engaged in commerce maintain private shrines in his name.

While Newar merchants are known throughout the region for their business acumen and penchant for profit, Sankhu Newars in particular have a reputation for pursuing wealth through the most crafty means. I was frequently cautioned by friends, acquaintances and colleagues from other Newar settlements against the unscrupulous characters in Sankhu – often with reference to a Newari saying that warns, '*Pvahya jāḥle nya keni, sakvamiyā jāḥle manu keni'* (Fish get caught in the nets of fishermen, humans get caught in the nets of people from Sankhu). A woman of the Shrestha Merchant caste from Kathmandu who had married into a Sankhu household explained the sentiments behind this saying in this way:

> I consulted with a few friends [about my marriage]. They acknowledged that people from Sankhu are generally not good. From the beginning we Newars have not looked favourably on people from Sankhu. Compared to the people from other places, Sankhu natives tend to cheat others, to trick them, to go to any length to make themselves better off, to tell lies, and to do mischievous things.

In fact, I expect it would be difficult to document a relative excess of 'greed' or 'deceit' or 'crafty business practices' among Sankhu Newars. The point is not that these sayings and claims provide evidence, but rather that they suggest a special significance of the town's commercial history in shaping how it is perceived in the wider community of Newars.

Money-lending: 'Killing the Poor'

Money-lending is one domain through which Sankhu merchants have earned this reputation. Tamangs from surrounding hill areas to the north have historically fared particularly poorly at the hands of Newar merchants. Through trading relationships, the latter not only profited from the purchase and resale of Tamang produce, but also burdened the Tamangs with large debts and regularly confiscated their land and other forms of wealth held as collateral. Until the institution of land reforms (extending the rights of tenants) and laws governing money-lending in the mid-1960s, merchants were basically free to draw as much profit from lending money (and renting out land) as the local economy could bear. One left-leaning Merchant-caste Newar who had helped nearby Tamangs organize a tenants' movement in 1958, characterized these relationships in this way:

> Before 1958 the merchants [*sāu*] used to take collateral, like land titles, even for very small loans. So [as a borrower] you could lose your land for not being able to pay back those small loans. In those days, the Tamangs didn't even have enough money to buy a *kātro* [Nep., white cloth used to cover the body of a deceased person during mortuary rituals]. They would have to come to the *sāu*

for even such a small loan. And on top of that, the *sāu* would never make a loan before the borrower did some menial labour in his own house ... . In those days the Tamang households really had absolutely nothing. I'd say they didn't even have 500 rupees worth of wealth, like pots, farming tools, that kind of thing. All of their wealth – their land, their gold, their farming tools – fell into the hands of those *sāu*. How the *sāu* used to kill the poor back then! [8]

The deepening of the cash economy and the opening of alternative transit routes to and from Sindhupalchowk and Helambu loosened the grip of Sankhu Newars on the economies of neighbouring Tamang villages.[9] While many Newar merchants have closed their shops on the old trade route, some continue to mine those areas for profit through money-lending and wholesale grain marketing.[10] The daughter of one such Newar merchant explained how her father used his familiarity with the region to assist a friend in finding 'an investment' (*lāy*): 'My father has arranged one of those investments for his friend Raj Dev who doesn't own any land; from lending money [to Tamangs] Raj Dev gets enough interest payments in grain for him to eat [rice] for the whole year.' Even within Sankhu, professional money-lenders have long profited at the expense of their less affluent neighbours. I asked one low-caste man, whose family rents agricultural land to supplement a butchering business, how the richest *sāu* in his neighborhood made their fortunes. His reply (paraphrased from my notes):

Well, by killing poor people like us, of course! In those days they'd give people like us a lot of hardship and earn their fortunes that way. Whatever work they had, they'd give it to us [debtors]. Or they'd take interest, and deplete our wealth that way. Or they would pay us so little for our work.

A poor Merchant-caste tenant elaborated on the nature of money-lenders' power prior to the land reforms of 1964:

In those days, the *sāu* used to have a *lot* more power; because yields were so low, the demand for loans was very high. Instead of 10–12 *muri* rice yields now, then we were getting only 4 *muri* on the same land, which was not enough even to pay off all of our rent plus interest. Those days my family ate only wheat, corn and millet, though we were cultivating rice.[11]

During the Rana period in particular (and prior to land reform), the high demand for credit in the absence of regulatory oversight allowed money-lenders to wield their power with usurious interest rates and other extraordinarily onerous terms. In addition to paying 25 per cent interest rates per growing season (1 *pāthī* interest for every 4 *pāthī* of grain borrowed), borrowers had first to supplicate the *sāu* with *ghiu khāne* (Nep.) – gifts of fruit, eggs, sweets, clarified butter and such – in order to express deference and win the attention and favour of the lender. Even small, in-kind, seasonal loans required collateral deposits – usually land – which were promptly seized in the event of default. Alternatively, the lender might permit the borrower to work off the loan through bonded labour, or, according to the son of one of Sankhu's most notoriously usurious money-lenders, detain and punish them in makeshift private jails. 'In some cases', explained a man from a nearby Parbatiya village that also had commercial relations with Sankhu, 'if you were born the son of an indentured servant, you had no home or no land, so you just moved into the *sāu*'s house and stayed there as a bonded labourer'. One Farmer-caste man whose household had been notorious for 'killing the poor' recalled that indentured servants were sometimes exchanged between households as part of a woman's dowry.

Although regulatory reforms and shifts in the geography of transit in Sindhupalchowk and Helambu have undermined the power of Sankhu merchants, their legacy remains in the unfavourable terms on which loans are made even today. Fifty-three per cent of the borrowers in my randomly sampled survey of 157 households reported borrowing from money-lenders. At the time of this research the local interest rate was either 36 per cent (NRs 1/NRs 1,000/day [Nep. *dhyāke byāj*] or, less commonly, 24 per cent (NRs 0.02 /NRs 100/month) [Nep. *choke byāj*] – compared to the legal maximum of 10 per cent. When loans are repaid in kind, a practice which is in decline, the interest rate can exceed 100 per cent, at 4–5 *pāthī*/NRs100/6 months.[12] For loans over a few hundred rupees, most professional money-lenders still take collateral in land or gold; some still expect gifts of *ghiu khāne*, an exchange which I was able to witness on one occasion; and some still 'allow' their borrowers to work off their interest in unpaid labour, as one low-caste woman explained:[13]

We had a very large loan with Ram Bahadur's father. Well, we only borrowed money for two baskets full of fertilizer. But with all the interest they kept adding on, over the years, we have had to work off the loan with our labour, very slowly. Mostly in portering services, but also in planting rice, or other work in their fields, or just doing any work that they call on us for. They killed us with that interest, but now we have managed to pay it off all at once, when my son went as his porter to Gosainkund.[14]

Money-lenders are able to maintain these practices owing in part to the lack of competition from formal sources of credit. The Nepal Bank opened a branch in Sankhu in 1968, but is renowned for long delays, inaccessibility (especially to the poor and women) and obscure lending policies. In addition, legal prohibitions against interest rates over 10 per cent are easily circumvented and enforcement is lax. When writing a contract for 10 per cent interest, for instance, the lender can simply over-report the amount of the loan or take an amount in collateral equal to the principal plus interest payments at 36 per cent for 10 years (the period after which the money-lender has a legal right to confiscate collateral).[15]

Remarkably, the exploits of money-lenders have not provoked collective moral outrage (with the exception of the 1958 tenants' uprising noted previously). Such practices are generally considered a normal and accepted part of community life. As Jonathan Parry (1989: 78) notes about the complacency surrounding the avarice of merchants in Benares, India, '[m]erchants may not be liked, but their rapacity is somehow part of *jāti* [caste] *dharma*, of the code of conduct which is an aspect of his nature. You might as well get worked up over the propensity of scorpions to sting.' In Sankhu, a common expression similarly likens the relationship between a debtor and his *sāu* to a buffalo facing slaughter by a butcher: 'There is not much point', explained a Shrestha Merchant-caste man with ample experience as a borrower, 'in begging for mercy'. A Butcher-caste man made the association between debt and death more explicitly:

If I owe you money, right, and you come for it, then in our culture we say, 'I had a brush with death!' [Nep., *kasto kāl āyo*] What words do you think might come to my lips in that circumstance? Because as soon as you see me, of course you'll say, Bring the money! Well, that's like death itself coming.

Another saying compares the experience of being trapped by a money-lender to an eclipse, when the moon 'catches' the sun; 'so firm is the money-lender's grasp', elaborated a Brahman priest with whom I was discussing the meaning of eclipses, 'that it will follow you into death'. The same priest continued:

In the same way, when you go to the jungle and you see vines wrapped around a tree, smothering it so, or a tree bending over so it is almost snapping in half – that also is a tree that has been snatched by a money-lender. The tree is still living, right, but even though the tree is still living, the money-lender has not let go of it. He is saying, 'Bring me my money!' He has come to collect his debts.

One further indication of money-lenders' power lies in the prohibition – by royal decree (dating from the Malla period) – on collecting debts during festivals: 'Otherwise', explained the Shrestha man who had made the analogy to buffalo slaughter, 'if I have lent you money, you will always be hiding from me; during the festival you will think, "Should I go out or stay hiding at home?" And then who is going to turn up for doing the work of the festival?' Even today the royal proclamation banning money-lending is re-enacted on festival occasions by a man bearing a royal sword. Designated as the representative of the crown, he traverses the town's procession route prior to the festival, announcing its onset and the prohibition on collecting debts (among other customary rules).

The deepening of the cash economy has expanded options for borrowing in the informal economy, but even these alternative sources of credit are fraught with peril and deceit – only in these cases it is typically the lender who faces the greater risk. The poor and middle class often turn to friends and relatives for small, short-term, interest-free loans (Nep., *sāpati*). This option, pursued by 25 per cent of the borrowers in my survey (20 households), keeps capital within more circumscribed communities, but puts a strain on those relationships when the borrower cannot repay and the lender has no legal recourse (because no contracts are written).[16] In the commercial sector, *udhāro* (credit) loans enable people to make purchases on credit – to buy now and defer payment. The *udhāro* system runs entirely on trust, with no collateral taken, no interest charged and no contracts written. The logic is that default results in loss of supply, since it takes a long time to build new *udhāro* relationships. But buyers in Sankhu routinely keep large 'accounts', deferring payments indefinitely, and dwindling markets leave sellers with little leverage.

Finally, the *Ḍhikuṭi* (Nep., treasury) bidding game is a recent financial innovation that also provides ample opportunity for cheating and wilful default. *Ḍhikuṭi* became very popular in urbanized areas of the Kathmandu Valley in the early 1990s; Newars adapted it from Thakali (an ethnic group in north-central Nepal) rotating credit schemes of the same name, which had long been used to finance the Thakalis' own long-distance trade. Newars looked to *Ḍhikuṭi* as a novel means to finance weddings, funerals and other kinds of social investments growing increasingly costly with the influx of 'modern' commodities and practices in the 1980s. In the monthly rounds of bidding, the highest bidder wins the kitty, while the other players contribute equally to make up the bid. The game relies on those who have already 'won' to continue making payments until every player has had a 'turn' at winning. The three *Ḍhikuṭi* in Sankhu of which I was aware had failed because participants had abandoned the game after taking the kitty – even in cases where players were close friends and neighbours.

Sankhu Newars are also notorious for cheating and deceit in other kinds of business (again, the *practice* may indeed be pervasive in other areas of the Kathmandu Valley, but the *reputation* for cheating attaches particularly strongly to Sankhu). Licensed dealers of state-subsidized staples like sugar, kerosene and fertilizer, of whom there are 25 operating in Sankhu, turn an easy profit by illegally charging market rates. Likewise middlemen [*bañjāri*] who buy grain from growers in Sankhu and its outlying villages for resale in Kathmandu, are known to mix lower grades of rice (purchased in Kathmandu) with the high-value varieties grown locally. Mill owners have their own tricks for increasing their shares of milled grain beyond the established ratios, while shopkeepers are regularly suspected of tampering with their weight measures. Like money-lenders, merchants who succeed in these schemes are not generally condemned for robbing the state or deceiving their customers. At worst they are resented for being *camkha*, clever; more typically they are accorded the same grudging respect as money-lenders.

Land Tenure: 'Eating the Land'

Land tenure is one form of economic disparity that has provoked collective resistance, and the exploits of Sankhu's landlords have earned the town notoriety in this regard as well. Vast disparities in access to land were established after national unification through the feudal system of revenue farming and land granting described in Chapter 3. Land and taxation powers were granted to local functionaries in exchange for administrative oversight and/or political patronage. This system fostered a local elite who could take advantage of their political position to reap impressive economic rewards. In Sankhu the most powerful local functionary was the *duāre*, who collected taxes on *pharmaisi birtā* grants (large grants to royal patrons and benefactors)[17] and administered local justice. In so doing, the *duāre* and his council of merchants (*sāu mahājan*) heard cases and meted out penalties, ensured the proper execution of local festivals and rituals, oversaw the work of other local functionaries, and enforced the state's system of *corvée*-like compulsory labour (*jhārā*).[18] Another functionary, *jimiwāl*, oversaw the collection of taxes on *raikar*, state-owned land cultivated by tenants.

The *duāre* and *jimiwāl* were compensated for their services by a small proportion of the taxes levied. The greatest benefits, however, accrued from their political autonomy in administering the town. They were able, for instance, to enrich their own land holdings by 'eating the land', confiscating land of those unable to meet onerous tax burdens. The person who held the post of *jimiwāl* up until 1950 when the Rana regime was overthrown is said to have acquired 11 houses in this manner. The *jimiwāl*'s responsibility for ensuring that new tracts of land be brought into cultivation provided further opportunity for expanding his personal landholdings. The *duāre* and *jimiwāl* were also entitled to non-material benefits, such as the right to exact unpaid compulsory labour, *bethi*, for their personal needs.

Various other functions of governance were carried out and remunerated through *birtā* land grants. *Ka birtā* (also know as *rakam*) remunerated agents of specific governmental administrative tasks. The *bumbhāri* monitored and resolved disputes surrounding the division of inherited agricultural land, while the *chembhāri* performed the same service with respect to the division of household property (houses, sheds and moveable wealth).[19] These positions, too, accorded considerable opportunity for personal gain, since they involved the allocation of property. The last person to occupy the *chembhāri* post had a reputation for 'eating the land' of the poor and for having used his official position as a stepping stone to one of the most lucrative money-lending enterprises in Sankhu. *Kha birtā*, another kind of *rakam*, went to those who performed local, often ritual services, such as many of the caste-based occupations;[20] the person responsible for providing the palace with special stones used to grind spices;[21] and the person overseeing compulsory labour in the service of the nearby gunpowder factory. Holders of *ka* and *kha birtā* were exempt from the *jhārā* labour tax.

Those who acquired landholdings too large to manage could rent out parcels for additional income, and so there emerged a fundamental class distinction between tenants and landowners. Through to the end of the Rana period there were no legal controls on rents. Collected in the form of unhusked paddy rice, rents varied dramatically by tenant – ranging from half the yield (*adhiyā* rent), to fixed amounts that could even exceed the yield in a bad crop year. One man of the Butcher caste, who had endured the later years of the Rana regime as a tenant, described the landlords' power this way:

The landlords would charge impossibly high rents, often 100 per cent of the yield, and basically kill the tenant to the point where he stops paying rent and gets kicked off the land. It was easy for the landlord to just replace him with another tenant. Our rented land yielded 16 *muri* unhusked paddy rice and that is exactly what we paid in rent. The tenant would usually be willing to do this, because at least he could get the wheat or corn or other [winter] crops grown on the land for himself. At that time, we only ate *ḍhiḍo* [a thick cereal made from wheat, corn, or millet – considered to be low-status food], rarely rice.

In the Tamang areas north of Sankhu, tenants reported in some years having only straw and grass left over after paying rent and the *ghiu khāne* (supplicatory gifts) that even landlords were in the habit of demanding. The high rents also bred cycles of debt: the tenant might borrow against next year's crop or work the landlord's fields to pay off rent.

In fact, it was Tamang tenants of Newar landlords who first instigated collective protest in the Sankhu area.[22] In 1958, 35 Tamang households pledged to pay no more than half their rice yield in rent and no more than 10 per cent interest on loans; to stop providing day labour for their landlords; to refuse – with an arsenal of stones to be used as necessary – admittance of Sankhu landlords to their village (lest the landlords confiscate property or collateral); and to prohibit – by the same means – women and children from the landlords' households from collecting fodder and firewood in the forested area surrounding the Tamang's village.

The landlords attempted various strategies for breaking up the small Tamang movement – including threatening the lives of its leaders – but the movement survived until 1964 when land reforms strengthened by the force of law the provisions that the tenants' movement had succeeded in enforcing locally. In addition, land reform classified agricultural lands by levels of productivity and fixed rents accordingly, required landlords and tenants to register their lands, put a ceiling on land ownership, and allotted tenants a 25 per cent cash share of land sales (or tenancy rights on sales for which they do not take a cash share).[23] Sankhu landlords are said to have vehemently protested the reforms – travelling *en masse* to the palace to air their views. Though their protest did not succeed in thwarting land reforms, the legacy of exploitative tenancy relations can still be felt in Sankhu today. The descendants of Rana government functionaries are currently some of the wealthiest and most landed households in Sankhu, some of which have yet to observe the rights of tenants secured over 30 years ago. Some still have not registered their *birtā* land, making it difficult for tenants to claim their rights.[24] Others do not provide receipts for rent payments, especially to poor, uneducated tenants who are not well apprised of the law. Without receipts, tenants have no legal rights. Land reform has, however, enabled tenants to hold an advancing real estate market at bay. Were it not for the claims of their tenants, many landlords in Sankhu today would have sold their land in order to take advantage of the booming suburban real estate market which has sent land values sky-rocketing even in the farthest reaches of the Kathmandu Valley. The value of one *ropāni* of land along the motorable road as it reaches Sankhu, for instance, increased from NRs

2,500 just 30 years ago, to NRs 300,000 in 1993, and NRs 500,000 in 1995. Since land speculators categorically refuse to purchase land on which tenants have cultivation rights – their purpose being development and not agricultural production – tenants have taken advantage of their leverage to demand 50 per cent of land sales (instead of the 25 per cent legally due to them). For the moment, then, the subsistence needs of tenant farmers have largely sheltered the land from the reach of the market, but it may be only a matter of time before a 50 per cent share of a rapidly escalating land market tempts even the most risk-averse tenants.

Cooperation and Competition between and within Households

In Sankhu, as in Newar society in general, the household is the fundamental economic (and social) unit. Competition and distrust between households can be extremely fierce, even among blood relatives, but also within households ideals of cooperation are often compromised by practices of self-interest and deception. Newars typically reside in extended joint family households, comprised of a couple, their sons, daughters-in-law, grandchildren and unmarried daughters. Descent and inheritance are reckoned patrilineally and residence patrilocally; women, that is, move from their parents' to their husband's household on marriage; brothers usually reside together as extended family until the death of their parents, when they divide the family property and establish separate households (although the division may take place before their parents' death). Within a joint family household of adequate means, each nuclear family has a private room for sleeping, but cooking, eating, religious observance and finance are managed communally through a rigid sexual and age-based division of labour.[25] The senior man is the unequivocal household head, although for business purposes he usually acts in consort with co-resident brothers and sons.[26] The senior woman designates work responsibilities among other married women in the household and possesses the coveted keys to the family store room.

Declan Quigley (1985) aptly likens Newar merchant households to corporations, with the father and each of the brothers acting as 'managing directors' of multiple 'subsidiaries', and women and children as 'junior partners'.[27] Households, that is, are often multi-occupational, often engaging in as many enterprises as there are sons to undertake them (the average and maximum number in my survey being three and ten respectively). A single household might draw income from agriculture, rice milling, shopkeeping, several different service occupations and various home-based enterprises such as wool-spinning and carpet-weaving. The corporate structure offers incentive for diversification and defence against risk. Because each son can rely on the household's collective resources, he is able to experiment with specialized 'subsidiary' enterprises. It must be noted, however, that in spite of this favourable arrangement, Merchant-caste Newars in Sankhu are distinctly non-innovators: they tend to 'experiment' only in businesses in which others have a track record of success (a phenomenon which Quigley [1985] calls 'the copycat principle' and which is readily visible in rows of identical shops lining the Sankhu bazaar).

With respect to outsiders, households practice a fierce solidarity, expressed spatially with the most private domains of the household (both economic and ritual) being located on the top floors of the house and those domains that admit guests and lower-caste patrons on the lower levels. Important financial decisions, life-cycle rituals and ceremonial meals take place strictly within the confines of the upper levels of the household. In addition, household members are each formally initiated into the lineage of the household head (sons and daughters as children and daughters-in-law after marriage) – a privilege which grants admittance to the most secret space of the household, the altar housing the lineage deity.

In economic affairs, outsiders are generally regarded with intense distrust.[28] Joint ventures and partnerships are extremely rare. Merchants explain that they would rather endure low profit margins (often reported at less than 5 per cent) and compete with numerous identical businesses for a dwindling base of customers than risk financial partnerships with unreliable relatives, friends and neighbours. When I inquired about the benefits of reduced overheads and purchasing costs that come with collaborating in business, merchants routinely volunteered accounts of having been cheated by business associates, even friends and relatives. As one Artisan-caste man explained (having unsuccessfully attempted partnerships in a movie hall and a petrol dealership):

Even your closest friends can turn against you when money gets involved. As soon as one person senses an opportunity for personal profit, even if he causes harm to the others, he will take that opportunity. Many people who were once very close friends are no longer speaking to each other after their partnerships have failed.

Because there is no tort law in Nepal (and no strong litigious tradition), the victims of failed partnerships have no legal recourse for reclaiming lost investments and must instead find retribution through vigilante-style acts of subterfuge. One informant described how he resorted to seizing the motorcycle of a delinquent partner and sold it to recover part of his losses from a failed joint enterprise.

The scepticism among Sankhu Newars toward cooperation in business contrasts starkly with their penchant for cooperation in ritual and religious matters (discussed at greater length below). A Merchant-caste young man put it frankly: 'We Newars work together for feasting and festivals all the time, but when it comes time for business, well, we don't get along.' Or, in the words of an elected local leader of the Painter caste:

In the social sector, for doing social work, if anyone dies or something, when such a difficult thing happens, there is a [cooperative] system for managing the cremation and the expenses. But in the economic sector – how to pull that sector ahead – no one has thought about it enough …

Many directly attribute the declining economic condition of Sankhu, its visible decay and stagnant markets, to an inability to cooperate in matters of commerce and economic development. A woman who had married into one of the wealthier Merchant-caste households in Sankhu posed her assessment of the relationship between Sankhu's reputation for unsavoury business practices and its lack of development rather starkly: 'Sankhu has such fertile fields, plentiful water, good soil, but because people there can't get along with each other, because they are always cheating … that's why you don't see any development there.'

It is within the joint family household that cooperation is said to prevail. In the idealized scenario brothers pool their incomes at the household level for distribution and allocation by the household head. As one of the wives in a multi-enterprise Merchant-caste household explained:

Because Bhakta Krisna [household head] is the one who manages the household wealth, … he also has the responsibility to take care of the whole family, including each of the brother's children … . According to our custom, after collecting the brothers' earnings, he has also to give it out, for clothes, school fees, food, and different investments.

If a brother moves away from Sankhu, until the formal division of the household property, he is still expected to contribute income and entitled to draw on the family store of rice, potatoes and other agricultural produce.

Even *within* the household, however, individual practices of squandering resources – or suspicions that others are engaged in such practices – often belie these normative representations. For example, in an attempt to stockpile resources for the eventual break-up of the joint family, a brother and his wife might withhold income for their personal savings from the household pool. The same Merchant-caste woman speculated about her brother and sister-in-law when I asked about intra-household cooperation:

It's the husband and wife [within the joint family] who are more like a cooperative, right? ... Like Govinda and Maili earn money from their teaching, see. No one knows exactly how much they earn or how they earn it .... If someone asks how much they have saved, they can simply say, we have no money. That way they can avoid contributing very much to the family income ...

She continued, implicating the joint family household structure more generally:

Among the brothers, it is very common to hide moveable forms of wealth, like money, gold – not to distribute it equally ... to conceal the wealth and take it later [after the division of the household property] for themselves. You know how I have a safe in my room? In our custom, it is common to keep gold and money in a safe, to keep tight control over the key .... Even if some wealth falls into your [a brother's] hands, you don't tell anyone in the household that you have it; it's common to *cheat* like this a lot and so to accumulate wealth for yourself.[29]

Likewise in the distribution of household expenditures norms of cooperation and solidarity often break down. The household head responsible for distributing resources might spend disproportionately on a favoured son or (in the event that brothers co-reside after the death of their father) on his own nuclear family – resulting in extraordinary inequalities even within the same household.

The tensions and suspicions resulting from these practices come to bear with particular force on the moment of dividing the family property and separating households, each headed by a brother of the formerly joint family. According to custom (and the law), on this occasion each brother should get an equal share of household assets, including both moveable (e.g. money savings) and immovable (e.g. land) property. In the event property is divided before the death of the parents, the oldest and youngest sons receive an additional share in order to underwrite their customary responsibility to care for and perform costly death observances for the father and mother respectively (or, less commonly, a surviving parent may take a share in his or her own name). Tales of unequal divisions and swindled victims of brothers' deceit, however, are practically legendary: one brother promises to take care of his mother in order to get her share of the inheritance, and then so neglects her that she dies an early death; one brother promises to take the inheritance of an infant brother in trust until he matures, and then never cedes the property to him; one brother claims a right to a bigger share because he has more children, or he contributes more to the joint family income; or one brother siphons off so much income from a family enterprise for so long that he ends up being much richer than the others. Once the inheritance has been divided, however unequally, brothers establish separate households and enter into the more openly competitive relationships that characterize the wider society.

SOCIAL INVESTMENTS AND THE NEWAR HONOUR ECONOMY

The ethic of private gain in Sankhu – and the resulting uneven patterns of accumulation – do not inspire much open dissent or public debate, even if it is privately acknowledged and resented. To explore this apparent contradiction, it is necessary to consider another dimension of Newar cultural economies – the enormous social investments to which individual gain must be directed. For while markets in money and land are key sources for the generation of wealth, it is through gifting, feasting and other forms of social investment that one can uphold the good reputation and honour necessary for economic security, indeed survival, within Newar society.

Honour, then, or *ijat*, fuels the system of social investment and must thus be recognized as a most significant currency in the Newar marketplace of value (see also Cameron 1998; Liechty 2003; March 2003; Miller 1992; Rahcja and Gold 1994 on the significance of *ijat* in other South Asian contexts). Anthropologist Sarah Miller's (1992: 396) appraisal of how social identity in urban high-caste Parbatiya society is reckoned in terms of reputation applies with equal force to Newars: 'Identity seems to be delivered back to you from others. "What are they saying about us?" … could be an icon for an identity based on *ijat* and prestige, on repute and renown.' Conforming to the criteria of rarity, demand and desire, honour is thus a form of symbolic capital in the sense expressed by Bourdieu. As such it shares some qualities with material forms of capital: it can be produced and consumed, hoarded or expended; it can cost a great deal of money; and it provides a return on (social) investment. Unlike material forms of capital, however, a person or a household's honour is 'sayable' (Miller 1992): as already noted, households (and individuals) go to great lengths to shield their financial status and ambitions from public scrutiny; reputation, on the contrary, is unequivocally a matter of public record. As such, *ijat* cannot merely be accumulated like a possession; rather, it depends on relations with others. Honour must be conferred by society, and is achieved through subscribing to its cultural calculus. Thus one's honour must be continually defended and replenished by meeting numerous religious and social obligations. These networks of obligation create a web of community ties that work to encircle Sankhu in a space-based social, emotional and economic interdependency.

The Newar Feast

Feasts, as already noted, are a distinguishing feature of Newar society; they are a primary means for accruing *ijat* because they punctuate most important social obligations. Occasions for feasting come around with remarkable frequency and impose no small burden on household budgets. First, there are the life-cycle rituals: depending on one's caste, religious affiliation and gender, up to seven rituals associated with birth; two initiation rituals; betrothal; marriage; three old-age initiations to the status of gods; and the 13–45-day intensive series of mortuary rites. Each of these entails not only the requisite feast, but also elaborate, costly and time-consuming preparations for the ritual itself, involving both the prescribed configuration of kin and an entourage of ritual specialists. The ancestors, too, must be worshipped – fed, clothed, housed and comforted as integral members of the social group – through mortuary rites performed regularly by the living. These occasions for worship also require the preparation of a feast to which the appropriate kin and ritual specialists must be invited.

Community and national festivals propitiate deities ranging from the town's patron goddess Vajrayogini, to Bhimsen (patron deity of commerce), to the gods of the distinct lineage groups (*digu dyo*). All festivals, which number approximately 35 during the calendrical year and which range in duration from one day to one month, each entail at least one domestic feast of some measure, as well as varying levels of household participation in their collective community-wide dimensions. Even ghosts – the spirits of those who have died and never passed to the land of the dead – must be appeased with their own special offerings, dietary observances and public rituals. Failure to perform any of these rituals or prepare the associated feasts does not just incur the wrath of gods, ancestors and ghosts; one's honour is at stake and, as we will see, there is a lot to lose.

The actual consumption of a feast transpires ceremoniously, with guests seated in a line on long, narrow straw mats, and those of senior status seated to the right of their status juniors. Hosts steadily ply their guests with multiple (and mandatory) helpings of food and drink – employing the requisite gestures of deference and generally trying to prolong the affair as long as possible in order to establish their credentials as hosts. As one prominent local merchant proudly described it:

At a Newar feast, the hosts lovingly serve each dish in a particular order and place them in a particular spot; and how many dishes there are! I bet you have never eaten a *real* Newar feast. Oh, hosts show their guests the greatest respect.

For guests, attending feasts is a remarkably time-consuming affair. Since the straw mats can usually only accommodate 20–30 bodies at once, guests must be cycled through in shifts; within a single shift no one may rise before their status seniors – usually older men with not much better to do than tarry over a big feast. When the time finally comes to seat a new group, guests weary with waiting their turn can often be seen jostling to make the next shift as if trying to board an overcrowded bus.

Feast content is thoroughly prescribed, entailing several meat, vegetable, and lentil or bean dishes, *baji* (beaten rice), fruits, sweets, curd and plenty of home-distilled alcohol – all of which, as any host will bemoan, amounts to no small expense of money and labour time.[30] The specific composition of guests is also prescribed according to the kind of celebration at hand. For marriages and girls' or boys' initiations a household must assemble its entire social universe: joint family members, lineage members, relations through mothers and married sisters and daughters, friends and neighbours. These feasts must be of an appropriate scale, encompassing not only prescribed kin and close associates, but also whenever possible those whose very presence can reflect favourably on the host's social standing (such as politicians or businessmen). Lineage deity feasts involve only heads of lineage households. Mohani (Nep. Dashain, annual harvest festival) and *śrāddha* require the presence of *mhyāy masta* (married daughters, married sisters and their husbands and children, often travelling from homes in other Newar communities), while several of the purificatory rites for newborns involve a special role for the brothers of the infant's mother. Feasting patterns thus provide a trace on the social geography of the town, as well as its links with neighbouring towns and cities of the Kathmandu Valley.

The expense can be enough to sink even those with the basic material comforts of home, land, and regular business income, as one Merchant-caste woman remarked:

We Newars are such a good-for-nothing bunch! My family just had to go and spend 135,000 rupees for my younger sister's wedding party. So, sure, we have this rice dealership and this potato dealership, that land and this house, but we are always having to spend everything we earn and more on these events.

The average cost of a wedding party or son's initiation among the 150 households surveyed in my research was NRs 64,000 – a formidable expense when compared, for example, to the monthly salary of a university professor in Kathmandu at the time of this research (NRs 6,000). It is acceptable, and indeed desirable, to enlist the help of neighbours and relatives in the tremendous work effort necessary to stage a large feast such as a wedding party (in the absence, it must be recalled, of basic indoor plumbing). Most households cannot carry off the event without recourse to *sāpati*, small loans from friends and relatives. In general, however, the objective is to display as much financial capacity and material wealth as possible. As one Merchant-caste woman put it, 'The whole purpose is to show that you can make the expense!' In these highly public contexts, saving money or otherwise cutting corners might suggest an inability to pay – and any hint of poverty imparts its own, relentless shame (*bejat*).

Newar *Guthis*

Many obligations associated with feasting are organized and enforced under the auspices of the characteristic Newar *guthi* associations. As corporate bodies that enable households to fulfil their social and religious obligations through group action, *guthis* thus play a crucial role in regulating social life within Newar communities (see also Quigley 1993). Every household (through a senior male representative) should belong to at least two *guthis* (a *digu dyo guthi* and a *sī guthi*), through which worship of lineage deities and performance of mortuary rites are organized respectively.[31] Temple and festival *guthis* ensure the propitiation of deities presiding over a particular locality (such as Vajrayogini) or the performance of a public ritual (such as *ihi*, the girls' initiation rite); about half of the approximately 80 temple/festival *guthis* still functioning in Sankhu are related to the work and worship of Vajrayogini.[32]

Guthi members adhere to a rigid organizational structure that facilitates monitoring of compliance with social norms: responsibility for managing *sī* and *digu dyo guthi* functions (including the *guthi*'s own mandatory round of feasting) rotates annually among the membership, while authority within the association is vested in the senior two members; the leadership enforces a rigid system of penalties and fines intended to punish noncompliance with *guthi* rules or absence from *guthi* functions.

And much of the *guthis'* ritual practice transpires in secrecy behind closed doors, in order to express a vigorous exclusion of outsiders (and, as discussed in Chapter 5, in order to reproduce caste and gender hierarchies). As such, *guthis* exercise an important stabilizing role in Newar society. Located only 17 km from the capital city and being well integrated with the city's electronic and telecommunications media, Sankhu's residents know well the allure of modernity, especially since the post-1995 trade liberalization and market deregulation. In the face of competing ideologies of mobility and development, *guthis* are viewed by many (and especially those with direct interests in preserving the established distribution of power and resources) as the surest mechanism for protecting 'traditional Newar culture' against 'outside' influences of modernization. Indeed, the tendency toward such practices of hermetic cultural reproduction has characterized Newar society since nation-building efforts of the still-reigning Shah dynasties first threatened political and cultural colonization in the mid-eighteenth century.

In addition to nominal annual contributions from members, *guthis* (especially temple and festival *guthis)* are often sustained financially through land endowments. The land is rented out to tenants and thus generates income to finance feasting and ritual activities (the average *guthi* landholding in my survey was 2.2 *ropāni*). In the case of some temple and festival *guthis* (such as that of Vajrayogini) the land is held in public trust and its income is managed by the National Guthi Corporation; these are *rāj guthis*. Lineage deity and death *guthi* land, on the other hand, is privately owned and managed, and may or may not be registered as *guthi* lands. Not all *sī guthi* and *digu dyo guthis* are endowed in this way, however. Initial donations of land may have been lost to land reform or to divisions of household property over the generations. And many families, of course, never possessed the land to pledge as *guthi* endowments. Given the increasing scarcity of land, many *sī guthis* have developed some kind of revolving loan system as a means for accruing and managing *guthi* capital. Members can obtain small loans for their personal use and the interest helps defray *guthi* expenses.[33] In fact, borrowing from the fund at interest is often an obligation that rotates with other managerial duties of the association; the high interest rates do not reflect true costs of lending, but are rather intended to ensure *guthi* income.

These financing strategies notwithstanding, *guthi* membership exacts extraordinary (financial) costs on individual households (like all forms of social investment). In Sankhu, where the scope for profiting from commercial enterprise is in decline, *guthi* obligations are weighed gingerly against forms of investment that might yield a more direct financial return. Yet the costs of foregoing *guthi* participation – tantamount, in some cases, to excommunication from Newar social life (Nepali 1965) – remain prohibitive, as the following comments of a *guthi*-less merchant caste man suggest:

> If you don't do your *guthi* work, then society really holds you in contempt. Our *guthi* has many members; my grandfather eventually had to drop out because he could not afford to offer the feast when his turn came around. After that everything, including our business, became difficult; it was even hard to arrange for me and my brothers' marriages because the first thing they always ask: which *guthi* do you belong to? (See also Joshi 1992)

In the calculus of the *ijat* economy, that is, *guthis* fulfil a crucial economic as well as social function, by ensuring the sound social standing of households who meet the arduous (and expensive) round of obligations. As such, *guthis* are distinctively place-based organizations. Membership roots an individual in a particular town, in a particular neighbourhood (*tvaḥ*), as a descendant of a particular lineage. Membership also commits an individual to social obligations that are distinctively *local*: the rounds of feasting, worship of lineage deities and performance of mortuary rituals on the death of any adult belonging to a member household – in addition to other forms of sociality spawned by such obligations – create a web of community ties that encircle the town in cross-cutting and overlapping interdependencies.

Dāna and Newar Spiritual Accounting

One of the most symbolically potent forms of social investment among Newars is *dāna*, a gift, presented to a ritually designated recipient that enables the donor to alleviate misfortune or sin by ritual means. In a manner that reflects much of the ethnographic evidence from caste societies in northern India, *dāna* is offered most commonly to a Brahman or Vajracharya priest in the form of coins serving as surrogates for items prescribed in the scriptures (like the auspicious cow).[34] The offerings are made on a routine basis during life-cycle rituals when it is necessary to dispose of accumulated evil (*pāp)* and inauspiciousness (*daśa*), or upon chance encounters with *daśa* – states of disorder (*asānti*) that cause disruptions (like household discord or falling profits).[35] But one can also give *dāna* to relieve ethical burdens associated with unscrupulous business practices, such as charging high interest rates, or mixing grades of rice, or withholding receipts from tenants. On these occasions, astrologers are likely to prescribe *dāna* offerings as a means of removing *daśa* and *pāp*.[36] So, for instance, one might be instructed to ward off an affliction from *daśa* by giving *dāna* to a Brahman priest on a particular day of the week for a certain period of time. These strategies are widely understood to be an integral part of negotiating life in a hostile and competitive world – in which one may encounter inauspiciousness, but also accrue it through one's own actions.

Priests, in turn, have the unpleasant but unavoidable duty of receiving these 'gifts'. While evidence from north India suggests that evil qualities transfer directly to the priestly recipient (see especially Parry 1980), Newars stress that *daśa* and *pāp* may be dissipated through various means to 'digest' (*pacay yaye*) them, such as the repetition of mantras. One practising Rājopādhyāy Brahman in Sankhu explained how he resolves the moral peril of accepting *dāna* in this way:

> Accepting *dāna* is extremely difficult. You cannot just take what is offered and use it or the inauspiciousness [of the donor] will fall upon you. So you have to accept the *dāna* with *kuśa* [a grass considered to be ritually purifying]. Actually, it is the *kuśa* which accepts the *dāna*. You must also do *jap* [telling the beads] right there after taking the *dāna* with the *kuśa*. Otherwise the inauspiciousness falls upon you and you will become very ill. It is very dangerous.

Different kinds of *dāna* entail different levels of peril, but all require the basic routine of diffusing the inauspiciousness with *kuśa*, *jap* and mantra. Offerings of sheep or buffalo (or, more commonly, their coin surrogates) just before someone dies require more mantras than offerings of cows as *dāna*; salt is the 'strongest' form of *dāna*, and requires the Brahman priest to do his *jap* while standing waist-high in water, lest he be overcome by evil and sickness. Even in more Buddhist interpretations of *dāna* – when the emphasis is on acquiring merit (*punya*) – a materialist view of sin prevails. During the *Pañcadāna* festival, for instance, *dāna* is offered exclusively to Buddhist priests, who process *as monks* (*bhiksu*) through the town along with a chariot bearing the image of the Buddhist goddess of fertility, Basundara.[37] The ideology of *dāna* dictates that the priest (Hindu or Buddhist) should receive *dāna* in a disinterested fashion, as part of his *jāti dharma*. In this respect it must be contrasted with *dakṣiṇa*, cash that is 'put directly in the hands of the priest', given as remuneration for service. In practice, though, *dāna* prestations provide a much-needed supplement to the priest's otherwise meagre income.

What is remarkable to an outside observer is that it is the *priest* who is derided for greed in this exchange relationship (for their material interest in *dāna*), while the donor earns a reputation for religious piety, regardless of his sins or misfortunes. In spite of the moral peril entailed in accepting *dāna,* the prevailing view among patrons of priestly services alleges that the priest has gotten 'something for nothing' in a world where expectations of material reciprocity govern the idea of the gift (Parry 1989). Even though priests hail from some of the poorest households in Sankhu, on numerous occasions I heard Merchant-caste people speculating among themselves about how much they can earn per day during the astrologically prescribed auspicious 'seasons' for household rituals requiring *dāna* offerings. Or they may point out that, although the emphasis in *dāna* transactions should be (according to religious doctrine) on the ritual rather than material dimension of giving – because, as one priest explained, 'it is not possible to buy *dharma*' – priests violate this truism by favouring wealthy over poor patrons and sometimes even by requesting a fixed amount of cash as *dāna*. During a household purification ritual orchestrated by a Brahman I asked a fellow observer the Newari term for the priest's complex hand movements that accompany his utterance of mantras; the reply, in a loud voice: 'He is doing that just as a way to ask for more money [*dāna*].' Even the proverbs capture the popular discomfort surrounding the perceived profit accruing to priests in receiving *dāna* offerings: evoking the conditions of duress under which the donor commonly offers *dāna*, one Newari proverb laments, 'Distress for the layman is fortune for the priest' (Lall 1991). As in the north Indian case described by Parry (1980, 1989) it is thus priests and not merchants who are derided for and associated with greed.

Dāna gifts should not only be received but also *given* in a disinterested fashion. The donor should seek neither a material nor a spiritual return. But here again a contradiction arises, for in practice people expect gifts of *dāna* will serve them with relief from sin or misfortune, and even with the reputation of exemplary religious devotion. One money-lender known particularly for his crooked accounting methods and retention of debtors in makeshift jails described the moral cleansing he enjoys from giving *dāna*:

I myself acknowledge that I have killed the poor [with high interest rates]. But I am not like some money-lenders who do not uphold their religious obligations (*dharma*) or give offerings of *dāna*. Even if they do not treat the poor as badly as I do, those other money-lenders [who do less *dharma*] are suffering now. Their businesses are failing while mine is thriving.

Thus in fact the ideology of *dāna* as an unreciprocated gift promises the donor an honourable reputation for religious piety and disinterested generosity, notwithstanding unethical business practices or other self-interested pursuits. In Buddhist and Hindu spiritual accounting, giving *dāna* offerings is an act of *dharma* that ultimately gets weighted against *pāp* in determinations of *karma* (fate) upon rebirth.[38] Given the capacity of *dāna* to hedge against sinfulness and greed, then, it is no surprise that Sankhu's most wealthy and 'clever' merchants are also some of the most benevolent patrons of Brahman and Vajracharya priests.

NEWAR ECONOMICS OF PRACTICE[39]

The ethnographic evidence from Sankhu reveals a strong ethic of private gain governing practices of commerce, land tenure and householding. The force of this ethic lies partly in the legacy of the profitable trans-Himalayan trade, from which much of the material wealth in Sankhu derives today – even if, practically speaking, opportunities for profit have fallen dramatically with the changing geography of transit. As revealed in proverbs as much as in practices sanctioning the acquisition of wealth, self-interested economic pursuits do not inspire any particular moral condemnation – even if profit results from cheating vulnerable clients. In the calculus of the *ijat* economy, however, finance capital must be transmuted into symbolic capital through social investments in religious piety, hospitality, feasting and local associational life. Material forms of wealth in themselves do not secure a high-class position in Sankhu; rather, status derives as much from symbolic as from material forms of wealth. And symbolic wealth, the honour of a good reputation, accrues only by meeting the heavy requirements of social investment that accompany important life-cycle, social, festival and religious occasions.

Sankhu Newars describe such social investments as a kind of welfare system: the generosity and hospitality that goes along with religious and social duties such as *guthi* membership, works to redistribute resources and level economic differences; 'No one goes hungry in Sankhu' is a common refrain, or 'Nothing goes to waste: even leftover food and clothes of the dead get put to good use.' Indeed, obligations to kin, *guthi*, neighbours, priests and other ritual specialists encircle the town in tight webs of interdependence that ensure basic levels of provisioning for all social citizens who conform to the logic of the honour economy, however much gender-, caste- and age-based hierarchies may endure. Even the materially wealthy cannot afford to isolate themselves from the town's dense networks of social obligation. For those lacking in finance capital, it is the honour generated through hosting feasts, performing *guthi* tasks, offering *dāna* and making other prescribed social investments that guarantees against the threat of economic destitution. The honour that accrues from fulfilling these social obligations is one's best economic guarantee – the shame in forsaking them, one's surest demise.

Anthropologists working in the Polanyian tradition have suggested that cultural economies, like that of Sankhu, with heavy requirements for social investment differ fundamentally from more deeply capitalist contexts (e.g. Bloch and Parry 1989; Steedly 1993). In the honour economy, an ethic (and indeed practice) of private gain is permitted to flourish in the short run, at the scale of the transient individual life. But individual acquisition is embedded within, and in fact subordinate to, a longer-term 'transactional order' concerned with social and cosmic reproduction. Maurice Bloch and Jonathan Parry (1989: 29) have suggested that such embedded forms of acquisitive practice can be contrasted with a more fully capitalist system which conflates short-term and long-term transactional orders: in western capitalism 'the values of the short-term order have become elaborated into a theory of long-term reproduction', based on the principle that '*only* unalloyed private vice can sustain the public benefit' (emphasis in original).

I wish to emphasize a more analogous relationship between capitalist ideology and the principles of social investment governing the honour economy in Sankhu. First, as Parry (1989) himself notes with respect to the Indian context, the capacity for social investment in Sankhu is premised on an ethical evaluation of finance and trade seemingly even more conducive to the 'spirit of capitalism' than existed in medieval Europe, where usury and other non-productive sources of wealth were branded corrupting and immoral. More importantly, both systems require redistributive social investments to mask the fundamental contradiction between profit premised on inequality and an ideal of social protection for all promised by their legitimating ideologies, whether in the form of an articulated economic philosophy (such as the neoliberal claim that market competition will generate optimal social outcomes and that wealth will trickle down) or normative beliefs about social interdependency (through Newar caste patronage, *guthi* membership and other forms of social obligation). Social investments, whether in the form of state welfare policy or patterns of feasting and hospitality, may mitigate extreme hardship for the poor, but they also provide moral justification for acquisitive behaviour and a social order maintaining uneven accumulation. In Sankhu, patterns of sociality woven through various forms of social investment may work to redistribute resources, but they also lock people into particular social locations – the wife of a usurious merchant, the low-caste client of a Brahman priest. Tight webs of interdependency make it very difficult for individuals to shift that location, especially to shift their status in an upward direction.

5   CASTE AND GENDER ECONOMICS

In addition to demanding an onerous regimen of social investment, the honour economy functions to maintain and defend caste and gender hierarchies. This chapter investigates how these relations of inequality underpin the Newar cultural economy in Sankhu, stressing the disadvantages faced by low castes and women in the accumulation of symbolic and material capital. Drawing on a practice-theoretic framework that engages concepts from Gramsci and Bourdieu – habitus, doxa, symbolic violence, ideology and critical consciousness – as well as insights from feminist geography and anthropology on the cultural and spatial dimensions of oppression and resistance, the chapter considers not only the ritual dimensions of caste and gender (as is often the convention in the anthropological literature on South Asia), but also the socio-spatial dimensions.[1] It examines concrete dominating practices mediating opportunity within the honour economy – the cultural work of enforcing caste and gender hierarchies through the regulation of social space, the division of labour and the built environment, as well as discourses of legitimation. Here the reader gains an understanding not only of dominant caste and gender ideologies (for example, the logic of purity and pollution), but also how prevailing anthropological theories about them express a politics of ethnographic representation.

The emphasis here on cultural *production* raises questions about how ideological constructions occupy the minds – and bodies – of those in subordinate positions. To the extent that they assume postures, behaviours, and roles that mark their own subordination or affirm an ideal of hierarchy as common sense (Bourdieu's doxa and habitus respectively), low castes and women are complicit in their own disadvantage. But they are not solely constituted by hierarchical premises; they are not merely *Homo Hierarchicus* (as Dumont 1970 would have it; see Parish 1997). Low castes, for example, negotiate the stigmatizing dimensions of caste patronage to meet their material needs, while seeking to maximize symbolic capital under conditions of constraint. Women, likewise, have invested their dowries (culturally coded as women's own property) to amass considerable material wealth for their families, even as they adhere to norms of seclusion and modesty. The chapter thus rejects notions of false consciousness that critics allege to be implicit in Gramsci and Bourdieu and defends the potential they claim for individual and collective reflexivity, by exploring how low castes and women recognize the established order as a constructed political order and manipulate material and symbolic resources to advance their interests. In so doing, it illustrates the contradictions of caste and gender ideology and highlights the critical resources available within culture.

ECONOMICS OF CASTE

Caste Ideology

It is simply not possible to understand the Newar cultural economy without recognizing the significance of caste, 'one of the most enduring hegemonic enterprises in all human experience' (Parish 1997: 209). Although caste was outlawed in Nepal in the 1955 Civil Liberties Act (which prohibited discrimination on the basis of *varna*, race, caste, tribe or ethnic group), the state has tacitly permitted caste to persist as an important customary marker of social identity (see Höfer 1979). In Sankhu the caste system serves as a moral and symbolic order structuring social and economic life. As such, caste functions ideologically to justify an uneven distribution of material and symbolic capital in Newar society.

The idiom of purity and pollution operates as one key structuring logic of the caste system: low castes 'suffer for the city', as Steven Parish (1997: 28) puts it, 'soaking up' its inauspiciousness and filth. Their contact with the impurities of human existence allows high castes to maintain levels of purity sufficient for their charge of worshipping the gods, engaging in commerce, ruling and waging war, and ensuring the transcendental purity of values. Three corollary principles accomplish these distinctions: *separation* in matters of marriage and contact; occupational *interdependence* by which each caste fulfils particular professional and ritual roles; and *hierarchical ranking*. This widely repeated formulation first appeared in Célestin Bouglé's *Essais sur le régime des castes* (1971 [1908]) and was extended by anthropologist Louis Dumont (1970) into a theory of caste resting on a fundamental opposition between western and caste societies. By Dumont's reckoning, in western liberal societies those forms of hierarchy (such as race) that express a fundamental breach of the core values of individualism and egalitarianism get classified as discrimination and arouse severe moral condemnation. Caste, on the contrary, operates as a mode of distinction in the context of fundamentally 'holistic' and 'hierarchical' societies and, as such, cannot be evaluated by western rights-based standards of justice. Here the individual has no sociological autonomy and hierarchy results not in inequality but 'consensual interdependence'. In Dumontian fashion, Marriott (1976) argues that Indian persons are 'dividual', rather than individual, to capture the extent of interdependency. The Indian person's 'divisibility' rests also on the principle of 'biological substantialism' by which he or she is subject to transformation through the exchange of coded substances (such as food or *dāna*).

Informants of any caste standing asked to characterize the caste system in Sankhu will indeed at once produce a list of designated caste positions, with Priests at the top, Untouchables at the bottom, and other castes ordered by professional rank in the middle. Yet evidence from Sankhu suggests considerably greater scope for individuality (and individual recognition of injustice) than a Dumontian framework would suggest. The limitations of a Dumontian interpretation of caste become further apparent in Newars' own preoccupation with the political construction of caste. For example, because considerable confusion and contest surrounds the precise ranking of castes, the ranked list of named groups varies from informant to informant. Thus (Merchant-caste) Shresthas might include named Shrestha sub-castes in sketching the caste hierarchy, but gloss over internal divisions of another caste group or even rank a group of lower castes together at the same level. Members of the lower artisan castes are thus often lumped together as a single group by those not interested in the details of rank at the lower levels. Artisan castes themselves (for example, in Sankhu: Painters, Oil Pressers, Blacksmiths) take special care to specify a hierarchy among themselves, with each representing their own caste in a superior position. Such competing cognitive maps make it virtually impossible to generate *the* definitive caste hierarchy and demonstrate the lines of discord within Dumont's perceived holism.

Newar ethnographer Robert Levy (1990) attempts to resolve such distortions of perspective by designating 'macrostatus levels', castes or clusters of castes whose collective social and ritual function is important for the symbolic constitution of the city. Thus, we have an idealized rank ordering of six macro-status levels as in Table 5.1 (named caste groups within each level are also noted, but not ranked, as relative status of castes within levels is highly contested).[2]

Table 5.1 Idealized rank ordering of six macro-status levels

'Pure' castes

I. Priestly castes; note that the hierarchy is 'double-headed' (Gellner 1992) with Brahman and Vajracārya Priests providing ritual services to the Hindu-leaning and Buddhist-leaning laity respectively.

Vajracārya	Buddhist Priests	**Rajopādhyāya Brāhman**	Hindu Priests
Sakya	Goldsmiths; Buddhist		

II. High-level (Chathariya) Shresthas (Merchants); levels I and II are entitled to tantric initiation and, in the case of Hindus, to wear the Hindu sacred thread.

Jośī	Astrologers and Saivite Tantric Priests
Śreṣṭha	Merchants

III. Low-level (Pāñcthariyā) Shresthas (Merchants) and Jyapus (Farmers)

Śreṣṭha	Merchants
Jyapu	Farmers

'Borderline Pure' castes

IV. Artisan castes – groups who call on a different set of ritual specialists than levels I–III and from whom orthodox members of levels I–III will not accept water.

Nau	Barbers
Bhā	Funeral Priests
Kau	Blacksmiths
Citrakār	Painters of religious images
Sāymi	Oil Pressers
Gathu	Gardeners
Duim	Palanquin Carriers, Trumpeters
Chipā	Dyers

'Impure' castes

V. Those from whom castes I–IV will not accept water, but whose touch does not require purification.[3]

Nay	Butchers, Musicians, Barber for borderline pure castes
Jogi	Death Specialists for pure castes; Midwives; Musicians
Danya	Death Specialists, Barbers, and Funeral Priests for Jogis
Dom	Drum players and Duck Raisers

VI. *Untouchables*

Those from whom 'Pure' and 'Borderline Pure' castes will not accept water and whose touch requires purification.

Po	Sweepers, Fishermen, Beggars, Guardians of mother goddesses

---

Source: Derived from Levy (1990).

Here Levy relies on the Dumontian distinction between status and power to explain the superior position of Priests relative to those, such as Merchants and Kings, wielding secular power. In this formulation, the status of Brahmans ranks higher than the power of kings. Note that here we have power construed simply in terms of force, rather than power in the Gramscian sense as working through the culture to influence everyday common sense and practice (see Quigley [1993: 30–1] for a thorough discussion of this aspect of Dumont's theory).

This representation of caste ideology runs into trouble, however, if one considers a fourth principle underlying the caste system revealed in Gloria Raheja's ethnography of ritual prestations in a north Indian village (1988): the *ritual centrality of dominant castes*. Brahman and Vajracharya Priests not only worship the gods, but also (as discussed in Chapter 4) perform the ritually precarious work of absorbing inauspiciousness and evil through gifts of *dāna*. Priest castes thus share with the Borderline Pure Nau (Barbers) and Bha (Funeral Priests), Impure Jogi (Death Specialists), and Untouchable Po (Sweepers) this obligation to receive ritually defiling and precarious biomoral substances of their patrons (although occasions for performing this service and strategies for 'digesting' the inauspiciousness differs among them). In this regard, as Declan Quigley (1995) and Jonathan Parry (1980) have pointed out, Brahmans occupy a morally 'pure', and therefore high, status not because of their association with the priesthood, but in spite of it (and the same can be said for Vajracharyas).

Raheja's study suggests that the essence of the caste system is best captured not through the idiom of purity and pollution, but in terms of obligatory transfers of inauspicious qualities. Her representation of caste as an ideological construct thus emphasizes the ritual centrality of the dominant caste – in her case, the farmer caste. By this reckoning, Shresthas' dominant political-economic position constitutes the centre of a circle of ritual patronage in the Sankhu context (here a generalization of Shrestha dominance cannot be extended as the composition of the dominant caste varies by the (considerably variable) caste distribution within Newar towns). Shresthas are patrons (*jajamāna*) of other castes, high and low, who provide both material and symbolic services (see Table 5.2, Figure 5.1).

In all instances, when dominant castes engage the services of client castes to remove ritually defiling substances such as hair or food for the dead, and when they give their sin- or inauspiciousness-bearing substances to client castes as payment for their services, they are simultaneously acting out economic dominance and symbolically constructing moral superiority. Thus for Raheja power *and* status reside at the centre of networks of ritual prestation (though greater attention to the dynamic of power might suggest placing the dominant caste at the 'apex', not

Table 5.2   Castes with obligations to remove ritually defiling substances from their patrons

---

Brahman and Vajracharya [Priests]:
Accept *dāna* during life-cycle rituals, unpropitious planetary arrangements, and other occasions for unloading sin and inauspiciousness.

Nau [Barbers]:
Cut hair; cut and clean the toenails of high caste *jajamāna* during the preliminary purificatory rites for festivals and life cycle rituals.

Bhā [Funeral Priests]:
Impersonate the spirit of the dead when they accept a large *dāna* offering from the deceased's family on the 11th day of funerary rites.

Jogi [Death Specialists]:
Likewise incarnate the dead (in the state of a ghost [*pret*] before the deceased attains the status of ancestor [*pitri*]) when they receive offerings on the seventh day after death. Thereafter, Jogis accept a share of every feast in their *jajamānas'* household, which is set aside in the name of all deceased in the *jajamānas'* family.

Nay [Butchers]:
Perform the ritually defiling tasks of cutting the umbilical cord of high-caste newborns and playing music in high-caste funeral processions; if children in the *jajamāna's* family repeatedly die young, Nay – as a 'rough' or 'hard' caste – may be asked to 'buy' the next newborn child so that ghosts and demons will be less likely to attack the child; at the time of caste initiation, such children are again 'sold' to the *jajamāna* so that they may participate as full members of their own caste.[4]

Po:
Accept a form of *dāna* considered extremely difficult to 'digest' on the most inauspicious and ritually defiling occasions, such as eclipses. They also perform the most defiling mundane tasks for dominant caste *jajamāna*, like cleaning toilets.

---

the 'centre' of the Newar social geography of caste). Her view rejects Dumont's vision of a simple linear hierarchy with Brahmans' high-status position at the top and Kings (or Merchants, in Levy's formulation of the Newar context) wielding secular power at the second-level ranking.

Raheja's model has the advantage of alleviating some of the ambiguities surrounding the exact position of intermediate castes in a purity/pollution continuum; in the ritual centrality model the emphasis is on their orientation to the dominant caste, rather than on a rank among them. Of course, elements of both logics come to the fore in different contexts as Lerche (1993) points out, so neither can claim to have captured the essence of caste society. More significant for our purposes, however, are the critics, such as James Laidlaw (1995), who argue that Raheja's model is too

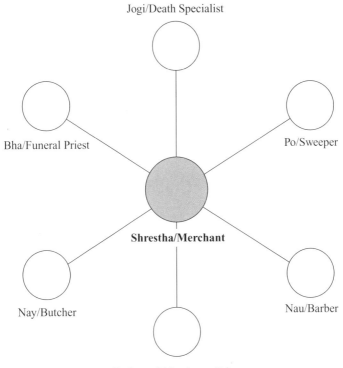

Figure 5.1 The caste system as a circle of inauspiciousness-removing patronage (adapted from Raheja, 1988)

reductive, presenting caste patronage as a total social system structuring relationships in determinate ways. Here again we have a formulation that eclipses individual agency and posits a fundamentally different kind of person, whose interdependence, and indeed interrelated biomoral constitution, produces a disposition to acquiesce to the collective interest, especially that of caste and family – and that, as Mines (1994) points out, creates a myth of the South Asian as Other, the radical antithesis of the western individual.

Thus, while I find the macro-social models of Dumont, Levy, Marriott and Raheja useful for interpreting Newar cultural ideology, an epistemological framework emphasizing the economics of practice is more compelling for encompassing not only the realm of ideology, but also the zone of people's experience, reflexivity and indeed capacity for critical consciousness.

The focus in Bourdieu and Gramsci on the politics of culture, that is, can move beyond the moral relativism in Dumont, Marriot and Raheja – 'theirs is a fundamentally different society outside "our" frame of moral judgement' – by emphasizing not only where power resides in the caste system, but also how it moves through a range of cultural contexts and how it is experienced by differently positioned social actors.

CULTURAL PRODUCTION OF CASTE

Urban Space

However encompassing caste ideology may profess to be, it can never be homologous with an essential Newar 'culture'. It must be continually created and maintained as a legitimating concept of reality through concrete cultural practices. The construction and regulation of urban space is one sphere of cultural practice through which dominant castes have attempted to naturalize caste distinctions and make them seem moral and just to those in disadvantaged social locations. The chronicles (dating from the Malla period) dictate that impure castes reside in designated quarters outside the core areas of the town reserved for commerce and worship. Low castes were thus limited to building one-storey dwellings with thatched roofs and to wearing distinctive dress – for example sleeveless coats for Nay. Pure and Borderline castes occupied more central areas proximate to temples and shops; they could live in multi-level, tile-roofed brick houses and wear clothes befitting their higher status. Today, of course, spatial distinctions no longer enjoy politico-legal sanction and modern styles of construction and dress have eroded these kinds of material distinctions among castes. But a fundamental spatial ordering still prevails in Sankhu, with Pure and Borderline castes residing at the centre and Impure and Untouchables at the periphery, where the ghosts and spirits also reside. The latter are spaces of the city where high castes tread only at considerable peril. I noticed my Shrestha and Joshi hosts would become tense when passing by low-caste quarters, often coughing or spitting in disgust. In one instance a Shrestha research assistant became faint while conducting interviews in an Untouchable area; she fled and was later diagnosed as having been possessed by a ghost lurking in the area (see also Parish 1997: 23).

  Local sanction also bans low castes from entering certain temple complexes, the courtyards of Priests, and any shop whose wares they might contaminate with their touch. High castes restrict admittance to their homes based on caste ranking: Po are not admitted at all (except

to clean latrines on the ground floor); Impure castes can enter only as
far as the ground floor or, at most, the first-floor landing, and must wash
their own dishes if offered food or drink (lest the high castes come in
contact with their *cipa* – leftover, and polluted, food or defiled utensil);[5]
Borderline Pure castes, though historically admitted only as far as the
second-floor landing, are these days invited, along with Jyapu, Shrestha
and Priest castes to the kitchen level – though not as far as the cooking
hearth, which is reserved only for household members.

Caste division of labour

Caste ideology is also maintained through a rigid division of material
and ritual labour. Shrestha Merchants avoid stigmatizing manual labour
that would reflect poorly on their honour and prefer to concentrate in
commercial and service sectors. Priests and Borderline Pure castes
carry out their caste-prescribed occupations to various degrees, but
also commonly seek 'modern' forms of employment in the service
sector. Within the small social universe of Sankhu, however, Impure
and Untouchable castes are effectively confined to caste-designated
occupations, along with menial services for their *jajamāna* (high-caste
patrons), such as portering, delivering messages or running errands (see
Chapter 6 for a discussion of low-caste [spatial] strategies to resist their
low status by seeking employment outside Sankhu). The low status of
low-caste professions is reflected in low rates of remuneration, often in
kind rather than in cash, and often also on credit, *udhāro*, resulting in
many cases, in only partial payment for services rendered.

In addition to cultivating individual *jajamāna* relationships, each
caste plays a specific role in the 20 or so citywide festivals, crucial for
maintaining the cosmic and social order. During the Vajrayogini festival,
for instance, Vajracharya priests ride arrogantly alongside the deity,
expressing their high status as close-to-the-gods. Some Shresthas play
the role of 'gentlemen', *bhalādami*, strolling casually behind the drunken,
palanquin-bearing fray, as if to lend respectability and composure to the
chaos at hand; others participate in carrying the deities and playing music.
Nay perform stigmatizing animal sacrifices to feed the bloodthirsty gods
and goddesses. Jogi, Duim, Saymi, Dobi and Nay each play a special
kind of music. Brahmans and Joshis officiate for forms of worship not
handled by Vajracharyas. And Painters prepare and maintain the festival's
images and iconography. The Vajrayogini and Mohani festivals also
ceremonially reconstruct the medieval Malla court and designate roles

for representatives of the king and his functionaries, including the *duāre, bumbhare* and *chembhare*.[6] As noted in Chapter 4, caste-based ritual participation in the town's public festivals is underwritten by the system of *rāj guthis*. There are *guthis* that finance, among other things, the daily offering of flowers to Vajrayogini; a permanent guardian of the jewels which adorn her; the provision of whitewash, camphor, incense and rope for securely tying the goddess to the palanquin during the festival; and income for each caste participant of all major festivals. Although the 1964 land reforms have diminished the financial capacity of the *guthis*, the *national* scale of *guthi* administration reflects the state's continued official involvement in Newar ritual life and serves to legitimate caste as a key cultural axiom of social life.

Guthis *as regulators of caste*

Private *guthis*, too, are a most significant marker of caste difference in Newar society. Both mortuary (*sī*) and lineage (*digu dyo*) *guthis* are strictly segregated by caste and thus play a significant role in efforts to preserve caste purity against encroachments from 'below'. The ambiguity surrounding the precise ranking of castes introduces some porosity to the caste system, affording ample opportunities for households to claim higher status. One of the most common strategies is to marry one's daughter up the caste hierarchy, thus claiming status equality with her marital relatives. Mortuary *guthis* serve as a significant deterrent against such attempts at 'marrying in'. In Sankhu, marriages are still primarily arranged by the parents of the betrothed through a paid matchmaker, although with a first generation of TV-watching and college-going youth so called 'love marriages' are on the rise (resulting in significant stress on the caste system). If a household in Sankhu wants to ensure a 'Pure' caste marriage for their son, then a good place to start the search for a bride would be within the other lineages of one's mortuary *guthi* where caste pedigree can be assured.

Guthis also regulate against threats to the collective position of their members within the *jajamāni* system. For example, at the time of this research a Vajracharya Priest in Sankhu had recently begun offering priestly services to a Nay *jajamāna*, an Impure caste customarily ineligible for Vajracharya patronage. Even if motivated by acute financial necessity, this action was perceived as an affront to collective Vajracharya status, and, in response, the Priest's *sī guthi* excommunicated him, effectively stripping him of his Priestly caste status. Unable to endure the social costs of isolation from the Vajracharya community and its *jajamāni* networks (even weighed against the added income from Nay patronage), the Priest promptly renounced his relationship to the Nay *jajaman*, after which he was re-admitted to the Vajracharya caste and the status quo was restored. Thus, with its rigorous principles of excluding outsiders and regulating standards of social investment, the *guthi* system provides a means of coping with struggles over caste identification – and entrenching the principle of caste hierarchy.

Rules about commensality

Given the propensity for pollution and inauspiciousness to transmit through water and cooked food, practices of commensality are another key domain for expressing caste hierarchy. Boiled rice is considered particularly perilous; its consumption is limited to the kitchen area on the top floor of the house with one's immediate consanguineal relatives. Occasions for eating in more mixed company, such as feasts or rotating labour exchanges during planting and harvest, require the less precarious roasted and beaten form of rice called *baji*. Impure castes cannot attend the feasts of castes higher than their own, though they may be given a share of leftovers the following day (except Jogis, who must accept a share of the feast as a form of ritual patronage – delivered on the ground floor of the *jajamāna's* house before guests arrive – in the name of the *jajamāna's* ancestors). Untouchable Po are given *cipa*, polluted leftovers, food that has already been 'touched' and discarded. Rotating labour exchanges require similar precautions, as the host household should customarily provide an afternoon snack for all those participating. Farmers who belong to a caste higher than that of the host decline the snack and receive a small cash payment instead.

High-caste 'spin' on low-caste roles[7]

The doctrine of karma provides ample ideological justification for caste distinction and was evoked routinely by high castes in response to my naïve inquiries about the justice of a system that consigns some to absorbing the filth of the city and others to engage in 'benign' commerce. It was explained to me that low castes warrant their marginal status because they are dirty, sexually loose, offensive in their language and otherwise have failed to master acceptable patterns of social conduct. So sharp is low-caste speech, explained a Brahman Priest, that high castes should hear only the opposite of what they say: 'Because they were born into a poor caste, and because we sit much higher than them in society, their curse is our blessing; they curse us, and we on the contrary get blessed.' More fundamentally, low castes must suffer for the sins committed in previous lives: 'The conditions … of high and low castes', writes Parish (1997: 52), 'are … the *just desserts* for [past] actions for which persons were morally responsible; they get what they deserve and the status quo is justified.'

Interviewing low castes in the company of high-caste research assistants afforded an opportunity to observe high castes engaged in a sort of 'spin control', as Parish puts it, attempting to cast the negative consequences of hierarchy in a positive light. For example, while translating from Newari into Nepali during a conversation with a Po informant, one Shrestha interlocutor cast the Po's state of permanent pollution in these favourable terms: 'He never even has to purify himself like all the other castes, never has to worry about bathing or pollution; he is lucky that he can just walk around freely.' He continued:

Actually, for Pode [Po] begging is also a right, because just like we call on a specific *guruju* [Vajracharya Priest] to serve as our priest, we also have to give our *cipa* to a specific Pode. If another Pode comes to beg from us there will be a big fight [among the Po].

Likewise, in an interview with a Jogi, the share of high-caste feasts given pejoratively to Jogis as representatives of deceased ancestors was transmuted by my research assistant to become:

… the very most pure share of the feast; not even a fly should touch the *Jogi bva* [Jogi's share]; none of us [Shresthas] may eat until we have offered this share to *our* Jogi; it is carefully served in the most elaborate manner and should be received with great honour.

The expression, 'our Jogi', signals that the informant is a caste client of the research assistant's household. Such expressions of affection, along with other paternalistic gestures such as offering snacks, sending gifts on the marriage or initiation of their children and giving blessings and other ceremonial gifts during Mohani provide a deliberate palliative for the abuses of caste. They establish the *jajamāna* as fictive kin or benevolent patron – and represent caste obligations as benign guarantees for security and protection. Here we can recall Bourdieu's notion of 'symbolic violence', which cautions us to recognize in such gestures of kindness a form of domination that binds low castes more firmly to their high-caste patrons through feelings of trust and obligation. The very absence of coercion and overt violence signals that domination is secure.

Habitus: Low-caste Consent

To a certain extent ideological constructions and perceptions of the socially disadvantaged converge – as revealed in the domain of practice that Bourdieu calls 'habitus'. Low castes reflect their ascribed low status in the submissive, docile manner they assume and in the honorific forms of address they use in the presence of high castes, or in the myriad ways they self-regulate in matters of purity and pollution (such as by obliging the conventions of constrained mobility in temple areas, shops and high-caste homes). Low castes also valorize the fundamental caste principle of hierarchy in their attempts to establish social distance from and dominance over other low castes. For example, low castes reproduce stigmatizing discourse about the filth and roughness of those they wish to place in a relatively low-caste position, and they, too, exercise extreme fastidiousness in monitoring the defiling touch of castes lower than themselves through strict rules of isogamy and commensality. The concern with status and ritual pollution also manifests, as Quigley (1993) has argued, in low

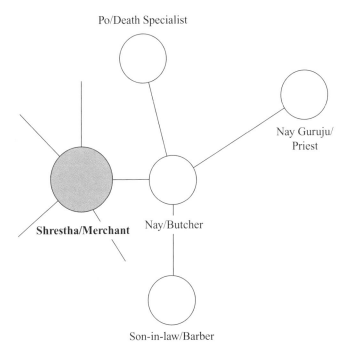

Figure 5.2   Replicated circles of ritual patronage

castes' attempts to replicate the dominance of Shresthas by positioning themselves at the centre of the inauspiciousness-removing services of other castes. For example, Nay enlist their own priest specialists (Nay Guruju) to officiate at life-cycle rituals and receive *dāna*;[8] a barber to clean their toenails (usually a son-in-law or brother-in-law); and a lower caste to accept a share of their feasts on behalf of the deceased (Po).[9] Figure 5.1 can thus be amended to reflect such overlapping circles of ritual patronage (see Figure 5.2), which suggest a collective cultural affirmation about hierarchy as an organizing principle of social life.[10]

Finally, low castes affirm the idea of hierarchy when they attempt to elevate their individual or collective caste status, such as by marrying daughters 'up' as has been noted previously, or by altering their position within the networks of ritual patronage, also noted previously in the example of Butcher-caste households cultivating the patronage of a high-caste Vajracharya Priest (instead of a caste-appropriate Nay *Guruju*). In the latter case, once the Priest was forced by his *guthi* members to stop serving Nay as *jajamāna*, the Nay in turn refused to perform their customary *jajamāni* work for him. This kind of jockeying for status reinforces the principle of hierarchy, even as it challenges the location of particular castes in the established social geography of *jajamāni* relationships.

Contradiction and Discontent

Understanding low-caste consent in terms of habitus offers only a partial view of life in caste society and reduces the ethnographic enterprise to descriptions of the status quo. Parish (1997: 34) argues instead for a more politically potent role for ethnographic research in giving due expression to the contradictions and discontents of caste (or other dominant) ideologies: 'We cannot ... simply substitute knowing a person's position in society for knowing the person. To do so risks doing some injustice to actors, reducing them to social constructions when they are more than this.' By this reckoning consent does not necessarily reflect total blindness to caste as a political construction, just as practical dominance does not necessarily reflect total hegemony.

On the contrary, low castes often recognize the stigmatizing effects of hierarchy *as* domination, and they participate and consent for strategic, not merely moral, reasons. A senior member of the Nay *guthi* that performs sacrifices and plays music during festivals described the *jajamāni* system to me this way:

Jajamāna traditionally means that if you are my *jajamāna*, then I have to do all of your work. If you have a feast then you have to invite us and give us a share. There are about 200 households of these *jajamāna* [to be handled by this particular Nay's lineage]. Sometimes this guy dies, sometimes that guy: it is a lot of work to manage all that! [Here he is referring to the role of Nay musicians in high-caste funeral processions.] And then there's also cutting the umbilical cords. And if there is a marriage, we also have to go there [to the *jajamāna*'s house] to slaughter a buffalo for the feast. But they would never give us the feast right then. A day later they'd say, 'Here, take the feast of yesterday.' Well, who wants to eat spoiled leftover food?!

Clearly, this man experiences his *jajamāni* obligations as onerous and distasteful, especially the subordination entailed in receiving the *jajamāna*'s feast one day after invited high-caste guests. Embedded in this description, too, is an economistic, rather than moral, interpretation of *jajamāna* relations: managing 200 clients and (later in the interview) collecting harvest shares as payment for services rendered. During a discussion about the decline of *rāj guthis* endowing public rituals, a Borderline Pure caste man (recently elected Chair of one of Sankhu's Village Development Committees) similarly stressed the economic significance of caste occupations:

The [Vajrayogini] festival and all the other *guthis* won't stop functioning entirely even if you try to abolish caste. See, caste-related work is the main source of income for a lot of people. I mean, you have the Nay caste, the Jogi caste, the Citrakar caste – they don't just work to fulfil the ritual function of their caste! Their caste is also their profession. And why does that Nay or that Jogi or that Citrakar do that profession? Well, it's his source of income. He makes a living from that income, right?

As a source of livelihood, patronage relations may be bought and sold, traded away for other assets or passed down as a form of wealth in divisions of household property – much as Peter Mayer (1993) and Jens Lerche (1993) describe *jajamāni* relations in late nineteenth-century north India and contemporary coastal Orissa respectively. The Brahman Priest officiating in Sankhu for most of the duration of this research had purchased 'patronage-time' from his cousins and brothers. Similarly, one Nau woman explained that on the division of her family's property, one brother agreed to inherit less land in exchange for more *jajamāna*. In addition to income, *jajamāna* relationships provide other material benefits. Thus when a Vajracharya Priest from a very poor household boasted of the high moral stature of his *jajamāna,* one of the most notoriously usurious and wealthy businessmen in Sankhu, his praise came down, ultimately, to the financial resources the *jajamāna* has to offer:

He is such a good *jajamāna*, the very best there is. He knows most of the Sanskrit verses and sometimes he'll even correct me when I make a mistake. I don't have to spend so much time teaching him what to do, like in the *śrāddha* [ancestor worship] you saw today. He also has *first class* materials for worshipping the gods, like that silver *argha*[11] and that beautiful bowl made from the horn of a rhinoceros. If you want to see how a good Buddhist *śrāddha* is done, all you have to do is come to his house because he does it the right way, taking no short cuts. And if I have any [financial] problems he will take care of them; I can always go to him for loans; I don't need to worry.

Consent to providing patronage services, then, may reflect a self-conscious balancing between the stigma of low-caste identity and security against poverty and hunger. As discussed in Chapter 6, if alternative means of subsistence can be found, sufficient to offset the social costs of defying caste norms, then low castes find no compelling moral obligation to honour their *jajamāna's* ritual needs.

The self-conscious nature of low-caste participation in caste relations is also evident in the contrasting representations they offer of their ritual roles vis-à-vis the *desa* – the ritual realm headed spiritually by a Newar king.[12] Here it must be recalled that caste organizes services not only for the *jajamāna*, but also for the collective cosmic and social realm. Nay, for instance, play music for festival processions and perform the sacrificial slaughter of animals. The same senior Nay man who earlier expressed his distaste for *jajamāni* work recounted with pride the significance of his caste for maintaining order in the *desa:*

In Sankhu, without us the [Vajrayogini] and Mohani [Dashain] festivals could not take place; they could not even begin without us, since it is we who assemble the people with our music, who announce the festival is about to begin; at that point, our word is the law.

In marked contrast to the continual negotiation and flux in *jajamāna* relations, moreover, Nay and other low-status castes have continued with remarkable consistency to perform their ritual work for the realm. They have maintained these commitments in spite of dwindling remuneration by the National Guthi Association. Here is how the senior Nay explained why his caste's music group has ceased playing for funeral processions of individual *jajamāna,* but continues to perform for city-wide festivals:

If someone [in the *jajamāna's* house] died, we had to go; if someone was born we had to go [to cut the umbilical cord]; that kind of work we have all abandoned. It became difficult for them [*jajamāna*] and difficult for us, so why should any of us bother? ... but the work of the gods, it's not okay to stop doing that; one must continue with one's own work in that regard.

Thus Nay consider themselves to share with all other caste groups an unconditional obligation – and collective subordinate position – with respect to the gods; but they do not always extend the moral dimensions of caste to encompass their relations with *jajamāna.*

Contradictions are at play, even within the hierarchy of ascribed caste roles. Low castes recognize that their labour, though ritually defiling, is crucial to maintaining the system as a whole. We have already noted the ambiguity of purity–pollution criteria for ranking castes – since Priests share with Barbers and Death Specialists the stigmatizing task of removing inauspicious qualities from the dominant caste, and since every caste requires this kind of ritual patronage by others whom they designated as lower status. The practice of tantra introduces further ambiguities which we can explore with recourse to Dumont's hierarchical ranking of the status of priests as a higher form of authority than the secular power of kings. In order to theorize the significance of tantra in the context of caste societies, Levy (1990) argues that power and status, rather than being separated along a secular/religious divide, constitute different *kinds* of religion in Newar society – the former having to do with tantra, kings' sacrifice to 'dangerous' female deities and esoteric rituals, and the latter with dharmic values, purity and pollution, 'ordinary' male deities and the dominance of Brahman priests.[13] In the religion of power, the ranking of purity and pollution loses its moral force, as Priests, Kings, Butchers, Death Specialists, and other tantric initiates participate together in the pacification of dangerous deities through esoteric tantric rituals.

This formulation offers some compelling explanations for the pride low castes take in performing citywide ritual services (and their relative irreverence for *jajamāni* obligations). The sacrifices performed by Nay during festivals risk being equated with murder and ordinary butchering, sin and stigmatized labour in the context of dharmic ideals. But in their ability to transmute sacrifice into a religious act, the Nay transcend the implications of impurity, and thus join the King (as sacrificer) and Priests (as tantric priests) in opposition to those trapped in the interdependencies of the city (Levy 1990: 345).[14] Even Untouchables, through the very fact of their 'toughness' – the fact that they don't even *need* tantra to accomplish the feats of managing defiling substances – elicit the respect, indeed the fear, of those 'confined' solely to the moral realm of purity and pollution. Thus Nay and other low castes enjoy a kind of privileged status through their association with tantric knowledge – and are reluctant to forego this status by withdrawing from the public rituals associated with their caste, even as their income from this work dwindles.

Critical Consciousness

For dominant castes, resolution of the contradictions of caste comes easily with recourse to ideologies that represent hierarchy as the natural and moral state of the world. For low castes, the contradictions can offer moments of insight into the arbitrary foundation of caste as a constructed political order. When they consent to the hierarchical implications of caste, they may do so strategically, engaging *jajamāna* relationships to meet their material needs. Recent strategies of abandoning caste patronage in favour of alternative sources of income (while preserving their association with the 'religion of power') reflect a more conscious will to resist the stigmatizing implications of caste, made possible (as will be explored in Chapter 6) by the emergence of new service-sector jobs in Kathmandu.

A clear legacy of critical consciousness is apparent in the stories low castes have told over the generations about the origins of their position in the caste hierarchy. By revealing the arbitrary foundations of caste, these stories create the possibility of alternative futures. A Nay account of caste origins, for example, attributes their low status to the capricious action of kings and to accident of circumstance:

Long, long ago we were the respected eldest son of the King – that's why our caste name is Shahi [respectful form for Nay]. Among the King's sons, none agreed to do the work of sacrificing or butchering water buffalo. Since the Kingdom required a meatcutter, the King proclaimed one day that the next morning whoever could be found defecating with their buttocks to the east would be selected to perform these tasks. The next day the King's army searched throughout the Kingdom for someone fitting the King's specifications, but came back empty-handed. Upon entering the palace, however, they found the King's own eldest son defecating as the King had described. What to do? How could the task of butchering fall on the King's eldest son? But the King honoured his proclamation and declared that from then on his eldest son would be designated sacrificer and butcher.

To assist his son in this task, the King allocated many servants to him: Chitrakaar for book keeping, Duiṃ for grazing the water buffalo, Chipa for kneading blood, Nau for burning off the buffaloes' hair, Bha for packing the meat, Kau for scraping the bones, Jyapu for transporting the meat, and Gubhaju [Vajracharya] for accepting *dāna* during death rituals. In this way, other castes were also formed.

All Shahi, as descendants of this eldest of the King's sons, are members of the Kashi clan. But we did not automatically become impure [of water unacceptable status]. In fact, the King regularly ate feasts prepared by his eldest son, even after he had become a butcher. One day, as the King was going to eat, he noticed a drop of blood in his water; horrified, it was at that point that he told his son he would no longer accept water from him.[15]

This story enables its tellers to represent hierarchy on their own terms, and not those of the dominant ideology – to resist its implications even as they operate within its parameters. The king's son assumed the responsibility of butchering only because he happened to be in the wrong place at the wrong time. He is not morally flawed or naturally subordinate, but a person caught up in circumstances beyond his control. Nor is there anything stigmatizing about butchering per se; rather, butchering is represented as socially necessary work that acquired polluting implications only through another chance occurrence. The story also asserts Nay pre-eminence over other castes, including Vajracharya Priests, who are represented here as the Nays' royally proclaimed servants. Hierarchy here is an imposition, not a natural fact, a cultural construction, not an objective reality. The story thus raises the possibility that social life might be organized according to alternative moral principles. By showing how their status is socially constructed, the story establishes distance between its tellers and the social identities ascribed to them by the caste system – a perspective which might, as Parish (1997: 140) suggests, 'keep actors flexible, preparing them to seek and accept … change should conditions allow it'.

ECONOMICS OF GENDER

Gender Ideology and its Production

The honour economy also has a pronounced gender dimension bearing directly on material opportunities available to women. A household's honour accrues not only by maintaining social investments, but also by managing the sexuality and ritual pollution of its women. The requirement to do so derives from ideologies attributing women with dangerous qualities, resulting from the ritual pollution they acquire through menstruation and childbearing and from their location 'in between' the lineages of their father and their husband.[16] During menstruation, the polluting qualities of menstrual blood place women in a temporary state of pollution, comparable to the permanent status of Impure castes, while the act of childbirth defiles an entire household.[17] These episodes of impurity can be managed by appropriate ritual procedures, but if mismanaged they evoke the danger of unrestrained sexuality. The moral peril in women's sexuality resides in its symbolic association with the perpetuation of the patriline and the protection of the spiritual solidarity of agnatic males. Thus while honour functions much like a possession for men (it can be gained and lost, nurtured or squandered), for women it behaves more like a character trait that reflects not only on themselves, but also on their household (Liechty 2003). 'A girl's body', explained a Butcher-caste man, 'is a reflection of her parent's honour'. It is primarily through sexuality and pollution (as opposed to integrity in maintaining social investments) that a woman's honour is gauged. If not properly managed, women's sexuality and routine bouts of ritual pollution can compromise the pedigree of an entire household or lineage.

The *production* of gender ideology, then, has largely to do with neutralizing women's 'dangerous' qualities. Such management is accomplished to a large extent by control of women's movement in space. As repositories of household honour, women's actions require considerable collective surveillance in the public spaces of the household and beyond. Although practice varies by caste, the high-caste norm of restricting women's movement outside the household only to limited occasions (visiting in-laws, meeting ritual obligations, working in the family shop or field) expresses the dominant ideology of women's seclusion to which most households aspire.[18] Recent brides face the greatest restrictions since their sexuality is at once most crucial and most threatening to the patriline. Thus, they may not leave the house unaccompanied or without the permission of their husband and mother-in-law. The only legitimate destination is their natal home or the home of another relative, from which they can return only with an escort and only upon being sent for by their husband. On a visit to her natal home in Sankhu, one recently married Shrestha woman described the extent of such restrictions within her marital household:

> They [husband and mother-in-law] don't send me outside at all. Not even to the store. If we need anything, he [husband] gets it, or my mother-in-law gets it. I expect they won't send me out for such errands for maybe one or two years. Usually a family won't let a new bride outside the house. They say they have to protect their honour.

Likewise, while anyone may fall prey to vicious and powerful gossip networks in Sankhu, women of any married status can assume themselves to be an automatic and special focus of public discussion when they are in the public domain – how do they look, what are they wearing, with whom are they walking, where are they going?

Guthi practices also construct gender difference. Membership is organized by *households*: all households of a given lineage in the case of *digu dyo guthis* and same-caste households of a neighbourhood in the case of *sī guthis*. Membership is inherited. In mortuary *guthis* households are represented by the senior male household head, while in lineage *guthis* they are represented by all male members of participating households who have been initiated into adulthood. In both cases, direct membership is expressed by who from a given household attends feasts (and in the case of lineage *guthis*, who receives *sī*, a designated organ of the head of a goat sacrificed for the feast). Women belong to *guthis* by virtue of their membership in households, but they participate in different ways. They do not enjoy full direct membership in lineage *guthis* because their ritual loyalty is considered more ambiguous, transferring as it does in marriage (along with residence) from the natal to marital household.[19] Likewise, because women's regular bouts of impurity associated with menstruation and childbirth are considered incompatible with mortuary rituals, they are excluded from highly valued ritual obligations of mortuary *guthis*. Women's participation occurs rather through the onerous labour associated with preparing ritual offerings and the associated *guthi* feasts.

While women's reproductive roles must be honoured and protected, women do not generally enjoy the same social status or property rights within the household as men. Newar customary practices (and, until 2003, the Nepal National Code) dictate that shares of family property should be divided equally among the father, mother and sons.[20] Typically (and by law up to the passage of an amendment to the property rights bill in 2002), a daughter inherits a share of her parents' property (*aṅgsa*) only if she remains unmarried until the age of 35, at which time she receives a share sufficient only to cover her living expenses until marriage (as well as the cost of her wedding feast and dowry). On marriage her share should be returned to her natal patriline, and divorced women have had rights in neither their parents' nor their husband's property.[21] Inheritance practices reflect a patrilineal reckoning of descent, a preference for patrilocal joint family residence, and concentration of status and power in male members of the household and lineage. Since married women reside with their husband's joint family (until it splits), their social universe straddles two households; the shift from the position of daughter in the natal household to daughter-in-law in the marital household normatively entails a fall in status. In the marital household, women generally face subordinating treatment until the birth of their first son, when they earn some status for their role in social reproduction. Sons are required to perform death observances for lineage ancestors, while daughters are singularly unqualified to perform this duty because menstruation places them in a state of ritual pollution that could compromise the spiritual future of the deceased. Infertility problems automatically get ascribed to women and are grounds at least for harassing and subordinating treatment, if not, even today, for taking a second wife.

As within many other culturally South and Southeast Asian societies, gender ideologies of sexuality, seclusion and pollution are also enforced

through a pronounced sexual division of labour that entrusts women
with responsibility for most domestic (household-related) labour and
limits their ability to accumulate material and symbolic forms of wealth.
In the absence of modern plumbing and reliable electricity, domestic
work alone becomes an extraordinarily time-consuming affair and as a
result married women enjoy very little leisure time. While campaigns
for 'girl child education' have evened out enrolments for boys and girls
at the primary levels (Shrestha 2002: 110), girls do not get the same
encouragement for studying at home or proceeding to higher levels
of education due to competing domestic responsibilities. Household
obligations thus lend practical force to ideologies of seclusion and
together they virtually preclude opportunities for outside employment
(except in teaching, a profession that is considered acceptable for women
not only because it extends their role in social reproduction, but also
because it enables women to return home by mid-afternoon to prepare
the evening meal).

In agricultural households women do the work of planting, harvesting
and weeding (the relatively 'light' labour that if done for hire earns them
a wage half that earned by men for ploughing – NRs 40/day with snack
for women, as compared to NRs 80/day with snack for men at the time
of this research). Commerce, meanwhile, is the conventional preserve
of men. Unmarried daughters and senior women may become involved
in various household enterprises, such as attending the family store, but
not usually in a management capacity or in large-scale transactions such
as wholesaling or banking. Harris-White's (1996) observations about the
limited roles of women in grain marketing systems of India hold true
for the Nepal context as well: the division of labour in production and
marketing reflects ideological norms about the gendering of tasks and
appropriate behaviour, and women are construed primarily as 'vehicles'
(through marriage alliances) for the transfer of commercial resources
between kinship groups. Like practices maintaining caste hierarchy,
seclusion and the sexual division of labour are justified with a predictable
'spin' on women's subordination: 'Newars treat their women well', is the
common refrain, 'because they don't send them outside the house; all
they have to do is cook and clean the house; we respect our women'.

Because the honour economy values displays of wealth as much as
exhibitions of moral integrity, *ijat* has a more material dimension that
also bears on the position of women in Newar society. A woman's very
appearance is considered to reflect on her household's honour. Only a
shameful household would allow their (married-in) women to walk around

'bare', without jewellery or the appropriate standards of dress, or even accept a bride who does not meet certain standards of beauty. Of course, in lending ideological weight to the notion that women should be well-adorned and dressed, the honour in wealth creates spaces for pleasure.[22] But it can also be experienced as a burden, to the extent that it limits women's freedom, exerts pressure to conform and invites collective social judgement. One Shrestha woman described how her husband's brother had objected to her marriage on grounds of her bad looks:

Actually, people only care about a woman having a pretty face. My face is not pretty. It is too dark. They [her in-laws] complained so much before I was married that my looks were not good enough. One brother-in-law even told me, 'My family will not accept you; we will not allow my brother to marry you, and even if he does, we won't allow you to stay in our house. No, we will not endure that kind of shame.'[23]

The sexual division of labour and restrictions on women's mobility are examples of cultural practices that defend dominant gender ideologies, represent them as natural and moral, and facilitate the accumulation of symbolic capital by men. Such conventions are not expressions of an essential Newar 'culture', but rather the outcome of repeated social practices in a specific geographic and historical location. Given men's and women's distinctive contributions to household honour, they express interdependency as much as hierarchy. At the same time, the *ijat* economy does serve as a particularly forceful deterrent to women's participation in kinds of market activities that require much social interaction or movement outside the household. Neither is it easy for women to make social investments independently, say in the form of hospitality or religious patronage, that yield symbolic capital and enhance economic security. Through the honour economy, we can thus recognize a dialectical relationship between gender ideology and social opportunity: ideological constructions of gender influence women's ability to compete in the honour economy; and the disadvantages women face in the accumulation of symbolic capital in turn inform normative understandings of women's roles and responsibilities in society. These patterns and relationships are inscribed in the organization of space through the paths women (are authorized to) trace among public and private domains and through the networks of sociality that encompass Sankhu in relations of interdependence. Women also act consciously on space, however, variously complying with and resisting dominant gender ideologies.

Women's Habitus

Of course ideology does not transpose directly onto consciousness – and it is the ethnographer's task to explore this realm of contradiction between the world as represented and the world as experienced. At times women's practices do often suggest a convergence between gender constructions and women's perceptions. In everyday bodily comportment, speech and action women, like low castes, often give expression to their ascribed low status – such as when they address their husbands honorifically, bow in respect to status seniors each morning before tea, or the myriad ways in which they self-regulate their movement in space. It is precisely these mundane and bodily manifestations of consent that Bourdieu suggests reveal the extent to which masculine domination – as a form of symbolic violence – has insinuated itself in women's consciousness and 'schemes of perception' as the natural way of things. Beyond these 'somatic expressions of the political' (Bourdieu 2001) are practices and behaviours that bear more direct material consequences. Consider, for example, common practices surrounding inheritance (*aṅgsa*). Although unmarried women over the age of 35 have had legal rights to inherit their father's property since the 1963 reforms to the Civil Code, social conventions among Newars dictate that landed property should pass exclusively to male heirs and that women should not enjoy the kind of autonomy that direct ownership of landed property would entail. Newar women meeting legal criteria for inheritance in fact have often declined to exercise this right and prefer to remain a dependent in a brother's household.

In such circumstances, when women's practices are structured in accordance with the dominant world view (Bourdieu's 'habitus'), the scope for progressive social change seems particularly narrow. The pathbreaking work of Amartya Sen (1990) on capabilities has relevance here for our interpretation of women's (and low castes') beliefs. Although that tolerance for subordination must be seen as a reflection of individual agency and 'perceived interest', it must not be confused with objective well-being resulting from 'positive utility' – as neo-classical economists would have it. For the satisfaction of subjective preferences is *not* a reliable indicator of life quality, because preferences, as Bourdieu would also agree, could be shaped by oppression and deprivation. Sen's moral economy thus suggests a warrant for action that will be explored in Chapter 6, founded not on expressions of preference (habitus), but on universal standards of life quality. If we probe the motivations of individual women in electing to place themselves in dependent positions vis-à-vis men, however, we find that women's choices often reflect modes of consciousness missing in Sen's sympathetic formulation, deriving from their strategic concerns for their own security. As one middle-aged and single low-caste woman explained to me, if a woman rejects the dependent status associated with being female, she risks falling outside the networks of (especially kin and *guthi*) obligation that encircle Sankhu, constituting Newar society and providing the ultimate protection against poverty and ill health (see also Agarwal 1994):

> Sure, I have a right to a share of my brother's inheritance. Still, I am not planning to take it. I'll just give my share to my brother. See, if I take my share, he and his wife might not take care of me later. Then who knows what could happen.

Tales circulating in Sankhu of women who *did* pursue legal rights to inheritance offer a ready understanding of 'what could happen' to an economically autonomous woman. Take, for example, the case of an unmarried Barber-caste woman who had recently died of physical complications related to malnutrition. Once she had become too old to cultivate her small (inherited) landholding, she no longer had the means to meet her basic subsistence requirements. Yet she also had no grounds to claim the assistance of her brothers, whose only obligations (in both legal and customary terms) lay with family members residing in their own households. She thus died alone – in a physical isolation that ultimately reflected the loss of social citizenship she had endured as an independent woman. A Shrestha neighbour of the woman described her struggle to me in the midst of an interview with another unmarried woman:

> After seeing the hardship of Tuli Santi Nini, I have seen enough of the fate of these women who do not marry! My god! She faced so much hardship, I couldn't even look at her.
>
> She did not get married, and she stayed there in her house of birth, taking her share of the inheritance. When she eventually got sick in her old age, and could no longer manage her land, she didn't have enough to eat. She died having gone through so much pain and hardship. *Hare Shiva Shiva*. She became sick and was lying on that mattress for two years. She stayed there in the small house behind ours. She stayed on that mattress for two years. We would sometimes hear her moaning.
>
> Sometimes we brought her biscuits, sometimes Horlicks, sometimes mung bean soup. 'Whatever has happened?', she would say, 'It is because of you that I am able to eat!' She had a younger brother but he scarcely even laid eyes on her. As if he was just waiting for her to die! Sometimes she would shit in her bed, right? She would tell her brother's family when she had to eat, but she didn't tell them about the shitting. So they beat her…. Her face swelled up this much. When we asked her what happened, she said, 'Shhhh. They hit me here; they hit me last night because I had shit in the bed.' She hadn't even realized it.

Having seen her hardship I am fearful for unmarried women who want to
take their share of inheritance. Even if they register it in their own name, it is
difficult.

Certainly not all cases of women inheriting family property result in such
extremes of abuse and neglect, but the account illustrates the threat for
women contemplating a path of economic independence. When women
choose to comply with normative gender beliefs, then, they (like low
castes) are not necessarily unaware of the nets of power in which they are
entangled and they do not necessarily accept those beliefs as legitimate
and moral. Their actions suggest consent, not blindness; acquiescence,
not total hegemony.

Material explanations can also be found in another instance of apparent
conformity to gender ideology, namely when women replicate the
principle of hierarchy by dominating other women as a means to increase
their own status. Women generally relish their sons' marriages for the
opportunity they present to control the labour and obligations of a new
daughter-in-law. A common Newari saying jokes in solidarity with the
mother-in-law of a new bride, 'Ah, now you can go all the way to the
jungle to do your shitting', because, that is to say, there is someone else
to do your household chores so that you will finally have enough leisure
time to indulge in private toilet. Young married women, for their part,
have a vested interest in conflict with their mother-in-law, as a means
for promoting the eventual splitting of the joint family household into
its component nuclear parts. For after such a split, a woman advances
from the undesirable status of daughter-in-law to become the senior
woman in a new household, in which she can acquire increasing authority
and influence through her relationships with her husband, sons, and
eventually her own daughters-in-law. The antagonism between mother-
and daughter-in-law contributes to sustaining gender inequality if only by
undermining the scope for solidarity among women within the space of
the household. Yet the antagonism is structural, rooted in fundamentally
material conflicts of interest. It reflects a desire to modify one's place
in an imperfect system, not necessarily (as it may appear) collective
consensus about gender hierarchy as a legitimate organizing principle
of social life.

Discontent, Strategy and Contradiction

In fact, those women who do comply with the ideals of marriage and
seclusion often speak explicitly about the subordinating implications.

One well-educated Shrestha woman who had managed to receive an inheritance (as an only daughter) explained to me that she married partly in order to retain a modicum of social embeddedness in the face of unbearable pressure to conform. She describes how her in-laws attempted to isolate her from any contact with neighbours when she moved to Sankhu as a new bride:

There is no chance to talk to anyone in that society! For one, when I was first in Sankhu, what they [in-laws] did was they told me, 'Don't speak with *anyone* in the neighbourhood … . The people here are not good, they are not to be trusted.' They told me these things right after I got married … . When they saw me speaking with the daughter-in-law of the house next door – she became my friend – they would get very angry. And they accused me of saying things that I hadn't. Then they told the neighbours not to talk to *me*: 'She is very bad; she does this; she does that' … telling lies about me. So in this way they prevented the neighbours from speaking with me. I guess these things are probably still circulating in Sankhu about me!

Another woman marrying into a Merchant-caste household that had fallen on hard times financially explained how even when women do conform to gender ideology – when they uphold household honour, fulfil household labour obligations, observe conventions of seclusion – they are nonetheless blamed for household misfortune when it strikes:

As soon as there is some wealth in a household, they say, 'Her husband is good; he has a good income; he is working according to his karma; he has luck (*bāgya*). When that is not the case, like with our house falling into disrepair, when there is no money, when there is no income, they are quick to make insults: 'His wife has to eat sweets; she walks around wearing nice clothes; where would she get such nice clothes? She has to eat so plentifully, that's why the house is ruined', they say. 'The house is ruined because of what a woman does. She has her husband under her thumb.'

Even a 'love marriage' – one arranged directly by the spouses – is subject to the same conventions of seclusion and gendered division of labour, especially when the young couple, often for financial reasons, resides with the husband's joint family. One recently eloped Shrestha woman explained with some bitterness to an unmarried friend how a woman should be sexually available to her husband (as I listened, tape recorder in hand because we had been in the midst of a formal interview):

A husband has a right to his wife. Before sex, he tells her she can have everything. After sex, she's at his mercy. Before, he says – 'Oh, we should be sure to educate you, send you to campus, make sure you get a good office job.' In the morning he says this, and after you've had sex, well then he changes his story. 'I need my breakfast, you can't go out today because *jeṭhi* (senior sister-in-law) needs help preparing the meal.'

Stronger evidence of individual gender consciousness can be found in the way women take advantage of spaces *within* gender ideology that grant opportunity to possess and wield power as well as enhance material status. Ritual and symbolic roles required of daughters in their natal home offer Newar women some crucial guarantees against abuse in their marital household (Parbatiya women, by contrast, must undergo a far more extreme split from their natal home upon marriage).[24] During the first year (when recent brides are particularly subject to ideals of seclusion and vulnerable to the exploits of senior women in-laws), the obligations are especially demanding. In addition to the regular round of festivals, a newly married woman must visit her house of birth (bearing the requisite food offerings from her marital household) on the first day of rice planting and the festival days for honouring one's mother and one's father respectively.[25] After (and including) the first year, each of the major festivals, as well as annual *śrāddha* (ancestor worship), annual lineage-deity worship and *sī guthi* feasts all require the presence of married daughters, and in some circumstances, of their husbands as well. Married daughters also fulfil crucial roles in the death observances of their parents.[26] A married sister must be present in her birth home for life-cycle rituals of her brother's children – especially those associated with birth, initiation and marriage. Finally, when a woman becomes pregnant, she is entitled to visits and feast offerings by her mother and sisters and, most importantly, to a month-long convalescence in her natal home for about four weeks after the birth of each child.

By thus occupying an intermediary position between two lineages, a woman can manipulate her connections in each to leverage material and psychological resources within them to her greatest advantage. Being the designated escort for such exchanges between several young brides and their natal home, I learned quickly how women covet these occasions for the opportunity to rest from the burdens and anxieties of life as a downtrodden junior daughter-in-law, and I was witness to many attempts to prolong visits in their natal home. Moreover, the mutual obligations of married daughters and sisters with their parents and brothers require a physical proximity of marital and natal households (no more than a few hours' walk or bus journey) that itself facilitates some oversight of conditions in the marital home by a woman's consanguineal relatives. The right of a woman's parents and brothers to intervene on her behalf is rehearsed symbolically during the marriage ceremony. The fathers of the bride and groom exchange ritualized words via their family priests: the bride's father apologizes in advance for any deficiencies in his daughter and pleads for her good care in her new home, while the groom's father promises to treat the new bride as his own daughter. Ritual assurances notwithstanding, physical proximity offers the best guarantee, as the Shrestha woman whose in-laws attempted to isolate her from her neighbours explained with reference to her sister-in-law, who had 'married in' from another household in Sankhu:

The big dominating the small is one *policy* we Newars have. But if you [a woman] can be sure that your house of birth is right there in the same town as your husband's house, then they [a woman's in-laws] cannot do things like tell the neighbours not to talk to you. Because you can go there [to your natal home] and tell your family what is going on inside your house. So they [in-laws] will treat you respectfully because they know you will talk and bring them shame.

More overtly material opportunities for women lie in the conventions surrounding women's customary rights to moveable property and privately earned income. Although Newar women do not customarily inherit property, they do receive significant wealth in the form of a dowry (*kvasah*) presented to them on their betrothal just before moving from their natal to their marital home.[27] In the Newar context dowry is unequivocally valued as 'women's own property' and thus contradicts the ideology of women's dependence embedded in patrilineal patterns of inheritance (*aṅgsa*). The accumulation of a suitably large dowry is actively underwritten by the bride's natal family through a feast held in her honour before betrothal. Invited guests must contribute to the bride's dowry, at a scale specified by the type of invitation received, in the form of sweet breads, *lākhāmari*. After the formal engagement, the bride's family sends a request to the groom's side for a fixed amount of *lākhāmari* – calculated on the basis of the number of guests to be invited for the bride's wedding feast. The bride's family then distributes the breads among friends and relatives as invitations to the feast – with the size of the bread indicating exactly how many household members must attend and the scale of gift expected. *Lākhāmari* is thus said to 'guarantee' a bride's dowry. Gifts are opened immediately upon presentation and meticulously logged on a list, *dalah pau*, which ultimately inventories the entire dowry. Throughout the feast the bride sits surrounded by close family members receiving the dowry gifts – the brass water urns, pressure cookers, steel pots, silver plates, copper vessels, brass utensils – that tower behind her in a prominent display of the wealth her family has leveraged through its wide social networks.

Once in her marital home a woman's dowry enjoys a special status as her exclusive private property. As one Funeral Priest-caste (Bha) woman incontrovertibly stated:

A woman should have total control over her *kvasah*, including in her husband's household. Others are not allowed to touch it without her consent. If the household head has to attend a [another woman's] wedding feast, he may offer to purchase an item from his daughter-in-law's dowry to put down as a dowry gift for the other girl, but he may not just take it. She must be paid for it.

In the event of divorce, all *kvasah* items must be returned to the woman (with the cost to the husband's family for staging a wedding feast sometimes being subtracted), according to the list compiled by the woman's family during the wedding: 'Even if a man has used just one notebook from his wife's dowry', a Shrestha woman emphasized for me, 'he must pay for it or replace it'. Here is one case where the *ijat* economy works in women's favour, since breaches to these norms would bring immediate shame upon a household; as one senior Shrestha woman put it: 'if we were to sell our daughter-in-law's dowry, our honour would be lost ... . The neighbours would say, "Oh, they don't have enough to eat; they had to sell their daughter-in-law's dowry!" '

In addition to being women's exclusive property, dowry wealth is subject to a different set of customary rules regarding its provenance and custody than men's inheritance. *Kvasah* affords Newar women some distinct benefits relative to the rights and obligations men accrue through the acquisition of *aṅgsa*. A man can rarely exercise complete autonomy in the dispensation of his inherited property because in most cases there are other male heirs – his sons, brothers, and/or parents – who have some legal claim. But a woman has no legal or customary accountability with regard to her *kvasah*. The strength of a woman's (otherwise dependent and subordinate) position lies precisely in the fact that she has no prescribed social debts or obligations to tie up her private property.[28]

Newar women generally exercise careful vigilance to keep their dowry wealth out of circulation – if not hidden entirely from view – within their joint family marital households. They take full advantage of the 'ideological space' within Newar customary ideas about dowry for the accumulation of certain kinds of private wealth. As one woman from a relatively poor household explained to me, 'If you just keep your dowry packed up like a bank note in a picture frame, what good is that? You have to put it to some good use.' To capitalize on their dowry, however, women must confront a fundamental (spatial) challenge: for norms of seclusion preclude any possibility of engaging in ventures requiring travel outside the household. Nor can a woman undertake enterprises *within* her marital household that would detract from time spent on household labour and the endless requirements of subsistence farming. One way women resolve this dilemma is by investing surplus dowry in money-lending or leasing out livestock (a traditional form of dowry wealth). Even women from families that are not well off can give accounts of how they had tripled or quadrupled dowry investments, as one woman described for the case of her aunt:

… when my aunt died, she did not know how to write her own name; she did not even know the alphabet; she really didn't know anything. But anyway, up to the time of her death, she used to keep a small fortune in her closet – money she'd earn from investing. She'd give someone a loan; interest would come; she'd reinvest the interest [through money-lending], and so on. From that wealth she provided her daughters with a nice dowry, and when she needed money for her own purposes, she could always take it from her savings.

Although few households in Sankhu raise livestock today, gifts of livestock were common for women's dowries up to a generation ago, when households relied more fully on subsistence agriculture. Older women I interviewed recalled making livestock loans with the goats (or sometimes cows) they received as dowry. They would board the livestock, usually with a Tamang family in a nearby village, and receive half of the offspring born each year, delivered on festival occasions when meat is required for feasting and animal sacrifices are required for worship. Or the livestock could be sold to leverage other investments, as one Shrestha woman explained:

I sold that he-goat when I arrived here [Sankhu] for 100 rupees; then I invested that 100 rupees in the Tamangs … . They said they had some troubles. They came to borrow 100 rupees and said they could give me 8 *pāthī* of unhusked rice every year in interest. That is much higher interest than you can get now. I let the loan go for six or seven years and I earned a lot of interest that way. When I asked him [the borrower] to return the principal, he said, 'Don't you have any shame?' And so I let the principal go. It is true that he gave me a lot of interest – double or triple the original NRs 100. Soon after that I stopped giving out loans because we divided the joint household and we had to worry about feeding ourselves then. I gave out the loans while we were living in a joint household.

Once a joint family splits, that is, women typically devote their private wealth to establishing and maintaining the nuclear family; under these circumstances they have less incentive to keep their wealth 'tied up' in private investments. In the absence of in-laws with whom to compete over resources, a woman might invest her *kvasah* wealth directly in her husband's business, as in the case of a Shrestha woman from Sankhu who recently married a man in Kathmandu with no brothers; her sister-in-law explained how she could do so even without her husband's knowledge:

She sold half of her dowry to invest in her husband's [retail] business. The wholesaler [who is from Sankhu] asks for payment before delivering the grains, right? From her husband's side [in Kathmandu], they are not willing to pay until the delivery is made ... . So, she pays the dealer [in Sankhu] with her own money. And the dealer is happy because the customer has sent the money at the time he placed his order, so the dealer feels obliged to send the order right away. Then her husband is happy because the order has come so quickly, so he sends payment immediately. The transactions all go through her hands; her husband does not know she has already paid the dealer, and she just pockets his payments ... . Otherwise, the dealer would never go out of his way to deliver the grains to his [her husband's] house, which is so far from the main bazaar in Kathmandu. She has invested in the middle. She is very clever.

Critical Consciousness

Although women often appear complicit in their own disadvantage to the extent that they assume postures, behaviours and roles that mark their own subordination, the discussion here suggests that their compliance does not necessarily reflect an acceptance of those practices as legitimate. It also suggests, as Mattison Mines (1994) has argued for the case of South India, that representations of South Asian identities as fundamentally collective, 'dividual' and thus homologous with normative caste and gender beliefs, overlook the role of *individuality* in South Asian social life – especially, I would argue, the capacity for reflexivity and critical perspective. Women do not consent to established norms without understanding the arbitrariness of the system, or recognizing opportunities to accumulate personal wealth and power. Occasionally such recognition can become the basis of critical consciousness – of explicit critiques of cultural ideology and musings about tactics for change. Thus the Shrestha woman who described being isolated from her neighbours speaks an explicitly feminist language of 'women's rights' and 'male domination'; she shared her thoughts with me about the need to build up physical and psychological responses to combat women's subordination:

If women and men are really equally capable, how is it that only women are denied opportunities? Women should also do all kinds of work ... . One source of motivation for me [in questioning these things] was reading, right? And on top of that, in my own experience, since I was young – well, my mother had only two daughters so there were no sons to dominate us. And my sister was not the type to resist, or protest, or fight, or go here and there ... . For that reason, I always thought that I should protect my parents, and defend their wealth.

From the very beginning, based on my reading and experience, I began to wonder how women could do any kind of independent work. As a woman, how should one take care of oneself and live a good life? What can women do to be strong? ... Not only in reading but also in practice I have searched for these things ... . I always tried to be better than men – I acted according to this principle . ... I read about the women in China, about the martyrs in the Chinese Revolution. Maybe you have heard of Lin Hu Lan. Their lives had a great deal of influence on me. She became a martyr at the age of 28. It is women like these whose lives really affected me. And Mao Zedong's wife, Yan Kaihui – it is women like her whose lives really affected me. And women in Vietnam or India like Laksmi Bai…. How did these women sustain themselves? These are the things I read about.[29]

One must always be able to protect oneself. Women must be strong. They must be of good health. When women become sick or weak, everyone dominates them. Because I believed that I should be strong, since I was a kid, I used to play sports in school, play in the open fields, take part in games, even at home, *exercise* a lot. Women must make themselves strong. If boys can make themselves strong, why can't women also? You should not just rely on the law … . If you are strong, then you can take care of yourself. You have to be able to take care of yourself in a real, physical way.

Thus, for example, on the death of her father this woman fought off the aggressive 'offers' by her father's brother's sons to perform the requisite mortuary rites. Instead she defied custom by taking birth control pills to ensure she would not menstruate during the 45-day observances. She was thus able to fulfil the male role of chief mourner and thereby secure the right to her father's inheritance under customary laws:

They [her deceased father's brother's sons] were very clever. The youngest son of my uncle used to come here a lot to wheedle my father into giving him the inheritance. My father would say, Sure, sure – but he did not in fact allocate his nephew the inheritance. When my father died they actually came to tell me that he had left them his property! Oh, the things they said. So I asked, did he put it in writing?

At that time they also came to do the mortuary rituals … after I had already made the preparations and begun the work. The Brahmans were all assembled on the ground floor of the house. The priest asked who was going to perform the rites. He asked me, and I said, 'I will do them.' He asked me if I was able to do the work. And I said, 'I will do whatever you ask me to.' You see, what the priests do is they like to pick quarrels! They ask for a lot of *dāna*. So I said, 'Whatever you need, I will give you … . I will do exactly what you tell me to.' I said this knowing his greed, and so he said, Okay … . And as soon as I said I would do the mortuary rituals they [cousins] became very angry with me. They knew then that I would not allow them to touch my father's wealth … . Oh, I spent a lot of money at the time of my father's death! I gave so much in *dāna*.

Then I had go to the *office* to declare proof of my relation to my father. In order to do that [in order for a woman to inherit property] a closely related man must sign my declaration, saying: 'This is the only child; she is not married; all the wealth will be in her name', etc. I had to go to that office for 4–5 years. If I had not fought, done the mortuary rituals, registered at the office, and taken the wealth in my own name, then my father's brothers' sons would have come and taken all the wealth, arranged a marriage for me, sent me off, the end, finished!

Now, however much the practices highlighted in these last two sections – such as the expressions of anger and the strategic use of dowry and ties to the natal home – may express consciousness, even critical consciousness, of male domination, the problem Bourdieu raises in *Male Domination* (2001: 32) is that such practices ultimately constitute only 'weak weapons'. For they are:

… rooted in the androcentric view in the name of which they are dominated. These strategies, which are not strong enough really to subvert the relation of domination, at least have the effect of confirming the dominant representation of women as maleficent beings …

They are important as individual strategies, but they cannot by themselves transform the schemes of perception through which male domination (and other forms of oppression) are lodged beyond and below consciousness. Transforming the latter requires more collective modes of resistance – such as in the circulation of alternative origin stories among low castes – that challenge the stereotypes, break the doxa and 'put history in motion' by neutralizing the mechanisms that have neutralized and dehistoricized the relations between the sexes (Bourdieu 2001: vii).

NEWAR ECONOMICS FROM THE MARGINS

For planners and development practitioners, the point to emphasize here is that the *potential* for critical consciousness lies in the everyday experience of subaltern actors. The first step to facilitating collective projects for emancipatory social change is thus to recognize the basis for ideological critique within culture. As Steven Parish (1997: 69) puts it:

Understanding the dynamics of the moral and political imagination … is a necessary theoretical and ethnographic prerequisite to understanding processes of social change and political transformation. We can understand these fully only by coming to grips with what people actually think and feel, as complex and multiply-constituted selves, not by assuming they are entirely constituted by the social and political structures or 'discourses' in which they are 'embedded', although these may indeed shape much of what they think and feel, know and do. To understand commitment and resistance to cultural practices, we need a cultural psychology of ideology and critique, a cultural anthropology of the 'embodied knowledge' of social actors, that is sensitive to politics and economics.

In this chapter we have seen how low castes and women face disadvantages in the accumulation of symbolic and material capital, and how their subordination facilitates opportunities enjoyed by those in dominant social positions. To the extent that they assume postures, behaviours and roles that mark their own subordination or that they affirm the idea of hierarchy in their domination of others, low castes and women are complicit in their own disadvantage. Yet their testimony suggests that they comply not merely for moral, but predominantly for material reasons – out of fear of hunger, danger and chaos. And they do not comply without casting a critical eye on the system as a whole, without understanding its arbitrariness and its contradictions. The contradictory values of hierarchy and equality, fate and hard work, religion of power and religion of status, son preference and filial bond, *aṅgsa* and *kvasah* 'coexist in a mutually subversive complementarity' (Parish 1997: 11). When low castes recognize such contradictions, critical consciousness becomes as much a part of culture as conformity and belief.

The following chapters further explore the potential for locally situated social criticism to catalyse progressive social change. Chapter 6 considers the opportunities and constraints accruing for low castes and women as Newar cultural conventions articulate with new patterns of commodification and new labour markets resulting from the open-market policies introduced in the early 1990s. Chapter 7 concludes by theorizing a role for planning and development for facilitating more collective forms of critical consciousness.

6   GLOBAL–LOCAL ARTICULATIONS IN AN AGE OF NEOLIBERALISM

In order to imagine a role for planning in mobilizing the critical resources within culture, it is necessary to examine how local ideologies and practices are embedded in other scales of economic life. In the current global economic conjuncture, how specifically has neoliberalism, and its programmes of economic liberalization implemented since the early 1990s, articulated with the Newar economics of practice? Given what we know about the webs of sociality encompassing Sankhu and the contradictions of caste and gender ideology, we can consider how neoliberalism is experienced within the Newar economics of practice – not as a universally determining and uniform macroeconomic process, but as a historically specific interplay of local and macroeconomic systems. Without wishing to overlook the asymmetric power relations structuring this encounter at a world-historical scale, the emphasis here will be on how local logics of accumulation and investment elaborated in the preceding chapters contour the process of macroeconomic change, how they interact with the commoditization and emerging labour markets associated with Nepal's new economic orthodoxy, how the joining of local and macro produces an interplay of systems that reorders both, creating new social formations.[1] What new regimes of value and structuring ideologies emerge in these contexts, and what kinds of social relations and spatial practices result as cultural common sense assumes new parameters and new criteria? How do inter-scalar dynamics influence the way people in Sankhu construct place and conceive their world? In light of the concern here with progressive planning, what emancipatory and regressive political tendencies for women and low castes can be seen in these articulations of local cultural economies with macroeconomic processes?

164

MACROECONOMIC CONTEXT

Chapter 3 illustrates how the Kathmandu Valley, and Sankhu in particular, had been integrated with regional, even global networks of power and material exchange since the early centuries of the Christian era. While journalistic, tourist promotional and even some ethnographic texts emphasize the centuries of isolation and the exotic Shangri-la mystique associated with the region, we have seen how in fact the early monarchical societies of the Kathmandu Valley developed in relation to flows of traded goods and Buddhist doctrine throughout the Asian region. The modern Nepalese nation-state was similarly constituted, from the mid-eighteenth to the mid-twentieth centuries, in the vortex of the rise and fall of the British empire. Shah and Rana rulers engaged geographic isolation strategically to ward off British colonial and imperialist designs, yet their ability to do so, and to acquire political legitimacy on the home front, depended on political, economic and cultural integration with the British empire – in the form of markets for European exports and provision of Gurkha soldiers to quell rebellion in India. Until 1951 the terms of integration were closely regulated by the Shah and then Rana regimes: both kept British colonial designs at bay by prohibiting Europeans from travelling and residing in Nepal (on grounds of the moral peril they present for Nepal *desa*), while ruling through a strategy of distinction based on the conspicuous consumption of European goods – a paradoxical phenomenon which Mark Liechty (1997) dubs 'strategic exclusion'. Sumptuary laws denied peasant commoners access to the coveted foreign commodities (even those most proximate to the ruling elite in the urbanized area of the Kathmandu Valley), and prohibited them from engaging in activities deemed the exclusive purview of nobility: riding horses or elephants (and later, motorized vehicles), wearing European dress, stucco-ing their houses, or roofing with tiles. Meanwhile extractive taxation policies ensured that elite consumption of European goods was financed on the backs of Nepal's peasantry: 'Treating their entire state as a private feudal fiefdom', Liechty argues, 'the Ranas were able to mobilize resources such that their conspicuous consumption was of truly international dimensions' (1997: 59).

The year 1951 marked a threshold in Nepal's integration with regional and global political-economic processes – not so much in terms of ending an 'era of isolation', as the conventional representation goes (e.g. Panday 1999), but in terms of expanding and deepening access to foreign-ness and foreigners within the country, beyond the narrow circle of elites in Kathmandu. The Rana regime fell, suffering from ever-diminishing returns to power from the strategy of rule by distinction, and the Shah kings were restored as ruling monarchs (having secured safe haven in India as a resistance movement mounted in Nepal). The Shah dynasty presided over a short-lived experiment with multi-party democracy but then consolidated their power through the institution of a party-less *panchayat* system that prevailed until a 'democracy movement' ushered in a second multi-party parliamentary system in 1990. On the international front the government of Nepal could of course no longer rule by 'strategic exclusion' in the post-Second World War and post-Indian independence era; it thus entered into a series of contractual agreements that acknowledged the dominance of India on the subcontinent and the ascendancy of the People's Republic of China, while also establishing diplomatic relationships with extra-regional powers, most significantly the United States. Following two centuries of struggle with India and China, Nepal's territorial geography had by this time settled to the present national boundaries. But 'non-geographic political space' underwent dramatic change as Nepal opened its borders to more direct forms of foreign intervention and ceased its efforts to shield the Nepalese people from foreign influence (Panday 1999: 311). In the post-1951 period Nepal opened itself for the first time to mass media, public education, tourism and international development.

Foreign aid in particular transformed the economy and reached the far regions of the country, though not without entrenching existing lines of wealth and power, or creating new ones. The first of Nepal's Soviet-style five-year plans (1956–61) was financed entirely by the USA, India, China and the Soviet Union. By the fifth (1975–80), sixth (1980–85) and seventh (1985–90) plans, aid still averaged 50 per cent of total development expenditure, and the absolute volume of foreign aid increased steadily with each successive plan – the gross aid underwriting the seventh plan (NRs 28 billion) exceeding 75 times the amount received in the first plan (Tiwari 1992). Between the first and the eighth plan (1992–97), the literacy rate jumped from 5 per cent to 37 per cent; per capita income from US $45 to $1,186; and life expectancy from 35 to 55 years (NHDR [Nepal Human Development Report] 1999). Aid financed infrastructural growth (including the first motorable roadways linking Kathmandu to India, points west and south within Nepal, and Tibet; an airport in Kathmandu; postal and telecommunication facilities; and irrigation projects), social sectors (including schools, malaria eradication in the Tarai and integrated rural development projects) and economic development (stressing high-yielding crops, provision of agricultural equipment and import-substituting industries).

Throughout this period (and to the present) Nepal continually received pledges of aid exceeding even the donors' estimation of 'aid need' (Rana 1992). The excessive availability of foreign aid can in part be attributed to the timing of the country's emergence from isolationist rule – simultaneous with the consolidation of 'international development' as a mode of governance in the post-Second World War and postcolonial movements rejecting more colonial modes of intervention. But Nepal enjoyed particular appeal as a locus for development assistance, deriving from its geo-politically significant location between China and India. In the context of the Cold War and Indian imperialist designs on the subcontinent, Nepal soon became a battleground for influence among India, China and the USA, expressed through competing disbursements of aid (Panday 1999). Notwithstanding the divergent ideological orientations among these primary donors, the economic philosophies governing 'development' in Nepal (and indeed much of the so-called Third World) through the 1970s were fairly consistent, reflecting Keynesian, if not socialist, principles defending a role for the state in capital formation, import substituting industrialization, and the distribution of resources through subsidized credit, fertilizer and other productive inputs. However much aid financed (or determined) development expenditures, foreign trade occupied a small percentage of GDP during this period, with exports at no more than 5 per cent and imports remaining below 20 per cent of GDP through the seventh plan (Panday 1999). Exports in particular suffered from a restrictive Trade and Commerce Treaty with India, brokered by the Rana government in 1950 on the brink of its demise. The treaty stipulated that Nepal could export only primary products to India (including a ban on exports of goods from third countries, thus preventing Nepal from resurrecting a modern version of entrepôt trade) and must purchase all manufactured items from India (Panday 1999). Tourism, meanwhile, was limited through the 1970s to a relatively small trickle of largely low-budget hippies in search of drugs and dharma and did not enjoy significant state promotion. Thus, in spite of major shifts in economic and political space, foreigners, foreign commodities and industrial employment did not have a significant impact on daily life outside urban elite circles, tourist ghettos in Kathmandu, the few emerging trekking routes and the few state-owned industries (which by 1981 constituted only 0.48 per cent of the total workforce).

The mid-1980s marked a second turning point in the deepening and expanding of Nepal's integration with regional and global economies, characterized by an ideological shift toward economic liberalization and market-led approaches to development. The theory emanating from Washington and London from the early 1980s onwards stipulates that state-led development of the post-Second World War period created biased or 'distorted' incentive structures that 'got prices wrong' by sheltering goods and services from the calibrating effects of supply and demand. Withdrawal of state intervention would create more neutral incentive structures by opening pricing and interest rates to the 'free' market, thus generating an optimum allocation of resources. In Nepal, as in most of the Third World and Eastern Europe, economic liberalization proceeded, according to conditions on donor aid, through deregulating capital and labour markets, removing price controls, privatizing state-owned enterprises, liberalizing trade and introducing convertibility of the domestic currency (Sharma 1997). Following fiscal expansion financed by the World Bank in the early 1980s that resulted in enlarged fiscal deficits as well as dwindling reserves of international currency, the Nepalese government had little choice but to adopt a stabilization programme in 1985–86 supported by an IMF Standby Agreement – followed by Structural Adjustment Programs in 1987 and 1989 financed by World Bank Structural Adjustment Credits and an IMF Structural Adjustment Facility. After a gap of two years following the institution of multi-party democracy in 1990 (and a nine-month interlude of Communist Party rule), Nepal again entered into an arrangement with the IMF, this time under the Enhanced Structural Adjustment Facility, designed specifically to raise GDP growth, reduce inflation and reduce the fiscal deficit.

The finance sector (previously the domain of two state-owned commercial banks and two state-owned development banks) was an early and intense focus of the reforms – the locus of Nepal's 'most visible foray into economic liberalization' (Dixit 1995). In the early 1980s, the Nepal Central Bank first opened the banking sector to direct foreign investment by easing entry restrictions; three joint-venture banks came into operation by the decade's end, and another seven had been chartered to do business by the mid-1990s. It also facilitated the entry of new institutional forms, such as finance companies, merchant banks and mortgage lenders (by 1997, 35 enterprises had registered under the reformed Finance Company Act) and established the Securities Exchange Board to regulate trading on the Nepal Stock Exchange. In the mid-1990s Nepali politicians, spurred on by American development consultants, even devised an ill-fated plan to set up an offshore financial centre, relying on communications satellites to serve as 'the seaport that

Nepal never had' and to make Nepal the 'Switzerland of Asia' as a centre for financial investment (Dahal 1996: 24).

The finance sector is also significant for its marked shift in development philosophy embedded in a new approach to rural credit delivery. Through the 1980s 'small-farmer' programmes delivered credit and technical assistance at subsidized interest rates to male household heads as representatives of rural farm households. This model gradually gave way starting in the 1990s to microfinance programmes offering savings and credit instruments at market interest rates, specifically to women entrepreneurs deemed more likely to invest in the household economy. In the microfinance model of development, the onus for rural lending devolved from state-owned commercial banks to a separate class of rural development banks and 'grameen NGOs' (both modelled after the Bangladesh Grameen Bank), and women borrowers became the target of an aggressive 'self-help' approach to development. The switch to decentralized banking and its ideology of self-help made the finance sector a significant battleground of the People's War waged by a militant Maoist movement since 1996. However much microfinance professes local ownership, the state's role in promoting this mode of development (through low-interest loans, grants, permissive regulations and lots of propoganda) has not been lost on the Maoists. The ideological significance of microfinance cooperatives, village banks and savings and credit groups (of which over 2,500 have now been officially registered; Sharma 2003), not to mention the financial resources they harbour, have made microfinance branch offices in rural areas a favoured target of Maoist violence (Wehnert and Shakya 2003). And in regions of the country under Maoist control (primarily central-west), the insurgents have established a parallel network of village banks on terms alleged to be more favourable and more populist than state-promoted microfinance programmes.

The implications of financial-sector reform will be discussed in the following chapter on planning and development. More significant for our purposes here of exploring the articulation of neoliberalism with Newar economics of practice has been Nepal's trade liberalization policies, which have introduced new patterns of commoditization and new labour markets in Sankhu and its vicinity. In Nepal trade liberalization has entailed eliminating import licences, streamlining export procedures, abolishing the dual exchange rate and lowering tariff rates (Dixit 1995). While the volume in total trade grew from 16 per cent of GDP in 1975 to 40 per cent in 1996 (NHDR 1999: 15), in fact this expansion reflects primarily an increase in imports. Domestic markets were flooded with imported consumer goods over Nepal's 'adjustment decade' (1986–96) – ranging from basic housewares available to consumers at nearly all income scales, to clothing, to luxury goods affordable only to middle and upper classes. Fashionable shops in Kathmandu (as well as other commercial centres in Nepal) '[were] jammed with imported electronic consumer goods', reports Liechty (1995b: 166), 'making Kathmandu the "Hong Kong of South Asia"; televisions and VCRs have become standard features of urban middle class homes'. Motor vehicle registration in Kathmandu, another measure of foreign commodity consumption, jumped from fewer than 20 in the 1950s, to 70,000 in 1993, while annual new vehicle registration averaged 3,000 over the adjustment decade (clogging the city far beyond the capacity of its narrow, largely unregulated and unpaved streets; HMG 1996; B.L. Shrestha 1993: 30). From the early years of economic liberalization, the flow of imports – and the ubiquity of foreign commodities in everyday life – has skyrocketed, increasing nearly nine-fold between 1985 and 1995 (HMG 1996: 54–5).

Availability of imported commodities has been met by voracious demand. Although more than half the population fell below the poverty line, the marginal propensity to consume was high, at .867, over Nepal's adjustment decade. The high share of consumption in income can be attributed to rapid growth in private-sector consumption, at a compound rate of 15.4 per cent, over the same time period (NHDR, 1999: 13). High levels of consumption persisted in spite of low savings rates (gross domestic savings averaged 10 per cent over 1986–96), and the inflation (at double digit rates through the adjustment decade) and declining purchasing power resulting from currency devaluations, cuts in subsidies, increases in domestic tariffs and price increases following privatization of public enterprises (NHDR 1999: 14; Rimal 1996: 92). Between 1984 and 1994 the national urban consumer price index increased 184 per cent; of course, deflationary policies associated with liberalization made imports in particular more expensive (HMG 1996: 100). In Sankhu as much as in other communities throughout Nepal, people were buying more imported commodities and spending a greater proportion of their income on consumption, with a Nepali rupee that was declining in value.

Exports also increased over most of the adjustment decade (except in 1995 and 1996), although at a lower rate than imports; by 1995, exports were less than one-third of imports and the trade deficit had grown by 850 per cent, from NRs 5 billion in 1985 to NRs 47.6 billion in 1995 (HMG 1996: 54–5). In spite of donor-induced attempts to promote exports, the restrictive Trade and Commerce Treaty with India continued to hamper export-oriented industrialization, while the glut of imported Indian goods devastated even import substituting industries along Nepal's southern border (known as Nepal's 'industrial belt').[2] The export growth that Nepal did manage to achieve, meanwhile, was limited to a few narrow sectors that proved to be unsustainable beyond the adjustment decade. By 1990, hand-knotted 'Tibetan' carpets had surpassed tourism as the largest source of foreign exchange – comprising 57 per cent of all exports in 1994 and relying for its success on cheap labour and easy access to imported wools and dyes ('The End of the Carpet-Induced Boom?' 1994). Originating in the 1960s as a small-scale cottage industry geared entirely to the tourist market, Nepal's carpet manufacturing first found an international market (almost exclusively West German) in the mid-1980s. By 1992 Nepal had become the fourth largest exporter of carpets (following India, China and Iran) – with 200 large producing units and over 5,000 small-scale carpet factories registered in 1991 and 1992 alone ('Carpets: Recent Developments' 1992). For nearly a decade the carpet sector was a most significant generator of economic development in Nepal, dramatically boosting exports, foreign exchange earnings, spin-off economic activity and employment. By the mid-1990s, however, it faced irrevocable setbacks, owing first to a German film documenting the use of child labour and an ensuing consumer boycott on carpet production not adhering to international labour standards, and second to growing competition in carpet manufacture, particularly in India (NIIDR 1999. 15). The Maoist movement has dealt a final blow to the carpet sector, by making it a focus of ideological attack as a key locus of exploitation and a key product of western imperialism. Today all but the largest carpet factories sit idle.

The Nepalese garment sector represented 30 per cent of exports by the end of the adjustment decade, having received a large production windfall owing to Indian producers having saturated their US quotas. Although Nepalese garment producers contracted to fill US quotas enjoyed a short-lived protection of the guaranteed market, this sector, too, proved unsustainable. In the first instance, garment producers upset US buyers by failing to meet their quota allocation. And by the end of the 1990s, the General Agreement on Tariffs and Trade had severely undermined the garment sector by prohibiting quota agreements in international trade. For all they contributed to foreign exchange earnings in the short run, moreover, both the carpet and garment industries in Nepal relied heavily on imported raw materials and productive inputs; the scope for long-run sustainability was thus undermined at the outset by the lack of value added within Nepal (Guru-Gharana 1996: 27–8). Tourism was the third-largest generator of foreign exchange over the adjustment decade, peaking at 490,000 in 1999, an increase of 88 per cent from the end of the 1970s ('Carpets: Recent Developments' 1992; 'More Questions than Answers' 2000), a staggering figure when it is recalled that in the roughly half-century prior to 1925 a total of 55 Europeans had gained access to Nepal, primarily as invited guests of state. The increasing flow of tourists as well as airfreight at the height of the carpet boom turned Kathmandu into one of South Asia's busiest air transportation hubs. Tourism was allowed to expand in a primarily unregulated fashion (with dire environmental and cultural implications) through the 1990s, but never enjoyed the status of an export industry with strong state backing. Even with stronger public investment and planning, however, this sector was unlikely to have survived the burgeoning and increasingly militant Maoist revolutionary movement, which, combined with an ineffectual and violent government response, had undermined the entire Nepalese economy by the end of the 1990s.

All three industries – carpets, garments and tourism – concentrated in Kathmandu, and carpet production in particular was located largely in the Baudhanath–Jorpati corridor, just a few kilometres southwest of Sankhu.[3] As the largest employer by industry in Nepal – with an estimated 102,000 full-time workers and up to an additional 300,000 part-time and occasional workers – the carpet sector rapidly swelled the population in its areas of concentration in the early to mid-1990s. By 1994 total employment in the industry exceeded one-quarter of the population of the Kathmandu Valley, much of which was concentrated in the Bauddhanath–Jorpati area lying approximately midway on the motorable road between downtown Kathmandu and Sankhu ('Carpet Relocation Study' 1994). Once a meandering gravel lane far from the urban squalor of Kathmandu, the dusty corridor now bustled from dawn to late night with trucks, buses, cars, and three-wheelers hauling workers and supplies to and from this manufacturing centre. A brief stroll down any side lane brought into earshot the dull sound of hammers pounding away at row upon row of the hand-tied knots suspended on upright looms. Even though the German film documenting the role of child labour in Nepal's carpet industry severely crippled carpet exports by the late-1990s, in the Bauddhanath–Jorpati corridor the industry had generated enough spin-off economic activity to sustain a localized process of economic revitalization. Those able to participate in this rapid economic development, including low-caste migrants from Sankhu, found themselves in the anomalous situation of receiving steady infusions of cash through sales or income, but having few available avenues for productive investment. As discussed below, such localized cash surpluses contributed to the runaway consumerism that transformed the Newar economics of practice in the mid-1990s.

THE CHANGING LOGIC OF CASTE AND CLASS

The recent ubiquity of commodities in everyday life and the burgeoning labour markets associated with the carpet, garment and tourism sectors have particular implications for the Newar caste economy. In Sankhu some low castes have successfully engaged new service-sector jobs as channels to middle-class status in a manner that has posed a formidable challenge to their low status within caste ideology.[4] For the carpet factories, garment factories, hotels and offices opening in the wake of economic liberalization, all require a whole range of services compatible with low-caste occupations and below the rank and dignity of high castes. Thus, for instance, Po Untouchables from Sankhu have successfully found employment as janitors, 'peons' and septic tank cleaners; according to one Po man in Sankhu, the latter could earn up to NRs 4,000 at the time of this research for an annual cleaning of a large hotel or factory septic tank – a substantial sum when compared with the leftover feast the same service affords at the home of Sankhu *jajamāna* .[5] Likewise, a Nay (Butcher-caste) woman explains how butchering has become a more lucrative profession with the swelling population in nearby Jorpati:

My oldest sons have had a store in Jorpati for the last 10 years. Before there was not enough butchering work even for those [Butchers] already living in Kathmandu. Now there are a lot of people moving into Kathmandu and there is a lot of work. There is so much business that it is difficult to keep meat in the store. Some people [of the Nay caste] have even built houses in Jorpati from this business. My middle son who used to transport the buffaloes out to Sankhu has built a house in this way.

Such opportunities for low castes have persisted in Jorpati, in spite of the slow-downs in the carpet, garment and tourism sectors – largely as a result of the increased pace of urban migration among those displaced by the Maoist insurgency. Neither the Kathmandu Valley in general, nor Sankhu in particular have been the focus of direct Maoist intervention. (With the exception of some agitation among factory workers, Maoists have fashioned themselves after the Chinese and, unfortunately, Peruvian precedents, as a primarily rural, peasant movement.)

Now, to say that new market forms present opportunities for low castes in Sankhu is not to suggest that the terms of the emerging employment opportunities are in themselves ideal or just. On the contrary, the fact that those occupying low-end service-sector positions come from social positions customarily defined as 'low' and 'ritually defiling' itself enhances possibilities for exploitation, given the odds that at least some low castes will have partially internalized their low status. Hiring low castes for janitorial work, moreover, virtually guarantees an uneducated workforce (since only the present generation of school-going low-caste children have benefited from universal primary education in Nepal), unlikely to be versed in the details of labour law or to have experience in labour organizing.

Within the Newar economics of practice, however, low castes' new incomes enable them to participate as consumers in a new commoditized regime of value unleashed by import liberalization and the ensuing availability of foreign consumer goods. The commodity economy, of course, knows no caste distinctions. Within its calculus low castes can use their purchasing power on an equal footing with anyone else possessing the requisite cash savings. In the homes of those low castes who have successfully broken into the urban labour market for services, for instance, one finds the same televisions, telephones, electric fans and various other modern amenities that have become essential household items among status-conscious dominant castes. On this basis low castes have been able to climb toward the ranks of a newly consolidating urban middle class organized around a social logic of commodity consumption.

Honour remains the crucial currency within a commoditized regime of value, but strategies for building honour rely increasingly on the display of modern commodities – and rests less on building relationships and meeting social obligations. Class is thus emerging as a mode of social organization, an idiom of social life, that competes with the logic of caste by structuring hierarchy around competition in the calculus of commodity consumption instead of around initial endowments of *karma* and ritual purity. Historically, economic and caste status in Newar society have tended to converge – with dominant castes (Shresthas) enjoying relative material advantages compared to those castes patronizing them with ritual services. Indeed low-caste consent to a subordinating social system has been intimately bound up in their economic insecurity and dependence on high-caste patronage.[6] Today caste and class are becoming increasingly distinct idioms of social life, as an emerging commoditized regime of value presents an alternative to the old caste-based regime as a basis for the accumulation of material and social capital. Low castes even enjoy an advantage within the social logic of commodity consumption: because they have fewer social obligations than dominant and high castes (as a result of their ritually defiling condition), relatively less of their material wealth gets tied up in costly social investments. They can benefit from the material dimensions of *ijat*, without bearing as much financial burden for its social dimensions.[7] Thus the savings accrued by low castes earning cash incomes in Kathmandu's low-end service-sector professions have contributed in no small way to the phenomenon of runaway consumption that plagued Newar society through the 1990s – an inflation in standards of commodity consumption to be discussed at greater length below.

The new opportunities for low castes manifest spatially in two respects. First, jobs and businesses in Kathmandu enable low-caste men to physically leave behind many of the stigmatizing dimensions of low-caste identity, especially patronage relationships with high castes. Of course, their occupation may identify them as low caste in their new place of work and residence, but they are unlikely to enter into a new set of patronage relationships here. Rather, their physical distancing from the moral universe of Sankhu facilitates the strategy discussed in Chapter 5, of abandoning *jajamāna* duties while maintaining the empowering dimensions of their low-caste identity associated with the 'religion of power' (the tantric practices necessary for the worship of the 'dangerous deities'). The connections to Sankhu are almost never severed, as low castes like any other emigrants retain their ancestral residences; they use cash earnings to support ageing relatives, children, and women who have remained in Sankhu to carry on local butcher shops. But the physical distance offers greater freedom for low castes to set the terms of their participation in the Newar economics of practice.

Second, low castes' earnings have financed transformations in the landscape of Sankhu itself. As low-caste migrant men 'repatriate' their earnings to ancestral homes in Sankhu, their extended family households have initiated something of a construction boom – replacing single-storey, thatched-roof mud houses with multi-storey modern cement structures not affordable to many high-caste families. This transformation is particularly significant since low castes have long suffered the legacy of Newar customary laws (enforced until the 1950s) mandating their houses be constructed of mud and thatch, in contradistinction to the brick and tile of higher-caste homes. The new cement structures thus etch the narrowing (class) gap between high and low castes directly into the urban landscape (although the prescribed location of low-caste households at the town's periphery thus far remains unchallenged).

If the emerging logic of class provides an alternative framework for social mobility, low castes have, by and large, adjusted their practices at the scale of the joint-family household – claiming middle-class status by building a house, or sending a child to boarding school, displaying coveted modern amenities or abandoning stigmatizing services to their *jajamāna*. Occasionally they evoke the potential for *collective* strength presented in the new opportunities for wealth creation. The comments of one Butcher-caste man exhibit this kind of low-caste solidarity in response to my questioning about the implication for new work opportunities in Jorpati for Sankhu credit markets in particular:

We don't have to use the banks; we don't even need the big money-lenders any more because now there are plenty of resources right within our own [Nay caste] community. It used to be that we were all very poor, but now there are *sāu* [money-lenders and rich people] among us.[8] We have even initiated our own Bhimsen *guthi* [for worshipping the god Bhimsen who is associated with commerce] in the last five years.

The collective strategy to invest in pan-caste worship of the god Bhimsen suggests that the material processes set in motion by economic liberalization – the new patterns of commodification and new labour markets for Sankhu in particular – do not cause total cultural rupture. In this instance the Butcher caste is emulating dominant-caste practices both as a means to acquire cultural and finance capital within the prevailing regime of value and as an expression of their continued participation in the Newar cosmic order.

Dominant castes, meanwhile, are generally losing ground. The service-sector employment boom has not generally benefited professions that educated dominant- and high-caste Newars from Sankhu are wont to seek out – teaching, small-scale business and various professional government services such as described in Chapter 4. In fact, the comprehensive household survey conducted by anthropologist Bal Gopal Shrestha in 1996 revealed that only 49 per cent of men and 51 per cent of women in Sankhu are 'economically active' by conventional standards of income generation. Even accounting for unpaid productive work (performed largely by women) and for the fact that dominant-caste Shresthas comprise most of the 'economically active' population, these figures suggest significant levels of under-employment. Anecdotally, too, colleagues, friends and informants (especially those with more than a high-school education) from the Shrestha caste spoke regularly about their mounting frustration with the dearth of employment opportunities, not just in Sankhu, but also in Kathmandu.[9] Most dominant and high castes in Sankhu, that is, have not experienced the same relative increase in cash income or the correlative increase in purchasing power that many low castes have.

On the contrary, these groups have seen their purchasing power decline, not only with underdevelopment and double-digit inflation of the Nepalese rupee, but also with rapid inflation in material standards of *ijat* accompanying commodification processes. Within a commoditized regime of value, the material aspects of honour (deriving from displays of wealth) not only *matter more* (Liechty 2003), but also require displays of ever more modern, fashionable and valuable commodities. One domain where '*ijat* inflation' has hit particularly hard relates to shifting conventions surrounding the hosting of a wedding feast. Practices in Sankhu have been heavily influenced by a custom emerging among Newars in Kathmandu (where Parbatiya and Indian cultural practices can be more readily observed and emulated) of substituting the traditional *bhvay* (feast) with a modern 'party' (the English word is used). The difference in terms of both cost and meaning is significant. The consumption of a feast, as we have seen, proceeds rather ceremoniously, with guests seated on long straw mats in some order of rank hierarchy, eating laboriously prepared, home-cooked food served on traditional Newar leaf plates by ever-attendant hosts: the emphasis here is on relationships forged by hospitality. On the bride's side, the feast also entails offerings of dowry to the bride by invited guests, a process traditionally underwritten by *lākhā* (gifts of bread or cash from the groom's family to the bride's family): the bride's family requests *lākhā* (specifying bread or cash form), the groom side delivers, and then the bride's family either distributes *lākhā* in the form of bread as an invitation to the wedding feast (and an injunction to give a dowry gift to the bride) or (in the case of a poor family) expends *lākhā* in the form of cash to finance the feast itself. In either case, the emphasis is on the social relationships underwriting a material investment.

At a 'party', guests help themselves to food prepared by Kathmandu-based professional cooks and served buffet-style (a particular affront to the traditional sensibilities surrounding hospitality and ritual pollution); sit as and when they please on chairs rented from a Kathmandu-based catering company; and eat off rented plates with rented utensils; the emphasis here is on competing in the display of 'modern' forms of wealth. In the 'party' system, *lākhā* has fallen out of favour. Instead the onus is on the bride's family to demonstrate that they can afford to host a 'party' and leverage their daughter's dowry with their own material and social resources. The emphasis is on financial capacity, proving one's ability to survive the material demands of honour and respectability.[10] The first 'party' in Sankhu, hosted in 1994, set a painfully costly precedent among dominant-caste Shrestha households anxious to establish and preserve their respectability within an emerging social logic of class. Although most households simply cannot afford to 'measure up', many of them try, for maintaining *ijat* still takes precedence over protecting one's immediate financial position, even if that entails going into debt.

On the groom's side, too, inflation is felt particularly strongly in the increasing expectations about the quantity and quality of the engagement gifts that must be presented to the bride (in plain view of her assembled extended family) prior to betrothal. As one Shrestha woman lamented:

It is such a big burden these days to give those engagement gifts! You need a sari, blouse, all different kinds of make up, bracelets, a gold ornament, hair pieces, shampoos, hair dryer, lotions, cake – all the new things – as well as the old things like the betel nuts, *lākhāmari* [sweet breads], yogurt, and fruit.

Here again we can detect not only a quantitative shift in the amount of goods required but also a qualitative shift in meaning. In the Newar economics of practice, the 'old things' that this woman refers to symbolize the webs of sociality that sustain a household in a particular place (Sankhu). These things/relationships still matter, she is saying, but it is also important to establish one's ability to succeed in the calculus of commodity consumption. That capacity, too, must be symbolized in the content of the engagement gifts; when the gifts are delivered by envoys from the groom's side, the bride's relatives meticulously peruse the offerings, to indicate their concern that their daughter's future husband can afford the luxuries of modern living. Once again, if the groom's side cannot afford to meet these inflating obligations, it must simply 'find a way' to do so, as the same Shrestha woman put it, usually by borrowing money from friends and relations.

The heavy round of social obligations – and the inflationary tendencies within them – thus disadvantage dominant castes within the new regime of value, where social status must be achieved in the realm of commodity consumption and display. Many are acutely aware of their falling status, not only relative to large-scale business entrepreneurs (such as Tibetan carpet-factory owners in Jorpati), but also relative to low castes at home in Sankhu. In the words of one young, college-educated Sankhu shopkeeper with a particularly astute concern about economic development in Sankhu:

The middle class is declining in Sankhu.[11] It used to be that economic classes were segregated by occupation [i.e. by caste]; but now the lower class lives like the middle class ... . And the middle class continues the same extravagant lifestyle, with so many feasts and *parties*; increasingly middle-class people aren't able to meet all these expenses. No one realizes that they have to adjust their expenditures to fit their capacity. For example my younger brother just had a *birthday party*; he invited all his friends, served them beer [bottled beer, not the locally brewed variety] and fancy food; with that one *party*, more than a month's income from our store is just gone.[12]

In many cases the consciousness amounts to laments about the 'loss of Newar culture' – invoking culture here as ideology, as a fixed representation of the world that serves some interests at the expense of others. And for some, the anxiety surrounding cultural transformation finds expression in an explicit resentment and even animosity toward low castes, whose successes in a class-based social logic not only highlight their own financial woes, but also diminish the power of traditional forms of social capital. The exaggerated comments of a well-educated and underemployed young Shrestha man may be considered in this light:

Pode [Po, Untouchables] have an unfair market advantage; they have a complete *monopoly* on the market for cleaning septic tanks. Many of them have become very rich men. Those who work in the airports are especially lucky because they have a chance of finding some gold that smugglers may not have been able to hold inside.[13] I wish I could clean septic tanks!

Even as they may resent low castes and fear the loss of 'Newar culture', most dominant- and high-caste Newars in Sankhu claim that they cannot 'opt out' of competing within the commoditized regime of value, as a growing dimension of *ijat*. The risk of social isolation deriving from *bejat* (shame) and the lack of sources of economic security alternative to the webs of sociality demand their participation in the inflationary trends of *ijat*.

Yet at the same time that dominant castes are having to spend more on social investments without earning more, the value of their social capital is eroding before their eyes: given the competing logic of commodity culture, there are simply fewer contexts and narrower social circles within which old-style hospitality, caste patronage or acts of religious devotion are valued – and thus less chance that they will generate long-term *financial* rewards. Chapter 4 draws on anthropologist Jonathan Parry's research in north India to explore how the Newar moral valuation of finance and trade – and the possibilities for making ritual reparations for moral transgressions through *dāna* (ritual gifts) and for justifying the fortunes of the rich through the doctrine of *karma* – appears particularly conducive to the 'spirit of capitalism'. In the context of economic liberalization and the deepening of capitalist relations, however, we see these relations and this moral justification for profit eroding, as Sankhu's Merchant-caste Shresthas face diminishing financial returns on their social investments.

NEOLIBERALISM AND GENDER IDEOLOGY

Relative to low castes, the political possibilities opened up for women in the present macroeconomic conjuncture seem somewhat less promising. The recent proliferation of imported consumer goods, for instance, articulates with gender ideology in ways that subvert the progressive dimensions of *kvasah* for women. Young women report spending more of their private wealth on ever-changing fashion as a means of pursuing and upholding the status of 'being modern' or 'being middle class'.[14] The Shrestha woman who described her mother's and aunt's investments in money-lending and livestock loans, responded to my ensuing questions about contemporary uses of *kvasah* by noting that:

As far as I have seen, often women, modern women who have money, they usually invest their *kvasah* in doing a lot of *fashion* – they have finished off their money in this way, by buying a lot of gold [a traditional dowry investment], making different kinds of jewellery, *buying clothes*, then a few months later buying clothes again because they want to stay in *fashion*. (emphasis added)

Because consumption of modern commodities figures so centrally in an emerging class-based regime of value, women, as bearers of household honour, simply cannot afford to ignore the latest trends in clothing, make-up and hairstyle – whether they at times take pleasure in them, or experience them as oppressive or trivial. Linda Peake and Alissa Trotz (1999), drawing on the work of Appadurai (1996), have described such consumer expenditures as a potential source of pleasure that conveys agency, as 'experiments with self-imagining as an everyday social project' (Appadurai 1996: 4, cited in Peake and Trotz 1999: 118). In a context of financial constraint, however, agency lies as much in the stress of 'keeping up with the Joneses' as in the pleasure of self-indulgence. In one instance to which I was witness, for example, a young woman from a poor Astrologer-caste household had attempted to keep up to date with the fashions by working for days to design and sew herself a 'modern' wide-legged *surwāl kurta* (the Indian dress for unmarried women); when she first wore the new outfit on the streets of Sankhu, however, she was ridiculed up and down town for having chosen a colour not suitable for the particular style, and a fashion that had gone out of fashion. The woman was visibly pained by the experience and in conversation with me after the incident vowed to avoid leaving her house at all except under the most urgent circumstances. The hyperbole sounds amusing, but in fact I witnessed this young woman make an astounding retreat to the privacy of her home and shun public encounters over the ensuing few months.

The point to emphasize here is that because consumer commodities lose their value at such a rapid pace, women must continually make these kinds of (financial as well as emotional) investments. Fashions change, clothes wear out, and electronic goods and accessories eventually break down: as Liechty (2003: 125) argues, '[b]oth the commodity itself and its meaning are eminently perishable'. Using *kvasah* for purchases of consumer goods on a regular basis clearly leaves fewer resources for income-generating investments.

At the same time, there is some evidence that even the meaning surrounding *kvasah* is being renegotiated within the new commoditized regime of value. To begin with, dowries, like engagement gifts, have been subject to inflationary processes. For those attending the wedding feast at the home of the bride's parents, it is a matter of honour to give a suitably modern and suitably priced gift; parents and close kin of the bride especially face increasingly onerous obligations with regard to the contents of their daughter's dowry. A dowry these days should, like engagement gifts, include modern consumer goods that are clearly gendered female – cosmetics, hair-care products, fashionable clothes, jewellery; but dowries are also increasingly encompassing kinds of moveable property whose use is in wider demand by the extended family of a woman's marital home: sofa sets, televisions, steel storage cabinets and other commodities required for households to function at minimally accepted standards of modernity – even, in one instance of which I heard, a motorcycle.[15]

Now, as discussed in Chapter 5 this property is certainly *given* to a bride with the intention that it remain in her custody and function as an endowment for the conjugal couple's own nuclear household, even if the couple resides for some years in the groom's joint family household.[16] For many joint family households in Sankhu, however, marital gifts brought by women marrying in may also provide the first occasion for acquiring modern furniture and other consumer goods crucial for marking out claims to middle-class status. In a society where the calculus of class and commodity consumption is gaining new currency, it is increasingly common to find such dowry items appropriated for collective use – and display – in the more public spaces of the household. These tendencies directly undermine normative beliefs about *kvasah* as women's own property. One Shrestha woman compared these trends in Newar towns to the coercive north Indian dowry system,[17] in which the groom's family extorts dowry items from the bride's family:

It is really an Indian custom for a woman's marital family to use her dowry or for dowry to even include items that are in demand by men. At first it was not like that in Nepal. There used not to be a lot of *pressure* [on a bride's family] to give a lot of dowry. In India, and also in the Marwari society here in Nepal, the *tilak* system prevails. What happens in this system is that in order to marry their daughter, the bride's family must give as much dowry as has been requested by the groom's family … motorcycle, motor, house, whatever – the bride's family must give it.

KR: Has this custom influenced Newar society in any way?

In Newar society, wealthy families have tried to institute this practice.

KR: You haven't seen this in the Newar towns, though, have you?

What is happening in Newar towns now is that dowry items more often come to belong to whoever uses them [instead of exclusively to the bride]. So even in Newar towns, the groom's family may demand dowry items: bring a TV, bring one of those steel cabinets, bring this, bring that. Some people have started looking for dowry items with their sons' weddings in this way.

KR: Do they really request particular things?

Some don't really, but some do … . Now among the rich Newars, they have gone so far as to expect the bride's side to clean the house on the groom's side, paint it, repair it and so on before the wedding. The groom's side leaves all of the house preparations, decorations, curtains, everything – it is all considered to be part of the dowry. They'll consider it part of a woman's dowry to decorate the groom's house on the occasion of her marriage!

As the basis for honour shifts from old forms of social investment to participation in a commodity-based regime of value, households find the surplus necessary to finance the requisite consumer goods in forms of finance capital normatively earmarked as women's property. Dowry itself is no longer gendered exclusively female – with significant implications for women's financial autonomy within marriage or beyond divorce.

Some households have attempted to temper these shifts by instituting a practice of deferring the complete transfer of dowry items to their daughter's marital home until she has borne her first child or established a separate household with her husband; large items like furniture must be transferred upon marriage (since, as another woman from a poor Shrestha household explained, 'the whole purpose of this part of the dowry is to display to outsiders'). But more moveable forms of property, such as cash, brass kitchen utensils and gold jewellery, can be retained in a woman's natal home until she becomes firmly established as a permanent member of her husband's household and can thus be more firmly guaranteed of her rightful control over her own dowry:

These days it is like this: one does not know what the parents of one's son-in-law are like, right? So after you give your daughter to someone else's household, you can elect not to give all the dowry right away. Your daughter might take half when she gets married and keep the other half in her natal home. After she gives birth you say, 'Okay, now you can take all of your things.' And then you give them to your daughter. These days the custom is increasingly like that. After she's had kids, you can be pretty sure that your daughter will stay there in her husband's household.

These comments suggest an acute consciousness that the current trend of extended families using the dowries of their daughters-in-law as a means to accumulate modern commodities introduces new scope for disputes over the ultimate disposition – and meaning – of dowry items. To this point the will to resist the trend remains at the scale of the individual household.

New labour market opportunities, meanwhile, have not challenged gender ideologies restricting women's mobility in the same manner that they have begun to erode the status prescriptions of caste hierarchy. Among low castes, for instance, when men migrate to Kathmandu women often take over family enterprises in Sankhu (such as butchering services of the Nay/Butcher caste), a practice which rejects the ideology of the male household head; when male migrants return to Sankhu for extended periods, especially for ritual and festival occasions, however, patriarchal principles are quickly re-established and continuity of gender ideology assured (for similar findings about the relationship between male migration and gender ideology in Indo-Guyanese communities, see Peake and Trotz, 1999).

In general, the customary preoccupation with ritual purity and pollution reduces possibilities for introducing market forces into the domain of domestic work within the household (and thus for freeing women to enter the labour market in new ways). Prescriptions against ritual defilement require that food must be prepared by a woman officially initiated into the family lineage. The implications for women's employment opportunities are twofold. First, Newar families do not hire labour to perform domestic tasks involving food processing, cooking or cleaning of eating and cooking utensils in the same way that they hire agricultural labour, or porters or builders to renovate their house.[18] Thus, second, if married women are to find employment, it must not compromise their obligation to prepare two home-cooked multi-course meals each day. As a corollary to the ideology of purity and pollution, the customary concern with women's seclusion narrows employment opportunities in some households even further. Women of all castes commonly take up various forms of home-based work; the most common at the time of this research was knitting sweaters for the tourist market. Wholesalers from Kathmandu contracted large orders to 'middlemen' in Sankhu – typically young women whose father or brothers had strong business connections in Kathmandu. The contractors in turn subcontracted piecework to their friends and relatives in other households. Previous research has documented how these spatial practices of work increase the scope for exploitation of women relative to forms of production located outside the home (e.g. Mies 1982) – and indeed women in Sankhu earn a mere NRs 80–120 per sweater, leaving the wholesaler with at least a NRs 300 profit per sweater. This wage can be compared to the NRs 60/day earned at the time of this research by women for agricultural labour; knitting is not performed continuously due to interruptions from housework or schooling, so it is difficult to establish a time frame, but it generally takes 3–7 days to knit one sweater. Such forms of organizing work encourage women to compete for the subcontracting orders from Kathmandu (with lower and lower piece-rates) in a manner that narrows possibilities for the kind of collective identification that we have seen among low castes.

Even though the customary concern with seclusion still prevails upon marriage, Newar families in Sankhu have begun to look more favourably than in the past on sending their daughters to school. Given spatial requirements to work primarily within the marital household (and its enterprises), however, women with high-school and even college education are being compelled to let their new capabilities lay idle, or otherwise direct them toward domestic responsibilities. A study conducted in Kathmandu by Shtrii Shakti, the feminist NGO, similarly found that although indigenous Newar women residing in Newar communities of the old Kathmandu bazaar are highly educated relative to women of a multi-ethnic, suburban, immigrant area, the women from immigrant families are more likely to hold jobs outside the household than Newar women (Shtrii Shakti 1995: 57). Within the emerging class-based regime of value in Newar societies, then, 'educated women' in marriage are increasingly valued as icons of modernity, but education has not generally opened up new employment opportunities for women that might challenge ideological constraints on women's mobility. As Liechty (2003) argues with regard to Kathmandu middle-class culture more generally, Newars have thus modernized the concepts of girl and daughter in accordance with the development discourse on 'girl child education', but beyond marriage, in the context of the husband's family, the new freedoms of economic liberalization and political democracy hardly begin to challenge the deeply entrenched geography of social relations.[19]

GLOBAL–LOCAL ARTICULATIONS

This chapter has considered how local logics of accumulation and investment elaborated in the preceding chapters articulate with the forces of commoditization and the emerging labour markets associated with the current neoliberal economic orthodoxy – with special emphasis on opportunity structures for women and low castes. It notes the stresses on the Newar system of social investment posed by the recent inflation in material standards of honour. As material dimensions of *ijat* become more important (and more costly) in the Newar honour economy, social investments in *guthi* obligations, kin networks, caste patronage and religious observances offer fewer economic guarantees relative to the consumption and display of 'modern' commodities. As anthropologist Mary Margaret Steedly (1993) notes for the case of Karoland, Indonesia, when wealth is no longer preserved in social investments, its protective functions dissipate and the redistributive demands of kinship and community have narrower grounds to lay claim to capital and turn it back into social wealth; on the contrary, such obligations – which formerly guaranteed subsistence to all who participated in the Newar economics of practice but also maintained caste and gender hierarchies – become a burden within a commoditized regime of value.

In the emerging commodity-based regime redistribution has been accomplished by other means. For low castes, who can easily fill low-end service-sector jobs associated with the recent economic boom in Kathmandu, the macroeconomic context has provided an opportunity to transcend the subordinating implications of caste and geography, and to compete successfully within the new commodity-based regime of value. Although most households have responded individually to these opportunities, there is some evidence of a growing collective consciousness and the building of collective strategies among low castes. Meanwhile, commodity culture and caste hierarchy conjoin in a particularly disadvantageous manner for those who formerly enjoyed the material benefits of dominant-caste status. They face the dual constraints of under-employment and declining purchasing power, even as material standards for providing hospitality and exhibiting wealth are on the rise. For women across castes, on the other hand, the new commodity culture has intersected with Newar gender ideologies in a manner that subverts women's autonomous control over their dowry wealth. Although Newars have generally been relatively progressive in the area of girls' education, ideas and spatial practices surrounding women's seclusion have tended to preclude opportunities for even educated women to find employment in the fields for which they increasingly hold academic credentials, or to recognize and act on these constraints in a collective manner.

The findings presented here also offer several conclusions about the cultural politics of social change. First, the deepening and expansion of markets does not 'modernize' or 'develop' social groups in unilateral or predictable ways; nor can fixed cultural traits determine development outcomes or serve as models for replication. Rather, local economies of practice articulate with macroeconomic trends in a dialectical process reflecting both the agency of local actors and the structuring force of wider-scale economic processes – here the emerging labour markets in Kathmandu and new patterns of commodification. Social groups change through dialectical and culturally specific processes of material as well as ideological transformation. 'Market' values do not merely replace 'traditional' values; rather, new regimes of value articulate with old ones, creating different opportunities and constraints for differently positioned social groups, as well as shaping the parameters of labour markets and commodity circulation. Finally, the distinction between individual and collective responses of low castes and women contributes to elaborating a progressive agenda for planning and development in the following chapter.

7   PLANNING AND DEVELOPMENT

This concluding chapter brings the findings from critical ethnography of Sankhu's cultural economy to bear on the task of elaborating a theory of planning and development. In so doing it refutes the central tenets of a neoliberal, market-led approach to development rooted in Hayekian principles (and its corollary in the 'post-Washington Consensus'): the conceptual separation of the economic from political and cultural spheres; the rejection of planning as a 'dictatorship of ideals'; the instrumental interpretation of culture as a friction on market forces; the idea of self-regulating markets rendering optimal social outcomes; and the notion that social capital accumulating in civil society can be enlisted as an aid to the smooth functioning of markets. Drawing on Bourdieu's notion of an 'economics of practice' to emphasize the social and cultural dimensions of profit and exchange, it advocates a theory of development viewed not merely as economic growth through market deepening but as a process of embedding market rationality within a concern for social protections extended at various scales of state provisioning. I extend the Polanyian framework to argue that the expansion of human well-being (as an objective of development) entails approaching economic growth as only one among many *means* (and never an *end*) of development, but, above all, radically challenging existing cultural ideologies and cognitive structures. And I suggest that it is the task of planners – professionals engaged in community organizing, service delivery and/or economic development in disadvantaged communities – to facilitate those challenges by mobilizing locally situated social criticism.

CAPITAL ACCESS AS DEVELOPMENT ORTHODOXY

Chapter 6 noted that the finance sector has been an important and early site for neoliberal economic reforms, and in development those reforms have manifested in a faith that capital access programmes can achieve the dual objectives of creating opportunity for the poor and deepening the discipline of financial markets in rural, 'undeveloped' areas. The idea has been to draw the poor and marginalized into the market, by tapping the income potential in conventional householding and subsistence farming skills; small amounts of credit, that is, could spawn a vibrant new market sector in 'micro-enterprises' – small-scale businesses, like goat raising and basket-weaving, that draw on local knowledge and resources. Since many of the skills for such home-based enterprises are often gendered female in rural agrarian societies, and since economic development initiatives had for so long overlooked both women's productive capacity and their relatively greater levels of poverty, women have been a special focus of donor initiatives to promote micro-enterprise. Liberal theories of social capital play an important role in this recent 'feminization of development' (Rankin 2002), especially in relation to accessing the credit necessary to finance small-scale production.

The idea is that social networks can help correct for imperfect information about borrowers lacking in formal credit and employment histories and substitute for collateral by ensuring against default through social sanction and peer enforcement. Thus in 'microfinance' programmes that have now become a conventional technology of development, women borrowers are formed into 'solidarity groups' that, as the World Bank web page on social capital puts it, allows 'poor but closely-knit communities [to] pledge their social capital in lieu of the material assets that commercial banks require as collateral' (World Bank 2002a). Among the poor lacking in tangible assets, social networks and associational life are thought to enhance efficiency by facilitating cooperation among inherently self-maximizing individuals; as such, social capital represents a promising resource for linking the poor to market opportunity so that they may become the agents of their own development. For poor women, moreover, participation is said to yield not only an economic payoff in increased access to financial services, but also an 'empowerment payoff' in new forms of social capital that emerge within networks of borrower groups (Servon 1998). Donors thus consider microfinance to be a 'win-win' approach to development because investors can mobilize social capital to enhance the financial viability (indeed the profitability) of banking with poor women; and poor women gain access to both social and financial resources that allow them to help themselves through the market mechanism (Mayoux 1995; Morduch 2000; Rankin 2001a). It is a strategy that ultimately relies on ideologies of self-help and individual responsibility, as opposed to welfare and social rights.

I want to stay with the microfinance example a moment longer because it illustrates so well the instrumental way in which the idea of social capital has been deployed toward promoting market-led development. The first thing to note is that microfinance programmes replace a generation of state-subsidized development banks heralding from a bygone era of Keynesian 'development economics' that attributed to the state a responsibility to redistribute finance capital to the disadvantaged rural sector. Development banks provided credit at subsidized interest rates in order to engage the banking system as an instrument of social protection and embed it within wider community development initiatives. They targeted 'small farmers', conceived as male heads of subsistence family farms meeting fixed indicators of poverty, and attributed to the poor the subjectivity of citizen, having social rights to state protection.

Microfinance programmes, on the other hand, operate largely outside the formal banking sector through non-governmental organizations, cooperatives and other local associations, to deliver credit at market interest rates, primarily to women clients organized into self-regulating 'solidarity groups'. Donors have justified the end of credit subsidies (which they once foisted on relenting Third World governments) with recourse to liberal theories of social capital. Subsidy results in financial repression and elite capture, the argument goes; the best way to ensure that development benefits the poor on a sustainable basis is rather to mobilize existing social resources at the grassroots.[1] Thus borrowers receive credit on the basis of 'group guarantee' that substitutes social collectivity for collateral and is said to promote solidarity among women. Yet in practice, the financial imperatives for sustainability often lead microfinance programmes to engage the collective only in the most instrumental manner at the expense of the more time-consuming processes of consciousness-raising and empowerment. Microfinance programmes rarely take on the long-term process of challenging the gender division of labour, authority and ownership within households or addressing the social differences and hierarchies operating *among* women (e.g. Goetz and Gupta 1996). For from the lenders' point of view, the motivation for lending to women lies fundamentally in their greater propensity to pay back their loans. Indeed it is women's responsiveness to the discipline of weekly repayment schedules – and to a highly disciplinary institutional culture involving wearing uniforms, chanting slogans, singing songs and taking oaths – that may be credited for the extraordinarily high repayment rates of most microfinance programmes.

Thus microfinance, like other market-led development strategies, offer planners a way to shift the responsibility for development from the state to civil society. Here the subjects of development are construed not as citizens with social rights to subsidized credit, but as clients responsible to themselves and their communities. When poor women are viewed in a clientelistic relationship with the state in this way, the onus for development falls squarely on their shoulders, and their citizenship manifests not through entitlement but through the 'free' exercise of individual choice (see Rankin 2001a). Such instrumental uses of collective action and women's participation illustrate a key rationale for the way liberal interpretations of social capital have found favour in mainstream development circles, however much they also appeal to planners with progressive intentions (see, for example, Douglass and Friedmann 1988). For they enable the architects of neoliberal development policy to cast the recent shifts in poverty lending in progressive terms – local self-reliance, increased returns to human capital, reduced transaction costs. Social capital, that is, can be expected to fill the vacuum left by the restructuring of the welfare state in the shift from Keynesian to neoliberal economic philosophies. And it fits the mandate of the 'post-Washington Consensus' to 'get the social relations right' in order to enhance the smooth functioning of markets. When considered in articulation with Bourdieu's and Polanyi's insights about economy–society relations, ethnographic research from Sankhu detailed in the preceding chapters reveals the political dangers of embracing liberal notions of social capital that do not seriously question existing power relations and property rights.

IDEOLOGY AND OPPORTUNITY: LESSONS FROM SANKHU'S CULTURAL ECONOMY

Several key assumptions underpin market-led approaches to development as illustrated by the microfinance model, each of which will be refuted here with recourse to ethnographic evidence about the distribution of opportunity within Sankhu's cultural economy. The model assumes that once markets have been introduced they will function as an autonomous sphere that may rely on social capital for its sustainability, but can be managed by a professional staff of economic technicians concerned with the mechanics of price, supply and demand. Social capital is assumed to be a fixed input to the market and its quality and nature need not concern the development planner charged with assuring long-term financial sustainability. In fact, existing social networks and those forged in the formation of 'solidarity groups' (as well as in other instances of group formation, e.g. user groups, focus groups) are considered to be inherently benign, characterized by bonds of trust and reciprocity that promise economic and efficiency payoffs (see Rankin 2002). Families and communities are assumed to be the harmonious institutional frameworks within which the benefits of social ties and networks are enjoyed – a formulation that overlooks not only decades of feminist research on households, but also well-established research on the 'downsides of social capital' documenting the possibility that associational life might instil not cooperation but conflict (Portes and Landolt 1996). Finally, market-led approaches to development such as microfinance consider market access (including access to credit) *in itself* as the linchpin of opportunity for the poor and disenfranchised. This proposition is based largely on research documenting that women's status within their household and their authority to influence the disposition of household resources increases with their capacity to earn independent income (e.g. Drèze and Sen 1995).

Although it may indeed be the case that income correlates positively with household status, this relation does not tell us anything about the *process* of social change or prove that income is a sufficient condition for empowerment.[2] The question remains whether access to credit (or markets generally) *in itself* will suffice to alter opportunity structures. The first and obvious point to note is the important ideological and cognitive constraints women face in taking advantage of material opportunity. The notion of female seclusion, associated with such ordering principles in caste society as honour and ritual purity, limits Newar women's mobility and anchors their dependence on male household providers. It constrains women's capacity not only to carry out the purchasing and marketing dimensions of business, but also to transmute economic profit into social investments that could earn them symbolic forms of wealth so crucial to economic security in Newar society. As explored in Chapter 5, ideological constraints may be experienced so forcefully that women may decline substantial material opportunities when they arise. In cases where unmarried women have inheritance rights, for example, they must weigh the freedom of economic independence against the costs of probable social isolation and shame. Their compliance with normative views of women (in rejecting inheritance rights) reflects a consciousness of the ideological dimensions of opportunity as well as the material benefit in maintaining dependent relationships with men. Such ideological constraints are not simply 'imposed on' women by discriminatory cultures or calculating men; rather, women participate in reproducing dominant ideologies and cognitive structures through the myriad ways they consent to subordination and, as Bourdieu suggests women unwittingly do everywhere, somatize relations of domination in their very bodily dispositions (or perpetuate social hierarchy in their relationships with those in normatively 'lower' social positions). These examples illustrate the significance of ideological frameworks within which material opportunity transpires. If, as Bina Agarwal (1994) has persuasively argued, the material and ideological dimensions of social change are dialectically related, then development must attend to both; planners cannot assume a linear, causal relationship between market access and ideological change.

The second point to note in relation to the question of market access as a sufficient condition for social change has to do with the ideological space existing within Newar society for women to accumulate wealth. Women's investment of *kvasah* (dowry wealth; women's own property) in money-lending and other income-generating enterprises suggests rather interesting possibilities for integrating the *goals* of capital access programmes (and other market-led interventions) with actually existing cultural practices. In as much as they constitute an ideological justification for women's autonomy, dowries (as they function not only in Newar society but also among other Tibeto-Burman groups occupying more marginal socio-economic positions in the ethno-political landscape of Nepal) offer some potential to provide an entry point for social change. Yet this kind of strategic interface between the material and ideological dimensions of social change, between social institutions and economic behaviour, are rarely explored when planners regard markets as autonomous, disembedded spheres of development.

A corollary to this observation about existing ideological space must be an awareness of how local places are embedded in other scales of economic life, of how local cultural ideologies articulate with wider-scale macroeconomic contexts. In Sankhu the same material conditions – the changing patterns of commodification and new labour market opportunities resulting from neoliberal policies – have had different implications for low castes and women. An emerging social logic of class has introduced opportunities for low castes as a group to transcend the stigmatizing implications of caste, while having regressive implications for women of all castes in relation to dominant gender ideologies. For as the households into which women marry increasingly view dowries as an opportunity for acquiring expensive consumer goods, the potential of *kvasah* to leverage women's private income is severely diminished. Articulation with the macroeconomic context, that is, has generated very different opportunities for low castes and women; the difference lies not in material conditions, but in ideological frameworks.

The third point relates to the expectation that networks of social capital can enhance market access and thereby expand opportunity. The ethnographic chapters here have illustrated that social capital is indeed an important dimension of the Newar cultural economy, and a significant arbiter of opportunity. In Sankhu financial wealth alone does not suffice to achieve economic security. Rather it must be transmuted into symbolic forms of wealth – hospitality, religious patronage, *guthi* obligations and other modes of social investment – that establish one's honour and weave webs of interdependence upon which security ultimately depends. The heavily regulated system of social investment redistributes financial wealth, softening disparities and serving as a sort of welfare safety net. But it also locks people into particular social locations – a low-caste Butcher prohibited from entering the local tea shops, the recent bride of a high-caste merchant's son strictly confined to the confines of her marital household – from which it is very difficult to escape. Within this system, networks of reciprocity and obligation themselves can serve an ideological function, especially when they transpire between people occupying different social positions. For example, in the context of caste patronage, gifting and other gestures of kindness commit a 'symbolic violence' (*à la* Bourdieu); they act as a form of domination that bind low castes more firmly to their high-caste patrons through feelings of trust and obligation. In the context of highly stratified societies such as exist among caste Hindus, in fact, I have argued (in Chapter 4) that these kinds of social investments function analogously to welfare policies in advanced capitalist societies; in both systems social investments play an important role in ensuring social reproduction and providing moral justification for profit-making. The difference lies in the extent to which social investments mitigate class disparity in the two systems, not in their respective 'market' versus 'non-market' values.

In light of the hierarchical and coercive frameworks within which social capital can operate, one might wonder whether the 'solidarity groups' catalysed by capital access programmes could in fact entrench, rather than challenge, some already existing modes of subordination – *of* women but also *among* women. In Nepal, caste and ethnicity are obvious examples of the kinds of social distinctions that might structurally preclude women in some social locations from viewing their interests in terms of collective struggle with women in others. Chapter 5 illustrates how even among women within a single lineage, structural antagonisms extend across households over time as they expand through marriage alliances and contract with the splitting of joint families. Other ethnographic research in South Asia offers further cause for scepticism about the inherently benign qualities attributed to social capital in development circles. For example, women in microfinance programmes have been shown to self-select for group members with significant assets – such as 'husbands with income' – thus concentrating access to capital among relatively well-resourced households (Ackerly 1997). Groups also tend to self-select for members with identical caste and ethnic identities, limiting possibilities for gender solidarity across other socio-cultural differences (Rankin 2001b). When group members do vigorously monitor one another's consumption and repayment patterns in accordance with programme incentive structures, they can generate an environment of hostility and coercion that in practice atomizes rather than unites them (Ackerly 1997). In spite of the ethnographic evidence documenting the coercive dimensions of social capital, the Marxian perspectives advocated by Bourdieu are consistently overlooked in the context of development planning. I have argued (in Chapter 1) that this oversight reflects a deliberate hesitation to disrupt the ideological function of 'social capital' in development discourse, serving as it does to provide moral justification for the neoliberal restructuring of state–society relations.

THE CULTURAL POLITICS OF SOCIAL CHANGE

The ethnographic findings from Sankhu can be read iteratively with the synthesis offered in Chapter 2 of anthropologies and geographies of globalization to develop a theory about the cultural politics of social change, on which to construct a normative framework for planning. The task must begin by specifying an interpretation of 'culture' – an important and widely debated concept these days in development discourse. The ethnographic analysis and theoretical orientation offered here present an understanding of culture not as a fixed structure determining opportunity as is so often assumed even in the most liberal injunctions (*à la* post-Washington Consensus) to 'integrate culture into the design [of development projects]' (World Bank 2002b), but as the outcome of repeated social practices in a specific historical and geographical location. Those practices are shot through with power relations – even those practices such as gifting and reciprocity that appear to the most trenchant critics of capitalism as inherently expressing the virtues of solidarity and cooperation. It is thus the ethnographer's task to reveal how power operates through culture, by examining the production and consumption of ideology as much as the contradictions that ideology throws up for people to interpret and respond to on an individual or collective basis. Well-intentioned anthropologists and geographers have tended to impute progressive qualities to socially embedded economies, expecting that 'non-capitalist' forms of economic organization can offer critical perspectives on capitalist economic arrangements and inspire the imagining of alternative futures. Yet in the absence of an evaluative capacity, nostalgic idealizations of gifting and other non-monetized modes of exchange can translate into development projects that exacerbate already existing lines of hierarchy, coercion and exclusion.

It must also be noted that the most ardent advocates of structural understandings of culture as a fixed variable of opportunity can be found not only within the halls of the 'economic development' wings of mainstream donor agencies, but also among local cultural elites who have the most to lose from social change processes. Here we have only to recall the nervous lament about the 'loss of culture' among the Merchant-caste elite in Sankhu. For they experience the contemporary disintegration of caste patronage relationships resulting from new forms of low-caste mobility as a palpable threat to their status rooted in a 'traditional' honour-based regime of value. With the emergence of a competing commodity-based regime of value, there are simply fewer contexts and narrower social circles within which old-style hospitality, caste patronage or acts of religious devotion are valued – and thus less chance that they will generate long-term *financial* rewards. As they face diminishing returns to social investment, dominant castes recognize the relative advantage enjoyed by low castes with new service-sector incomes to compete in the logic of commodity culture. A view of culture as constituted through social practices thus establishes at once the power and also the vulnerability of 'tradition'; as Raymond Williams (1994: 601) puts it, 'Tradition … is … an aspect of *contemporary* social and cultural organization, in the interest of the dominance of a specific class. It is a version of the past which is intended to connect with and ratify the present.' And it is always vulnerable to reinterpretation as a form of resistance and counter-hegemonic work.

We have also seen that it would not be possible to adopt a practice-oriented interpretation of culture without an understanding of the spatial and scalar dimensions of ideology and social change. As the discussion of Sankhu's spatial organization in Chapter 5 suggests, cultural ideologies are inscribed in the organization of physical space and in the paths that people in different social locations are authorized to trace. Likewise, networks of obligation create a web of community ties that work to encircle Sankhu in social, emotional and economic interdependencies. Thus it is no surprise that progressive change could come most readily for subordinate groups – namely low-caste men – able to break the spatial bonds to place and community, while continuing to elude others – namely women – for whom ideologies of seclusion assume an explicitly spatial dimension. As the discussion in Chapters 3 and 6 suggest, moreover, local places are always constituted in relation to other scales of economic and political influence. Inter-scalar dynamics produce an interplay of systems that reorders both, creating new social formations. As in the case of Sankhu's emerging commodity-based regime of value, the articulation of local cultural ideologies with wider scales of influence has the potential to generate new regimes of value, altering the distribution of opportunity and changing the meaning of existing relationships. It is in these conjunctures that ethnographers must learn to recognize the emancipatory and progressive possibilities for those in subordinate social locations.

PLANNING AND DEVELOPMENT

For the task of developing guidelines for planning practice, we return to Polanyi's injunction to embed economic activity within a regulatory and procedural framework for guaranteeing social protections – at, we have added, multiple scales of the state. Polanyi's historiography has played a crucial role in refuting Hayekian rejections of planning as totalitarianism, by illustrating how capitalist markets have from their inception depended upon state intervention in the form of permissive regulation. Of course, neoliberal capitalism is no exception, however much it peddles an ideology that explicitly denounces state intervention and advocates the self-regulating capacity of markets. The information-theoretic turn in economics, now embraced by the post-Washington Consensus, has tweaked this ideology slightly in order to ward off criticisms of the social costs that must be paid when neoliberalism is applied in its pure form: it posits that a strong civil society with ample stocks of social capital can substitute for the 'interventionist' state as an alternative locus of *social* regulation that can help markets function more efficiently. In my view there are three ways to refute these propositions, each expressing or extending a Polanyian framework. The first is to note how under conditions of neoliberalism, the state continues to play a role in constructing markets and how the resulting social costs are often so severe as to produce counter-movements. This approach of exposing the 'myth of the self-regulating market' derives directly from Polanyi and has been duly exercised in Chapter 1. The second is to argue that World

Bank social capitalists have got the relationship between civic action and good governance backwards – that the conditions for people to participate in civic life must be *created by* 'a favourable political regime, characterized by political competition that is "constrained by mutually accepted ground rules", in the context of a "relatively egalitarian social structure" ' (Evans in Harris 2002: 62). And the third is to recognize the ideological and cognitive bases of inequality – embedded in social capital itself – that neither 'unregulated' civic engagement nor market access alone can resolve, and that points to some procedural requirements for progressive planning.

This final section explores the second and third assertions – which acknowledge that claiming a normative role for planning, as Polanyi did, involves at the outset not only recognizing the political constructedness of markets, but also actively participating in the political, social and spatial processes through which markets are constructed. It begins by noting the recent activism of Nobel laureate Amartya Sen, who defends a role for the state in providing social protections through his work on capabilities. Here is an example of an approach to concretizing Polanyi's vision in the context of the contemporary neoliberal orthodoxy and it is indeed cause for some optimism that Sen's work has been taken up by the World Bank (and not just the more progressive United Nations Development Programme [UNDP]). But close scrutiny reveals that Sen's vision, for all its injunctions to support human capabilities through strong public programmes, suffers, like World Bank social capitalism, from a reductive methodological individualism that overlooks the social struggle immanent in civil society. Thus the concluding paragraphs draw on the multidisciplinary framework advocated in Chapter 2, to consider *procedural* guidelines for planners wishing to address these forms of injustice – missing in the broad sweep of Polanyi's political theory.

The Activist State

Amartya Sen's capabilities approach comes close to justifying an activist state on Polanyian grounds of rescuing the idea of freedom from market rationality. Sen reached his position of *Development as Freedom* (1999) largely through his work on famines (e.g. 1981) and gender inequality (e.g. 1990), as well as his personal experiences of having grown up in present-day Bangladesh and surviving the partition of India and the Great Bengal Famine. On both accounts, Sen introduced a cultural dimension to what had been construed as largely socio-economic problems (see

Corbridge 2002). Thus he argued that famines result not just when food shortages arise, but when disadvantaged social groups lack entitlements to access the regional food supply. Likewise India's 100 million women 'missing' as a consequence of sex-selective abortion and early childhood mortality cannot be explained only by unfair resource distribution; other dimensions of women's capabilities, such as participation in public life or the freedom to make choices regarding marriage, childbearing and sexual expression are crucially significant. Thus, as Stuart Corbridge (2002), Martha Nussbaum (2000) and others have argued, Sen offers a trenchant critique of the utilitarianism at the root of neo-classical economics; for an approach rooted in individuals' preferences overlooks the accidents of history and geography that endow people with different, and unequal, resources and entitlements, and it offers those who are relatively well-off grounds to obstruct pro-poor government actions as compromising their utility.

For Sen, then, '[d]evelopment consists of the removal of various types of unfreedoms that leave people with little choice and little opportunity of exercising their reasoned agency' (2000: xii). Here freedom is construed not in the narrow sense of local self-reliance and 'getting the state off our backs', but in a much more expansive understanding of human and civil rights that would guarantee cultural recognition as well as socio-economic redistribution (in philosopher Nancy Fraser's [1995] formulation) and that would thus leave individuals free to pursue their chosen objectives. As such, freedom bestows the capability to earn an income and enjoy the resulting benefits of recognition, to be sure, but also the capability to express oneself freely, make choices about one's own body, and achieve other political-cultural aspects of a qualitatively '*good* human life' (Nussbaum 1995, emphasis in original). One of the greatest strengths of Sen's foundational approach to development as freedom is that it rejects the politically disabling forms of cultural relativism in essentialized accounts of 'Asian values' or 'the artisanal values of northern Italy' as much as in postmodern rejections of universalist moral positions. It reveals the dangers of cultural discrimination (such as, specifically, in orientalist distinctions of the West from the Rest) when culture is treated as a fixed attribute yet stakes out a firm moral stand about the cultural dimensions of justice. Most significantly, for our purposes of resurrecting a Polanyian approach to building economy–society relations, Sen's work 'leads to grounded interventions in the realm of social affairs and public policy', while also resisting the 'drive to normalize that James Scott described for the projects of high modernism' (Corbridge 2002: 9).

Given these political imperatives it might indeed be construed as a hopeful sign that Sen's work has been taken up by the World Bank (and is no longer only the preserve of more progressive multilateral agencies such as the UNDP). There a Culture and Poverty Program has been established with explicit reference to Sen and with an objective 'a) to improve poverty reduction efforts by mobilizing cultural strengths and assets and b) to improve the effectiveness of investment projects by integrating explicit attention to culture into their design' (World Bank 2002b; see also Sen 2000). But caution must be exercised in such applications of Sen's work. For, like liberal theories of social capital, Sen's vision has limited force as a political tool because it fails to address problems of entrenched power and symbolic violence that operate within culture. And it fails to recognize the significance of social struggles and contestational politics that have been historically necessary for people in most countries to achieve the redistribution of resources that are a crucial ingredient of freedom (Corbridge 2002). The capabilities Sen wishes to nourish are those of individuals (functioning freely within civil society), not of states or planners or even non-governmental organizations (NGOs) engaged in development work. Thus Sen's notion of development as freedom is rooted in the same reductive theories of methodological individualism that allow liberal theories of social capital to sit comfortably with neoliberal economics. The limits to Sen's formulation become especially apparent when he talks about progressive politics as a forum for raising diverse voices. Here a political space is imagined that encompasses only *cooperation* among individuals – rendered capable, it must be added, through good public services – and that silences the collective, often oppositional, action necessary to secure those services in the first place. It is a political space, as Stuart Corbridge notes that is 'more attuned to the comforting fictions of the World Bank than to many social realities' (2002: 50).[3]

The Praxis of Planning

Sen's analysis is extremely useful for identifying a role for the state specifically in ensuring basic levels of capabilities, through, for example, strong public health and education systems. But in the final analysis, Sen's framework maintains the dubious separation of the 'political' from other spheres of social life in his formulation of freedom as individual capabilities. The problem, as Stuart Corbridge aptly puts it, is that:

... to become 'developed' is not simply a matter of maximizing individual freedoms. Development also involves concerted struggles against the powers of vested interests at all spatial scales. It remains a difficult and sometimes dispiriting or even dangerous social project, as many poor people realize only too well. (2002: 53–4)

If we conclude that freedom of the poor is best expanded by collective mobilization at the same time as we wish to assert a role for planning in promoting progressive social change (at local as much as central scales of the state), then what is needed are some clear procedural guidelines, which are missing in Polanyi. The remaining paragraphs thus join the normative and multi-scalar thrust of economic and cultural geography with the emphasis on the politics of culture within strains of anthropology arising from the work of Gramsci and Bourdieu, to develop a more procedural dimension of Polanyi's normative framework. Based on insights from the critical ethnography of Sankhu, I advocate extending anthropological concern with 'practice' into the more activist domain of 'praxis'. In the domain of praxis, social science research itself becomes a form of practice with the injunction to make judgements, advocate change and empower informants to view their world critically.

The first step, then, is to recognize that planning must encompass an explicitly ideological dimension. Of course, social opportunity requires *both* material and ideological change; too often, however, market-led interventions, responding increasingly to donor injunctions for financial sustainability, focus on the material in isolation from the ideological, and consequently fail to bring about long-term progressive social change. Given the complex relationships between space, scale, individual practice and normative beliefs about caste and gender described here, it follows that access to markets does not in itself guarantee social opportunity or empowerment (although in certain circumstances they may be a crucial ingredient for them). Rather, culturally based schemes of perception, and the various ways they articulate with processes of macroeconomic change, play a particularly important role in structuring opportunity. For the case of Sankhu, introducing social change requires an understanding of how new commodity cultures articulate with a 'traditional' regime of value rooted in the honour economy and how this articulation creates different opportunities and constraints for differently positioned social groups. Small-scale credit projects are unlikely to alter these dynamics without building in a procedure for eliciting local perspectives on the ideological and cognitive constraints to gender transformation. The discussion here of ideology as spatial praxis suggests, moreover, that planners must have a tactical understanding of the role of space in challenging (or entrenching) dominant cultural ideologies: a recognition of the limits to undertaking change within fixed spatial boundaries of household or village (which will likely lead to diversifying experience, but not necessarily dismantling dominant ideologies), a caution against strengthening place-based institutions (local social capital) built on hierarchical premises, and an understanding of the tranformative potential when people 'get out of place' or are able to directly reform the built environment.

If one recognizes the significance of ideology and cognitive frameworks in social change processes, then the crucial issue for planners shifts from the search for *the* authoritative development model, to concerns about the locus and mechanism of social criticism. The question for *any* intervention – whether in credit markets, health, adult literacy or any other sector – must be: will it set off the critical mechanisms latent in experience of oppression necessary to sustain a dialectical process of material and ideological change? On the one hand, the findings here present development planners with some rather optimistic evidence about the scope for critical resources within culture to inform social change. In Sankhu the contradictory values of hierarchy and equality, fate and hard work, religion of power and religion of status, son preference and filial bond, *angsa* and *kvasah*, expose the arbitrary foundation of high-caste and male privilege. Even as they comply with normative caste and gender beliefs, the testimony of low castes and women reveals that they often recognize those contradictions and do not accept prevailing ideologies as legitimate or moral. Existing levels of individual consciousness, that is, can become the basis for building organized, overt movements for change, should planners learn how to recognize the critical resources available within culture.

On the other hand, as Bourdieu has argued, planners must be prepared to acknowledge that there are some aspects of ideology that people accept without knowing. And that relations of domination extend beyond the realm of mental representation into the very cognitive schemes through which people interpret their place in the world – making it very difficult to transform the 'instruments of knowledge' into the 'objects of knowledge'. Even when there is recognition, moreover, the exigencies of poverty and the need for economic security work to keep recognition at the individual scale; in *practice*, that is, the best strategy for securing individual needs often involves complying with normative beliefs about the division of labour, the organization of space and so on – and engaging principles of hierarchy to one's advantage in one's treatment of those occupying normatively 'lower' social positions. However much cognitive structures may be embedded in people's consciousness and bodily comportment, we can at the very least say that ideological and cognitive *change* (or the articulation of 'subordinate ideology' in Bourdieu's lexicon) requires more collective processes of recognition and action. As Bina Agarwal (1994) has argued, in the domain of ideology, collective strength is the most important transformative resource. Thus a role emerges for planners in eliciting the critical consciousness immanent in the contradictions of social life in a manner that facilitates recognition as a *collective* process and encourages people to move from individual and covert to collective and overt modes of action. In so doing planners must always negotiate the fragile balance between catalysing collective action on the basis of locally situated criticism, and avoiding the fallacy of false consciousness.

A first step, then, might be to draw on approaches in popular education that engage Freireian principles and tactics of consciousness-raising among groups of the poor and disenfranchised. Here practitioners require participants to critically address concepts and words with deep experiential relevance – such as dowry, property rights and marriage – as a mechanism to encourage collective critical evaluation of power relations and, crucially, to expand their organizational capacity. Similarly, planners might introduce strategies for 'conscientization' about the broader macro-regulatory context for development. Training in numeracy and basic banking principles can assume a political function as aspects of popular economics education, for example, if it seeks to foster a collective critical awareness of economic relations and policy affecting the lives of the oppressed. But, as Bourdieu has argued, the raising of consciousness is not enough to grasp the symbolic dimension of domination, '[b]ecause the foundation of symbolic violence lies not in mystified consciousness that only need to be enlightened but in dispositions attuned to the structure of domination of which [consciousness is] the product'. Thus 'the relation of complicity that the victims of symbolic domination grant to the dominant can only be broken through a radical transformation of the social conditions of production of [those] dispositions' (2001: 41–2).[4]

The task must therefore be to:

> … restore the paradoxical character of *doxa* while at the same time dismantling the processes responsible for this transformation of history into nature, of cultural arbitrariness into the *natural*. And to do so, one has to adopt the point of view … which is that of the anthropologist, capable of showing that the principle of division … which founds the difference between male and female [high caste and low caste, etc.] as we (mis)recognize it is simultaneously arbitrary, contingent, and also socio-logically necessary. (2001: 2, emphasis in original)

For it is the anthropologist who is most capable of thinking outside the schemes of perception that reflect the doxic consensus of any given society and make relations of domination appear self-evident and natural to both the dominated and dominant.

Planners, too, are often outsiders to the communities where they work, with the capacity to exercise this critical cognitive function. To the extent possible, then, planners could play a role in creating the social spaces for collective reflection on individual experiences of subordination and powerlessness. Such procedural considerations could facilitate the design of programmes – in any sector of service delivery – that encourage women, low castes and others in subordinate social locations to transcend individual, covert strategies of acquiescence and resistance and develop a collective social criticism of injustice. The facilitation of collective reflection, however, must not stop at the scale of the support group focusing on particular instances of domination – sexism, caste discrimination and so on. For the only way to expose the cognitive structures underlying dominant ideologies is simultaneously to engage in political action against multiple axes of oppression, that work, for example, to separate low-caste from high-caste women, or male from female low castes. Here planning must assist in building institutions – within the state as much as within civil society – that join critical capacities immanent in local experiences of oppression with the competencies of social scientific research. Such a joining of popular and scientific knowledge must work to identify the symbolic dimensions of domination, in order to create collaborative, critical projects bearing directly on public debate and *linking social analysis to political and legal reform*. This kind of social capital   a solidarity grounded in the joining of scientific with local analyses of dominant cultural and political ideologies – can provide a more emancipatory foundation for development – in contrast to dominant approaches that emphasize market deepening and capital access with little regard for the cultural politics of social change.

NOTES

INTRODUCTION

1. In this book I use the terms 'planning' and 'development' interchangeably, except in cases (specifically noted in the text) where it is necessary to consider the historical trajectories of these practices as institutionalized professions. 'Development', of course, conventionally refers to the specific relation of dependency of the 'Third World' on the 'First World' for financial and technical assistance, established in the post-Second World War era. In the context of the post-independence Third World, 'planning' has often referred to national economic development plans with a typical term of five years. As the planning profession has been institutionalized in the West, professional planners (who in fact work in non-governmental organizations, research institutes and local governments as much as serving on National Planning Commissions) have recognized the imperative to undertake 'development' work in disadvantaged communities of the 'First' as much as the 'Third' World – hence the expression 'community development' operative in North America. Professional graduate programmes in planning typically attract students with professional interests in both 'Third' and 'First World' contexts. 'Planning' and 'development' are thus used interchangeably here to denote the practice of professionals engaged in community organizing, service delivery and/or economic development in or on behalf of disadvantaged communities.

2. Liberal, that is, relative to the politically and numerically dominant Parbatiya (which literally means 'hill people', and is a term used by Newars and Tibeto-Burman groups in Nepal to refer to Hindu groups that South Asianists commonly call 'Indo-Nepalese' or 'Indo-Aryan' – namely, Brahmans [priests], Chetris [warriors], and their associated Untouchable artisan castes).

3. With the intensification of an insurgent Maoist movement in rural areas of the country, however, donors who have been forced to shut down development services in the rural hinterlands have recently sought to transfer their operations to populations of the Kathmandu Valley – and their justifications for shifting attention to an area formerly categorically excluded from their gaze tells a fascinating tale of 'the politics of need' (Fraser 1989).

4. I use the term 'cultural economy' to refer to the full range of economic practices – monetary exchange as well as the social and symbolic dimensions of profit and exchange. The term thus suggests not only that markets are embedded in cultural ideology and social institutions (*à la* Karl Polanyi), but also that symbolic and social goods and practices themselves are subject to economic calculation (*à la* Pierre Bourdieu). I thus use the term rather differently from its most recent currency in

economic geography to refer to economies competing on the basis of place-based images (see Scott 2001).

5. Newari caste names are capitalized, as are the English terms for their corresponding occupational status; thus, Shrestha (Merchant). When an occupation is referenced without denoting caste status, the lower-case is used; thus Sankhu merchants.

6. No adequate terminology has been developed to characterize relations among countries with differing access to resources and power. Most have pejorative implications: developed/developing, First World/Third World, core/periphery. Some have outlived their relevance, or the historical conditions of their emergence: First World/Third World. More politically neutral geographic terminology – North/South, West/East – do not always accurately capture the global distribution of power and resources. Here I have settled on the terms 'core' and 'periphery' to capture relative positions within a fundamentally unsustainable and uneven capitalist global system (though I resort to the term 'Third World' when I sense the language of 'core/periphery' could be misinterpreted as 'gradations of significance').

1 THE CULTURAL POLITICS OF MARKETS

1. Democracy, as such, has never been a central value of neoliberalism. Hayek argued that 'liberty and democracy can easily become irreconcilable if the democratic majority decides to interfere in the unconditional rights of each economic agent to have at its disposal … its property and its income' (Anderson 2000). On this point, consider a recent issue of *The Economist* addressing 'The Future of the State' in the world economy. Here it is argued not only that markets offer the best guarantee for individual freedom, but also that democracy will undermine capitalism: 'Democratic states', *The Economist* warns, 'may make such demands of capitalism, and place such burdens and restrictions upon it, that it will slowly fade away, along with freedom' (Crook 1997: 6).

2. A World Bank study commissioned to examine the 'East Asian miracle' controversially concluded that such interventions were 'market-friendly' and that free markets would have achieved the same outcomes more efficiently (see Wade 1996).

3. The limitations of this approach to understanding culture emerge already in the racist undertones of this evaluation of world religions.

4. More reliable empirical evidence from Italy, the geographic context from which Putnam developed his theory of social capital theory, in fact suggests an opposite direction of causality: that, as Harriss (2001: 62) writes quoting Peter Evans (1996), the ingredients for social capital to play a role in regional economic growth 'are the presence of "coherent, dependable public [that is, bureaucratic] institutions", and a favorable political regime, characterized by political competition that is "constrained by mutually accepted ground rules", in context of a "relatively egalitarian social structure" '.

5. The economy became disembedded within industrial capitalism when labour, land and money were turned into commodities, when their supply was organized as if they were items produced for sale, and when the price mechanism was allowed to determine their allocation and the income of their owners. The conversion of land, labour and money into commodities is the 'Great Transformation'.

6. The field of 'development studies' has a more controversial relationship with progressive politics, as Arturo Escobar (1995) and James Ferguson (1990) have revealed. While

some development theorists (most notable among them, Amartya Sen e.g. 1999) and nearly every mainstream development institution (most prominently, the World Bank) continue to profess a liberal view of development as alleviating poverty and creating opportunity for the world's poorest and most disadvantaged, in practice development has served to buttress the political-economic and cultural interests of the West far too much to accept these assertions at face value.

7. 'Governmental technology' is used here in the sense of Foucauldian governmentality studies that document the role of political and policy discourse in governing subjects, beyond the direct mechanisms of government (see Burchell et al. 1991).

8. 'Formalist anthropology' on the contrary argued that neoclassical concepts like 'scarcity', 'economizing behaviour', 'supply,' and 'demand' can be used to understand practices in 'ancient' and 'tribal' societies. The political implications of this position are stark: if the similarities between 'tribal' and industrial societies are more important than their differences, then micro-economic theory – and the policies derived from it – is relevant for all times and all places.

9. Gertler concurs: '[w]hen ... analysts resort to "cultural" influences to explain the behaviour of managers, firms and workers, this is normally tantamount to an admission of ignorance' (1997: 48).

10. For a sustained discussion on the cultural politics of value, see Graeber (2001).

11. In Polanyian fashion, this interpretation recognizes markets as socially constituted. For a similar approach that examines how 'markets' historically became naturalized as a sphere apart from 'culture' in the colonial Indian context, see Birla (1999).

12. See also Jeffrey (2001) for a discussion of Bourdieu's notion of symbolic capital in relation to caste society in South Asia.

13. In fact, Bourdieu argues later, in *Masculine Domination*, that the Kabyle of Algeria present an exemplary case of how male domination operates within people's 'schemes of perception' – a case that can serve as an objective archaeology of 'our own' western unconscious:

    ... [k]nowledge of the objective structures and cognitive structures of a particularly well-preserved androcentric society (such as Kabyle society, as I observed it in the 1960s) provides instruments enabling one to understand some of the best concealed aspects of what those relations are in the economically most advanced societies. (2001: vii)

    Here the caution of feminist anthropologists against the search for origins of gender oppression must be duly exercised.

14. On Bourdieu's structural interpretation of social capital, see also Foley and Edwards (1999) and Woolcock (1998); these sources do not, however, elaborate the broader 'economics of practice' crucial for understanding Bourdieu's specifically Marxian view of the socio-structural determinants of individuals' access to social capital.

15. For example the World Bank's web-based clearinghouse on social capital does not include Bourdieu either in its list of 'Key Readings' or its 'database of hundreds of abstracts of papers and articles on social capital' (accessed 24 August 2002, URL: http://www.worldbank.org/poverty/scapital/).

16. Here again I am drawing on Foucauldian governmentality studies (see note 7).

17. See also Fine (2001), Harriss (2001) and Rankin (2002). According to Ben Fine (2001: 173), even Stiglitz's relatively benign (i.e. 'market-friendly') information-theoretic economics proved too politically contentious for the World Bank (specifically when

he pressed for alternative policies following the crisis in East Asia) and his resignation in 2000 was shrouded in rumours of forced removal.

2 ANTHROPOLOGIES AND GEOGRAPHIES OF GLOBALIZATION

1. I use the terms 'practice anthropology' and 'anthropology of practice' interchangeably. By 'structural' here I am encompassing not only the structuralism of Claude Lévi-Strauss (which posits that all societies manifest a 'universal grammar of culture' that sets the parameters for the range of possible social forms and practices), but also the semiotics of Clifford Geertz (which views culture as embodied in public symbols forming 'webs of meaning' or 'psychological structures' that guide individual action) and the cultural ecology of Marvin Harris (which interprets culture in Darwinian terms – as the rituals, symbols and values providing adaptive strategies that ensure cultural reproduction in a given environmental context). See Ortner (1984) for this classification.

2. While some scholars have argued that the salience of 'hegemony' as an analytical tool is limited to historical conditions of its emergence in cultural Marxism (see G. Smith 1999: 239), others have noted its relevance for any context where overt violence as a mode of domination enjoys no political or social legitimacy, and where 'social practice is seen to depend on consent to certain dominant ideas which in fact express the needs of a dominant class' (Williams 1983: 145).

3. Ideology has assumed many different meanings within Marxian interpretations of culture (see Eagleton 1991). Even among Gramscian scholars considerable disagreement persists about the parameters of ideological forms of power. While I find the Comaroffs' interpretation particularly amenable to ethnographic research on the experience of domination, others have argued that it suffers from a naïve understanding of ideology as self-conscious and 'endlessly discussable' (G. Smith 1999).

4. James Duncan was an early critic of the 'superorganicist' tradition of Carl Sauer. His 1980 article, 'The Superorganic in American Cultural Geography', argued that in their exclusive focus on the material dimensions of culture, Sauer and his colleagues reified culture as a given set of beliefs that determine action; as such they overlooked social dimensions, and in particular an analysis of how power operates through cultural practices (Jackson 1989; Mitchell 2000).

5. Those participating in the 'reflexive turn' prompted by postmodern social theory have challenged the ability of anthropologists to authoritatively represent other cultures. They have agitated on the one hand for experiments in (and analysis of) ethnographic textual representations (to capture contingent and variable interpretations of the research process; Clifford 1988) and on the other for shifting the sites of ethnographic research to North American and European contexts – to 'exoticise the West' (Marcus and Fisher 1999).

6. I am indebted to Lauren Leve for discussions about this genealogical thread in anthropology.

7. Exceptions to this general observation can be found in the work of field-based geographers – such as Michael Watts, Gillian Hart, Judith Carney, Melissa Leach and Stuart Corbridge – whose interdisciplinary training and place-based field research illustrate the potential for an anthro-geography synthesis.

3   GENEALOGY OF MARKETS AND EXCHANGE

1. As David Gellner (1992) has pointed out, however, the census probably under-represents Newars because it assesses ethnicity on the basis of responses to questions about mother-tongue, and many Newars speak Nepali instead of their 'mother-tongue', Newari. The same point has also been made for Tamangs (a Tibeto-Burman ethnic group) by David Holmberg (1989).

2. Slusser (1982: 22) suggests that the Licchivi kings of Nepal descend from the Licchivis of northern India who controlled the flourishing Indian trade centred in Vaisali (the most opulent city of North India) around 500 BCE during the time of the Buddha; she speculates that as the Licchivis were assimilated by the Mauryan empire, one branch migrated to the Kathmandu Valley in the fourth century BCE, drawn by its prosperous markets.

3. See Gellner (1992) on the question of classifying Newars in relation to Tibeto-Burmese and Indo-Nepalese groups in Nepal.

4. As noted in Chapter 1, Parbatiya literally means 'hill people' and refers to 'Indo-Nepalese' or 'Indo-Aryan' groups – namely, Brahmans (Priests), Chetris (Warriors) and their associated Untouchable artisan castes (Tailors, Leatherworkers and Blacksmiths). On the question of pan-Newar ethnicity and its relationship to political-economic history, see Gellner (1992, 1997).

5. This reclassification notwithstanding, those journeying to the Kathmandu Valley from its mountainous hinterlands still sometimes say that they are 'going to Nepal'.

6. This classificatory system was legally codified in 1854 by the Ranas (who ruled Nepal through a feudal system of hereditary prime ministership from 1850 to 1951); see András Höfer (1979).

7. On the post-national political history of Nepal see Richard Burghart (1984), Michael Hutt (1994) and Rose and Fisher (1970).

8. As indicated earlier, Newari caste names are capitalized, as are the English terms for their corresponding occupational status; thus, Shrestha (Merchant), Brahman (Priest), Po (Untouchable). Diacritic marks are not given for ease of reading (except in Chapter 5).

9. Nepal is divided into the following nested hierarchy of administrative units: 14 zones, 75 Districts, and 3914 VDCs. The three VDCs that include different areas of Sankhu (as well as outlying villages) are Vajrayogini VDC, Pukhulachi VDC and Suntole VDC.

10. For a thorough elaboration of the town's physical plan in relation to ritual events see B.G. Shrestha (2002).

11. The figure, 85 per cent, is also drawn from Shrestha (2002) and refers to the per centage of households that own or rent agricultural land; since landless households can hire out members for agricultural labour, however, this figure in fact under-represents participation in agriculture. Only 23 per cent of the respondents to my survey reported growing enough rice for annual household consumption, the average duration of food shortfall per year being 8 months.

12. Only 36 per cent of the population reported agriculture to be their primary source of livelihood in Shrestha's 1997 survey, down from 71 per cent reported in 1969 in a study by HMG Ministry of Housing and Physical Planning (HMG 1969: 61 cited in Shrestha 2002).

13. This account is a variation on the well-known story about the formation of the Kathmandu Valley as a whole. For discussions of Sankhu's mythical and historical origins, see Zanen (1986) and Shrestha (2002).
14. Nepal's ancient and medieval history is recorded largely in such chronicles, dynastic histories detailing the acts of kings and the animate exploits of the gods and demons. A few of the most comprehensive chronicles have been translated into Nepali and English (from Sanskrit and Newari), but their oral tradition also persists. Bal Gopal Shrestha (2002) speculates that Sankhu priests retrospectively inserted the creation story of Sankhu into one of the chronicles detailing the origins of the Kathmandu Valley. The account here is a much-abridged version of the Manisaila Mahabadana, which is elaborated more fully in Shrestha's dissertation (2002).
15. *Bodhisattva* refers to one who has reached nirvana and returned to the world of suffering in order to assist others in reaching the goal of enlightenment.
16. The ancient and medieval history of Nepal has been pieced together not only from the chronicles, but also from coins, documents written on handmade paper, and inscriptions on stone slabs, pillars, sculptures, paintings and copper plates.
17. Scholars have used both transliterations, Sankhapur and Samkhapur.
18. NRs denotes Nepalese rupees; at the time of this research, the exchange rate was approximately NRs55 = US$1.
19. Inscriptions reveal that Licchivi kings Manadev (*c.* 465–505 CE) and Ansavarnam (*c.* 605–21 CE) did penance at and spent lavishly on the monastery (Slusser 1982: 165–7, 219, 271, 278). The Licchivi inscriptions refer to the monastery by its popular name, instead of with the Sanskrit nomenclature applied to Licchivi monasteries. Vajracharya (1972: 22–5) thus contends that the Licchivi kings must have perpetuated the name of a pre-existing monastery—as they did for many place names in the Kathmandu Valley. Slusser (1982: 275) offers additional evidence of the monastery's antiquity by noting that the stone *stupa* and caves on its premises are the closest equivalents in Nepal to the ancient Buddhist rock temples and cave monasteries of India.
20. Other documentary evidence of early trade in the Valley comes from fourth-century BCE statesman Kautilya who again referred to Nepal's woollen blankets in the *Arthashastra* (Kosambi 1965: 142).
21. In fact, Sankhu is a name applied by Nepali speakers. Sākva is the Newari name, which is still used amongst Newari speakers today. For a discussion of the competing interpretations of the genealogy of 'Sankhu' see B.G. Shrestha (2002).
22. *Stupa* (also *caitya*) are dome-shaped symbolic monasteries sacred to Buddhism.
23. This agreement allegedly explains the arrangement that Hindus can make blood sacrifices to Vajrayogini (a practice that would not normally be accepted by a Buddhist deity) by presenting her with the living creature and then performing the actual sacrifice at the Bhairav shrine outside and just below the Vajrayogini compound itself.
24. *Lignum* are symbolic structures sacred to Hinduism. The chronicles offer a more Hindu version of the story recounted locally—claiming that Sankaracarya defeated Vajrayogini and instituted the practice of sacrifice as a sign of that victory. See Daniel Wright (1958 [1877]: 71).
25. In his own inscriptions, Pratapa Malla claims to have previously captured Kuti, which no doubt provided a crucial bargaining chip in the negotiations of the 1650 treaty. See D.R. Regmi (1966: 60–72).
26. On the 1650 treaty and the commercial exploits of Pratapa Malla and Bhima Malla, see also Prem R. Uprety (1980: 20–12) and Perceval Landon (1993 [1928], vol. 1: 43–7).

27. Sankhu's significance in this regard was noted in 1811 by Colonel Kirkpatrick, who made the first official British exploratory mission into Nepal in 1793. Sankhu is among the few towns in the Kathmandu Valley to appear on his map, and is ranked among the few 'considerable places' in Kirkpatrick's informal survey of the population of the Kathmandu Valley (1986 [1811]: 160–1 and foldout map).

28. Drawing on Vajrayogini's wealth is considered inauspicious, however. Vajracarya priests in Sankhu claim that when the Kathmandu palace last dispatched representatives to withdraw Vajrayogini's treasures, they met an untimely death from the bite of a leech on the temple grounds.

29. In one instance a Vajracharya priest is said to have taken tea with the Dalai Lama in Lhasa; the priest suddenly began blowing into his steaming cup and glancing toward the south. He then astonished his host by sucking up his tea and forcefully spitting it in that direction. To the outraged Dalai Lama, the priest explained that he had engaged his tantric powers to transform that single cupful of tea into a rain so plentiful as to extinguish a fire that had at that moment been burning his house. Sankhu informants attribute this incident to a priest from Sankhu; Slusser (1982: 290), however, associates the story with a charred doorway in Musun Vihara, Kathmandu.

30. Regmi Research Collection, 'Check post officials and others in areas between Sankhu and Falam Sangu ordered to provide necessary facilities to Lamas returning from Kathmandu to Lhasa' (1812 [1869 V.S.]: 558). Translated from Nepali with assistance from Dhana Prasad Panday. 'V.S.' refers to Vikram Samvat (Vikram Era), the calendrical system used by His Majesty's Government of Nepal (HMG); Vikram Samvat was established in 56/57 BCE.

31. On the process through which the objects of Buddhist devotion and decoration – silks, gems, metalwork, amulets – entered into trans-Himalayan commerce, see Todd Lewis (1993).

32. The post-1950 period is addressed in Chapter 6.

33. On Sankhu's role in Prithvi Narayan's conquest, see Stiller (1975: 114); on the conquest more generally, see D.R. Regmi (1966: 249–57).

34. In Sankhu it is said that Prithvi Narayan's victory was accomplished by bribing a resident to admit the attacking army through an underground entrance to his home. Once admitted, Prithvi Narayan killed the man, a prominent merchant, on grounds that he was a traitor.

35. Though debased, the coins nonetheless had increased in value within Tibet due to their scarcity and usefulness in relation to other mediums of exchange.

36. Nepal considered the British a significant threat after they took control over Calcutta and began to operate as an arm of the British government.

37. The East India Company's regiments failed to reach the Valley before the last of the Malla capitals fell to the Gorkhalis. See Sanwal (1965: 69) and Oldfield (1974 [1880]: 272).

38. In fact, the first motorable road into the Valley opened only in 1959.

39. Other functions requiring *jhārā* labour included service during the Vajrayogini festival (such as carrying oil lamps, carrying the chariots of Vajrayogini and her accompanying deities) and daily provisioning of charcoal, firewood, and fodder to the nearby gun factory and magazine. On the latter see Regmi Research Collection, 'Order Regarding Supply of Charcoal to Magazine from Sankhu' (1799 [1856 V.S.]) and 'Unpaid Labor Impressed in Sankhu for Gunpowder Factory', 1833 [1890 V.S.]). Both sources translated from Nepali with assistance from Dhana Prasad Panday.

40. Regmi Research Collection, 'Order to the *Hulāki* in the Area Surrounding Sankhu' (1796 [1853 V.S.]: 218). Translated from Nepali with assistance from Dhana Prasad Panday; see Appendix for full translation. This is an order issued by the government to the recipient of the *jāgir* grant. In a similar arrangement, another government edict stipulates the payment of a government official's salary out of the customs duties on the Tibet trade: Regmi Research Collection, 'Payment of Salary to Mahendra Khawas from Revenues of Customs Duties on Trade with Tibet' (1794 [1851 V.S.] : 440). Translated from Nepali with assistance from Dhana Prasad Panday.
41. Regmi Research Collection, '*Ijāra* Granted to Ghana Shyam Upadhyaya for Revenue Collection in Sankhu' (1786 [1843 V.S.]: 117). Translated from Nepali with assistance from Dhana Prasad Panday. See also M.C. Regmi (1971: 127).
42. See Landon (1993 [1928], vol. 2: 283–5), Sanwal (1965: 286), Uprety (1980: 76–81) and Wright (1958 [1877]: 38). The same treaty also permitted the state to establish a factory in Lhasa and to conduct trading monopolies in certain products.
43. The term itself derives from the Sanksrit, Shrestha, meaning 'best', 'chief' or 'senior' (see Levy 1990: 79, n. 14). According to Kosambi (1965: 100–1), it was also applied to a class of financiers-traders emergent in sixth-century India.
44. Colin Rosser discusses this and other strategies employed by Newars to pass into the Hindu milieu – including the practice on the part of many Newar castes of changing one's name to Shrestha, which had by that time assumed an association with Hinduism. See Rosser (1966: 68–139).
45. A gravel road currently under construction is expected to link Sankhu directly with Malemchi and thus to restore Sankhu as the main thoroughfare to and from Sindupalchowk.
46. For a useful discussion of this Foucauldian approach to 'reading history in terms of our current practices', see Dreyfus and Rabinow (1982: 122–3).

4 NEWAR REPRESENTATIONS OF FINANCE: TOWARD AN ANTHROPOLOGY OF PROFIT

1. Tamangs are a minority Tibeto-Burman ethnic group residing in the hill areas of Nepal. Note that the discussion here of ideas about profit and wealth accumulation derive primarily from interviews from Shrestha Newars, and thus the conclusions cannot be claimed to apply to Newar society in its entirety. The discussion of social investment in the latter part of the chapter, however, is drawn from observations and interviews with low as well as high/dominant castes.
2. The term 'honour economy' is drawn from Liechty's '*ijat* economy' (2003). For a similar discussion of the regulating function of honour among caste Hindus in Nepal and India, see Cameron (1998) and Raheja and Gold (1994) respectively.
3. See Bloch and Parry (1989) for a survey of this literature.
4. Four *dam* is the equivalent of one *paisa*; there are 100 *paisa* in one rupee; at the time of this research, NRs 55 = US $1.
5. While most migrate to Kathmandu, a few young men have been lured recently by 'manpower' companies dealing in the export of Nepali labourers to work in the low-wage service sector in the Middle East. 'Economically active' is a conventional economic indicator used in the Population Census of Nepal, and refers to those over the age of 10 capable of participating in 'economic activities'. Like many such indicators used to convey economic statistics, the concept of 'economically active'

excludes from the purview of 'economic' unpaid domestic work usually performed by women, such as food processing and preparation (even though the latter clearly contribute to the household economy).

6. Translated from handwritten Newari with assistance from Madan Gopal Shrestha. See also the *Laws of Manu*, in reference to which much of customary Newar law was formulated (see Doniger 1991; Levy 1990: 381).

7. See Slusser (1982: 258–9 cited in Levy 1990: 254). In India, it is Ganesh who serves as the god of commerce.

8. 'Killing the poor' is an expression for exploitation, which was repeated on many occasions during interviews about money-lending. I have kept the literal translation in order to convey local perceptions about the extent of money-lenders' destructive power. As discussed below, Newars also liken the state of indebtedness explicitly to death itself.

9. The deepening of the cash economy can be explained by expanding labour markets in Kathmandu, increased agricultural yields (due to modern inputs like fertilizer and high-yielding seed varieties), and increases in the value of those yields (in 1978, for instance, 1 *pāthī* of grain (approximately 3.6 kg) was worth NRs 10; in 1995 its worth had increased to NRs 25).

10. These relationships can be compared to barter relationships maintained between some poorer Newar households and Tamang households; in such instances both parties refer to one another as *ista mitra* (Nep., friends and relations). Newars trade potatoes, peppers, spinach and other vegetables for the Tamangs' corn, millet and straw brooms; during the Vajrayogini festival Tamang *ista mitra* can expect to feast at the home of their Newar host in exchange for firewood: as one Tamang woman explained, 'It takes two hands to make good bread!'

11. One *muri* is equivalent to approximately 50 kg. Rent and interest were charged in rice, the most expensive of the cereal crops, leaving only lower-status grains for consumption.

12. It is commonly subsistence farmers who seek this kind of loan because their cash liquidity fluctuates with crop cycles, making inputs difficult to finance.

13. A surprising 30 per cent of money-lenders in my survey (19 households) reported engaging in this (very illegal) practice.

14. Gosainkund is a place of religious pilgrimage in the Langtang Himal, some three days' walk from Sankhu. One-third of the 63 households in my survey reporting money-lending accepted unpaid labour in lieu of interest.

15. Most loans, however, are negotiated orally, without a written contract: only 8 per cent of those who reported making loans in my survey claimed also to have prepared contracts (15 households).

16. At the same time more people are *making* loans: 40 per cent of my survey respondents reported having currently lent out money – by all accounts a significant increase from the cash-poor days when only a handful of powerful money-lenders were in business.

17. For example, Ananda Shamsher Rana, son of Bir Shamsher Rana, who was the younger brother of Prime Minister Jung Bahadur Rana (1846–56 and 1857–77), is said locally to have been granted approximately 8,000 *ropāni* (8 *ropāni* = 1 hectare) stretching north from Sankhu into Tamang areas of the Helambu region.

18. Recall that the *hulāki* or postal service associated with the Tibet trade was conducted through compulsory labour, as were various services during the Vajrayogini festival

and daily provisioning of charcoal, firewood and fodder to the nearby gun factory and magazine (see note 38, Chapter 3).

19. Since *chembhāri* and *bumbhāri* are derived from the Newari words *chem* (house) and *bum* (field) and since both individuals play a particular ritual role in the Vajrayogini festival, we can speculate that these functions may derive from at least the medieval Malla period.

20. They include land grants for the special instrumental groups of the Jogi, Duim, and Nay castes, and the ritual services of the Nau (Barber), Vajracharya (Priest), Brahman (Priest) and Joshi (Priest) castes.

21. 'Stone Contract Land Assignment in Sankhu', Regmi Research Collection (Kathmandu: Nepal National Archives, n.d.), vol. 11, reel E24131, p. 162.

22. According to the Merchant-caste Newar cited earlier who supported the Tamang movement, Newar tenants were difficult to organize because they were integrated into the social universe of their landlords. The Kathmandu-based Farmer's Organization, Kisan Sangh, also attempted to organize tenants in Sankhu. Like the Tamang group, the Kisan Sangh sought to control rents and interest rates, as well as limit the number of sacks of grain a landlord could transport per day for sale in Kathmandu. But local informants indicate that the Kisan Sang never enjoyed the same kind of local solidarity and support among Newars in Sankhu as the Tamang's more spontaneous initiative had in the surrounding villages.

23. For further detail on land reforms, see M.C. Regmi (1978). Following land reform, tenants in the Sankhu area were particularly organized about registering as tenants (and thus claiming their rights).

24. Legally, a tenant can pay the back-taxes on such property and claim title to it, but the cumulative taxes are often prohibitively high.

25. Of course, we are dealing here with ideal types to which there are exceptions. Poor families, for example, are often unable to accommodate the nuclear families of each married son and they tend to blur gender and age hierarchies out of economic necessity.

26. Rank among men within a household is expressed ritually on several feasting occasions throughout the year (*sīkāḥbhvay*), when the head of the goat sacrificed for the feast gets divided into eight parts and distributed among the senior men of the lineage (*phuki*) in rank order by age.

27. Quigley also notes that the evidence from Newar society contradicts conventional associations of the joint family structure with village subsistence economics (and of the nuclear family structure with urbanized and modernized contexts). In the Newar case the joint family system persists, indeed thrives, in an urbanized, heavily monetized and modernizing context—and in fact may have crucially contributed to the legacy of Newar commercial success.

28. In this regard Merchant Newars may be contrasted with Butchers who daily divide the meat of slaughtered water buffalo for sale in their separate shops and those agriculturists who have developed a rotating labour system to handle periods of intensive labour during the agricultural cycle. In these cases, as Gerard Toffin (1977) has noted with respect to Pyangaon Newars, it may be the lineage, not the household, which is the fundamental economic unit.

29. Words between * indicate that the speaker has used an English, as opposed to Newari or Nepali, word. Credit goes to Liechty (1995a) for developing this system of notation.

30. Newars use *baji* as the staple food in feasts because it does not transmit ritual pollution in the same way as cooked rice – a crucial feature when eating in mixed company.
31. In Sankhu lineage deity worship is actually organized by household (rather than household groupings called *guthis*), but in all other respects lineage deity worship resembles *guthi* practices and so it is treated as a *guthi* here. Gerard Toffin (1977), Declan Quigley (1995) and David Gellner (1992) similarly note that lineage deity *guthis* are in decline in Pyangaon, Dhulikhel and Patan, but that likewise the organization of the worship within a single family nonetheless reflects key *guthi* principles.
32. Some of these are *rāj* (state-owned) *guthis* and some are private. The land reforms of 1964 severely diminished the financial capacity of *rāj guthis*, to the point in some cases where local functionaries in Sankhu have stopped collecting income and operating funds; 38 *guthis* are listed for Sankhu in the National Guthi Association's Archival Section, and of those only 11 have active accounts at the Contemporary Records Section.
33. Of the 18 *sī guthis* in Sankhu on which I was able to obtain data, all but three had developed some kind of credit system. In most cases the funds are quite small—about NRs 2,000–4,000 (approximately US $36–72), with the largest reported to me in Sankhu being NRs 20,000 (US $363).
34. For the north Indian case, see Jonathan Parry (1980, 1989), Gloria Goodwin Raheja (1988) and Klaas W. van der Veen (1992).
35. Other routine occasions for offering *dāna* include birthdays (when offered to low-caste children), eclipses (when offered to people of the untouchable Po caste), and on neglecting to perform an important ritual (when offered, as a sort of apology, to a priest). The objective on all these occasions is also to remove accumulated inauspiciousness.
36. *Daśa* in particular is considered to accrue not just through people's actions, but in relation to their horoscope and the current planetary alignment; hence the need for an astrologer.
37. In the Vajrayana Buddhism practised by Newars, priests are householders – who undergo life-cycle rituals (such as marriage), as well as perform priestly responsibilities. *Pañcadāna* is the only occasion among Newars when priests assume the posture of monks – priests who have renounced this-worldly obligations and beg for alms, much like priests in Therevada Buddhist sects.
38. David Gellner (1992) notes that the Newar Buddhist view of sin as a material phenomenon 'is graphically illustrated' at Itum Bahaa in Kathmandu every year during the Sa Paru festival (Nep., *Gai Jātrā*) when a senior of the monastery uses a pair of scales marked on either side as *dharma* and *pāp* to illustrate how one's rebirth is determined by the balance of one's actions.
39. I am referring here to the 'economics of practice' *à la* Pierre Bourdieu (as elaborated in Chapter 1), in order to account for the social and cultural dimensions of profit and exchange in Newar society.

5   CASTE AND GENDER ECONOMICS

1. The term 'practice-theoretic' simply derives from 'practice theory' and is intended to denote the theoretical tradition rooted largely in the work of Bourdieu and Gramsci that emphasizes the production of culture instead of merely its fixed symbolic content (see Chapter 2).

2. Note that diacritics are provided for caste names in Table 5.1, but are dropped elsewhere for ease of reading.
3. Note that this category of touchable, but unclean is unique to the Newar caste hierarchy; no indigenous group is assigned this rank within the Parbatiya caste system – although the 1854 Law Code assigned it to outsiders like Muslims and Europeans. See Gellner (1995: 266).
4. David Gellner (1995), writing primarily on the basis of fieldwork in the city of Patan, attributes this function to Po Untouchables, not Jogis. The key criterion seems to be that the recipient caste be low and 'tough' enough to absorb the inauspiciousness of high castes without compromising its own status. A similar practice occurs on the birthdays of high castes, when high castes give *dhau baji* (sweet yogurt mixed with roasted, beaten rice) to the children of any Impure or Untouchable caste as a means of removing annual stockpiles of inauspiciousness.
5. Likewise, Impure castes patronizing tea shops in the Sankhu bazaar get served outside and are expected to wash their own utensils.
6. The roles of these functionaries are elaborated in Chapter 4. The King is represented by an appointed Shrestha household, while the ritual roles of palace functionaries are still performed by their living descendants.
7. I have borrowed this notion of 'spin' from Parish (1997).
8. There are no Nay Guruju in Sankhu; members of this caste must be summoned from Kathmandu when necessary.
9. Po, whom I interviewed in Sankhu, denied providing this service to Nay.
10. Quigley (1993: 114–70) suggests that the replication of circles of ritual patronage throughout the caste hierarchy reflects an attempt by the social totality to achieve political stability through strong kinship structures, in the absence of a stable political centre (king). Like Dumont's, his analysis concentrates at the level of the social structure and views ideology as a reflection of social reality. See *Interpretation of Caste*, (1993: 114–70) and Michael Moffat, *An Untouchable Community in South India* (1979). Note that 'Guruju' is here capitalized to denote the caste name, 'Nay Guruju', and must be distinguished from '*guruju*', one who is a Newar Buddhist priest by profession.
11. A conch-shaped vessel used for offering oblations to the deities. Asterisks denote English words used by interviewee.
12. Even though Sankhu itself may have never had a king, the concept of kingship is significant for the town's ritual composition, and the king is represented at major festivals by a sword sent as a representative of the Royal Palace in Kathmandu.
13. The religion of power and religion of status concern themselves with two different kinds of deities: 'dangerous' deities are attended by a special class of priests – Vajrācārya and Joshi, in Sankhu; they are offered blood sacrifice, meat and alcohol; and their icons are demonic, bestialized, predominantly female forms. 'Ordinary' deities, on the other hand, are attended by Brahman priests, are never offered blood sacrifice or alcohol, and their icons are in the form of idealized human, predominantly male, types. See Levy (1990: 207, 293–340).
14. See also Valeri (1985) on the ancient Hawaiian context where the sacrificer (ritual specialist, in our case Nay) serves as the substitute for the king on whose behalf sacrifice is performed, and thus acquires the status of a god in the context of the rite (even if he occupies a low status in the profane world).
15. This story was recounted to me on several occasions by Nay informants; questioning other castes confirmed that the story is known widely throughout Newar society.

A slightly different version of this story appears also in Nepali (1965) and Parish (1997: 123–4). A different, but equally subversive story of Nay origins can be found in Wright (1958 [1877]). In Sankhu, the Dom caste also has its own account of a legendary fall from royal status. On the interpretation of subaltern origin stories, see also Holmberg (1989) and Gyan Prakash (1990).

16. For a discussion of these phenomena with respect to Parbatiya and Tamang societies respectively see Bennett (1983) and March (2003).

17. During the first four days of menstruation, that is, women are 'water unacceptable' to members of their own family – they can not carry water, enter the family store room or worshipping rooms (or any other domain associated with the gods), or enter the kitchen, much less cook food. After four days and ritual purification, a menstruating woman can resume domestic activities associated with the hearth and eating, but it is not until the fifth day and another round of ritual cleansing that she may worship the gods. Birth generates ritually polluting conditions – for women from the moment of the birth, and for other household members from the cutting of the umbilical cord – until the purifacatory rites involving extended family members, usually six or so days after birth.

18. Among low castes, where prescriptions around ritual pollution are less rigid, women enjoy considerably more freedom of movement within their own caste community. Constraint on their mobility derives primarily from their caste status. See Cameron (1998) and Robson (2000) for similar arguments regarding low-caste society in Nepal and Hausa society in Nigeria respectively, and Peake and Trotz (1999) for a discussion of mobility constraints for women of Indian descent in Guyana.

19. A few lineages formally induct newly married women into their lineage *guthis*, but even in these cases women do not represent their household at *guthi* functions (unless no adult male members are present).

20. In the twentieth session (on 14 March 2002), the House of Representatives passed the Country Code (Eleventh Amendment) Bill, commonly known as the Women's Property Rights Bill, establishing the concept that daughters as well as sons are entitled to have inheritance rights by birth to ancestral property.

21. National Civil Code, as cited in Shtrii Shakti (1995: 164–5).

22. On this point see the related discussion in Peake and Trotz (1999: 114).

23. On women's beauty as a possession, see Miller (1992).

24. Lynn Bennett (1983) terms the role of daughters in their natal patriline, 'filiafocal ideology'. In the Parbatiya case that she chronicles the emphasis seems to be more on worship of daughters than on regular visiting of daughters to their natal home (and the resulting material advantages). See also Kathryn March (2003) on the significance of married daughters for their birth home in the Tamang context, as well as on the 'milk trail' – ties to the marital homes of one's mother and married sisters.

25. With the exception of newly wed women, on these days children of the deceased honour their parents with gifts to their priests which are considered nourishment for their parents' journey in the land of the dead.

26. Married daughters are uniquely qualified to perform these obligations because upon marriage, and the assumption of a primary ritual attachment to their marital household, the number of days they must observe pollution restrictions for the death of someone in their natal home is reduced from nine to four. They can thus undergo purificatory rites before any of the chief mourners, and perform tasks such as cooking that require ritual purity.

27. Technically, *kvasah* is translated as 'women's own property', including earned income. Since dowry usually comprises the bulk of women's own property, however, the term is often used synonymously with dowry. For a similar account of Tamang women's strategic use of personal property, see March (2003).

28. *Kvasah* must also be distinguished from the Parbatiya interpretation of dowry, *daijo*. Parbatiyas, however, distinguish between dowry, *daijo*, and women's private property, *pewa*; only the latter enjoys the same protected status as Newar *kvasah*, while *daijo*, may be considered the possession of the husband and even in some cases his co-resident joint family – a convention which has obvious implications for women's capacity to accumulate private property. See also Bennett (1983) and Raheja and Gold (1994).

29. After consultations with China historian Mary B. Rankin, I was not able to determine who Lin Hu Lan is; Yan Kaihui was executed after Nationalist government troops recaptured the city of Changsha from the Communist army during fighting in 1930; and Laksmi Bai is remembered for fighting against the British colonialists in India.

6 GLOBAL–LOCAL ARTICULATIONS IN AN AGE OF NEOLIBERALISM

1. See Liechty (2003) on the related question of how the transnational cultural flows associated with economic liberalization generate particular, and diverse, forms of modernity in Kathmandu as new processes of consumption interact with, and transform, cultural common sense.

2. As of 1996, a new trade treaty with India leaves little room for any non-tariff barriers (Panday 1999: 328). Articles manufactured in Nepal are now allowed preferential entry into India without any conditions regarding their labour or material content. The treaty also includes a facility for transit via Bangladesh, for streamlining procedures for Nepalese commerce at the Calcutta port, and for building a 5.4 km broad-gauge railroad line inside the Nepali border point at Raxaul (Panday 1999: 334). Unfortunately, exports remain low in spite of these provisions, owing to the current Maoist revolutionary movement and an ineffectual government response, which together have brought the Nepalese economy to a standstill.

3. The other centre of carpet manufacturing is the Jawalakhel area of Patan, also in the Kathmandu vicinity. The Baudhanath–Jorpati manufacturing zone particularly appeals to producers because they can draw from the waters of the Bagmati River just as it enters the Kathmandu Valley (untarnished and undiminished by competing industrial and commercial interests in the Valley). Production processes resulting in the depletion of the river's volume and indiscriminate dumping of chemicals and dyes have provoked heavy criticism of the carpet sector for exacerbating environmental degradation in the Valley (Guru-Gharana 1996).

4. The time period being referred to here is 1993–2000, when research for this book took place.

5. 'Peon' is a term, originating with the British in colonial India, for office servants who perform menial tasks ranging from cleaning to running errands.

6. I do not mean to suggest absolute congruence between caste and class, but rather that low castes have typically faced greater odds in accumulating wealth than dominant castes (Shresthas). Of course service-providing high castes, such as Brahman and Vajracharya Priests, are constrained by the same *jajamāna* relationships as low castes,

and so they, too, have tended to occupy lower class positions than the dominant Shrestha.

7. Untouchable and Impure castes, for instance, have fewer feasts to attend and a smaller social universe to entertain on their own feasting occasions. They do not perform the exceedingly expensive *ihi* girl's initiation rite and are generally less fastidious in matters of daily as well as calendrical religious observances. Liechty (1995a: 234) claims that the material dimensions of *ijat* are 'mattering more' relative to the social and religious dimensions within the new logic of class; whether or not this is the case – which would be difficult to document conclusively – low castes do indeed enjoy new opportunities to acquire *ijat* through material means.

8. In fact, the Naay *sī guthis* in Sankhu have substantial cash endowments – larger than those of most high-caste *sī guthis*. I discovered one Nay *sī guthi* with a rotating credit fund of NRs 42,000.

9. For an analysis of national under-employment trends in the 1980s see B.P. Shrestha (1990: 57–63).

10. Some informants explained that requesting *lākhā* from the groom's family invites ill-treatment for married daughters. One Vajracharya woman put it this way:

These days we think poorly of that *lākhā* custom. We say it is like selling our daughter. In the husband's house, they will give the bride a hard time. They will say, 'You are a woman we have brought here only having given away *lākhā* for your marriage! Do you think we just brought you here like that [freely]? No, we gave *lākhā* for you!' And so they might scold her or take her dowry. My sister did not accept *lākhā* for her daughter's wedding. She explained to her daughter that she would not accept the *lākhā* because later her husband's relatives would insult her. Now, after we have all discussed this issue, no one in my lineage will accept *lākhā*.

11. This man is speaking specifically about a middle tier of merchants – not the super-rich who have set up residences in Kathmandu, but those who operate established businesses and are able to live comfortably in Sankhu.

12. Such birthday parties are also a new tradition, displacing the relatively simple ritual of family feast.

13. Gold smugglers in Nepal are famous for their tactic of ingesting gold bullion before going through customs and then collecting it once safely inside the country when they defecate.

14. On the relationship between social practice and Bollywood cultural trends, see Liechty (1995b).

15. On the pressure to give adequately modern dowry gifts, see also Miller (1992).

16. See Goody and Tambiah (1973) for a discussion of dowry in the classical sense, of a *pre-mortem* inheritance given to daughters in order to endow the conjugal estate.

17. See Raheja and Gold (1994) and Agarwal (1994) on dowry in the north Indian context.

18. I know of only one exception in Sankhu, in a household where the wife of the household head had died, the daughter was studying in Kathmandu, and the sons had not yet married. In this instance, a 15-year-old Tharu girl was engaged to do the cooking. She was treated like bonded labour and denied basic levels of civility – her salary being paid annually to her father. Tharus are indigenous to the Tarai and have historically faced severe exploitation, including through this kind of indentured servitude at the hands of Parbatiya landlords who colonized the region after malaria was eradicated in the 1960s (see Rankin 1999).

19. Liechty's research in Kathmandu suggests that the trends in caste and gender ideology noted here are similar, only more exaggerated, in more urbanized Newar societies.

7   PLANNING AND DEVELOPMENT

1. Of course, development banks did suffer from problems of 'elite capture', but 'good governance' might have been applied with equal force to rectify these problems, rather than to discard the ideology of social protections altogether.
2. See Harris-White (1998) for similar conclusions based on her studies of Indian grain markets.
3. The silence here is particularly disarming given the attention Sen gives to the southwestern Indian state of Kerala as an example of the capabilities that attain to women and low castes when the state invests strongly in welfare and infrastructure – without duly acknowledging the prior accomplishment of land reform or the long electoral dominance of the Communist Party of India.
4. Nancy Fraser (1995) refers to this idea of dismantling cognitive structures informing cultural injustice as 'deconstruction', which in her view must be a crucial ingredient of the socialist imaginary.

BIBLIOGRAPHY

Ackerly, Brooke. 1997. 'What's in a Design? The Effects of NGO Programme Delivery Choices on Women's Empowerment in Bangladesh', in Anne Marie Goetz (ed.) *Getting the Institutions Right for Women in Development*, pp. 140–60. New York: Zed Books.

Agarwal, Bina. 1994. *A Field of One's Own: Gender and Land Rights in South Asia*. Cambridge: Cambridge University Press.

Allen, Michael. 1973. 'Buddhism without Monks: The Vajrayana Religion of the Newars of Kathmandu Valley', *South Asia* 3: 1–14.

Amin, Ash and Nigel Thrift. 1997. 'Globalization, Socio-economics, Territoriality', in Roger Lee and Jane Wills (ed.) *Geographies of Economies*, pp. 147–57. New York: Arnold.

Anderson, Perry. 1992. *A Zone of Engagement*. New York: Verso.

——— 2000. *History and Lessons of Neo-liberalism*. On-line. Available www.religion-online.org/cgi-bin/relsearchd.dll/showchapter?chapter_id=1432 (Accessed 30 June 2003).

Appadurai, Arjun. 1986. 'Introduction: Commodities and the Politics of Value', in A. Appadurai (ed.) *The Social Life of Things: Commodities in Cultural Perspective*. Cambridge: Cambridge University Press.

——— 1996. *Modernity at Large: Cultural Dimensions of Globalization*. Minneapolis: University of Minnesota Press.

Arensberg, C.M., H.W. Pearson and Karl Polanyi. 1957. *Trade and Market in Early Empires*. New York: Free Press.

Barnes, Trevor. 1992. 'Reading the Texts of Theoretical Economic Geography: The Role of Physical and Biological Metaphors', in Trevor Barnes and James Duncan (eds) *Writing Worlds: Discourse, Text and Metaphor in the Representation of Landscape*, pp. 118–35. London: Routledge.

——— 1996. *Logics of Dislocation: Models, Metaphors, and Meanings of Economic Space*. New York: Guilford.

Bennett, Lynn. 1983. *Dangerous Wives and Sacred Sisters: Social and Symbolic Roles of High-caste Women in Nepal*. New York: Columbia University Press.

Birla, Ritu. 1999. *Hedging Bets: The Politics of Commercial Ethics in Late Colonial India*. PhD diss., Columbia University, New York.

Bista, Dor Bahadur. 1978. 'Nepalis in Tibet', in James F. Fisher (ed.) *Himalayan Anthropology: The Indo-Tibetan Interface*. Paris: Mouton.

Bledsoe, Bronwen. 1998. *Vajrayogini and the Kingdom of Kathmandu: Constructing Polity in Seventeenth-century Nepal*. PhD diss., University of Chicago.

Bloch, Maurice and Jonathan Parry. 1989. 'Introduction: Money and the Morality of Exchange', in J. Parry and M. Bloch (ed.) *Money and the Morality of Exchange*. New York: Cambridge.

Bouglé, Célestin. 1971 [1908]. *Essays on the Caste System*, trans. D.F. Pocock. Cambridge: Cambridge University Press.

Bourdieu, Pierre. 1977. *Outline of a Theory of Practice*. Cambridge: Cambridge University Press.

—— 1990. *The Logic of Practice*, trans. R. Nice. Cambridge: Polity Press.

—— 1993. *The Field of Cultural Production: Essays on Art and Literature*. Cambridge: Polity Press.

—— 2001. *Masculine Domination*, trans. Richard Nice. Stanford, CA: Stanford University Press.

Bourdieu, Pierre and Terry Eagleton. 1992. 'Doxa and Common Life', *New Left Review* 191: 111–21.

Boyer, Robert. 1996. 'The Convergence Hypothesis Revisited: Globalization but Still the Century of Nations?', in S. Berger and R. Dore (eds) *National Diversity and Global Capitalism*, pp. 29–59. Ithaca, NY: Cornell University Press.

Brenner, Neil. 2000. 'The Urban Question as a Scale Question: Reflections on Henri Lefebvre, Urban Theory and the Politics of Scale', *International Journal of Urban and Regional Research* 24(2): 361–78.

Britton, John. 1978. *The Weakest Link: A Technological Perspective on Canadian Industrial Underdevelopment*. Ottawa: Science Council of Canada.

—— 1988. 'Economic Change and the Region Question', *Canadian Journal of Regional Science* 11(1): 167–79.

Buck-Morss, Susan. 1995. 'Envisioning Capital: Political Economy on Display', *Critical Inquiry* (21): 434–67.

Burawoy, Michael et al. 1991. *Ethnography Unbound: Power and Resistance in the Modern Metropolis*. Berkeley: University of California Press.

Burchell, Graham, Colin Gordon and Peter Miller (eds) 1991. *The Foucault Effect: Studies in Governmentality*. Chicago: University of Chicago Press.

Burghart, Richard. 1984. 'The Formation of the Concept of Nation-State in Nepal', *Journal of Asian Studies* 44(1): 101–25.

Cameron, Mary. 1998. *On the Edge of the Auspicious: Caste and Gender in Nepal*. Chicago: University of Illinois Press.

'Carpet Relocation Study 1994', *Eco-News* 5(3): 1–5. [USAID, Nepal.]

'Carpets: Recent Developments 1992', *Eco-News* 4(1): 11–13. [USAID, Nepal.]

Cassidy, John. 2000. 'The Return of the Price Prophet', *New Yorker* 7 February: 44–51.

Castells, Manuel. 1996. *The Rise of the Informational Society*. Malden, MA: Blackwell Publishers.

Christopherson, Susan. 1993. 'Market Rules and Territorial Outcomes: The Case of the United States', *International Journal of Urban and Regional Research* 17: 274–88.

Clifford, James. 1988. *The Predicament of Culture: Twentieth-century Ethnography, Literature, and Art*. Cambridge, MA: Harvard University Press.

Coleman, J. 1990. *Foundations of Social Theory*. Cambridge, MA: Harvard University Press.

Comaroff, Jean. 1985. *Body of Power, Spirit of Resistance: The Culture and History of a South African People*. Chicago: University of Chicago Press.

222 *The Cultural Politics of Markets*

Comaroff, Jean and John Comaroff. 1991. *Of Revelation and Revolution: Christianity, Colonialism and Consciousness in South Africa*. Chicago: University of Chicago Press.
—— 1992. *Ethnography and the Historical Imagination*. Boulder, CO: Westview Press.
Corbridge, Stuart. 2002. 'Development as Freedom: The Spaces of Amartya Sen', *Progress in Development Studies* 2(3): 183–217.
Cornia, Giovanni Andrea. 1987. 'An Overview of the Alternative Approach', in Giovanni Andrea Cornia, Richard Jolly and Frances Stewart (eds) *Adjustment with a Human Face: Protecting the Vulnerable and Promoting Growth*, pp. 131–46. Oxford: Clarendon Press.
Cox, Kevin R. 1997. 'Introduction: Globalization and Its Politics in Question', in Kevin R. Cox (ed.) *Spaces of Globalization: Reasserting the Power of the Local*. New York: Guilford.
Crang, Philip. 1997. 'Cultural Turns and the (Re)Constitution of Economic Geography', in Roger Lee and Jane Wills (eds) *Geographies of Economies*, pp. 3–15. New York: Arnold.
Crook, Clive. 1997. 'The Future of the State: A Survey of the World Economy', *The Economist* 20–26 September: 5–48.
Dahal, Madan K. 1996. 'Outward-oriented Economic Nationalism: A Model for Development in Nepal', in Madan K. Dahal and Horst Mund (eds) *Social Economy and National Development: Lessons from Nepalese Experience*, pp. 1–36. Kathmandu: Nepal Foundation for Advanced Studies.
Dalton, George. 1965. 'Primitive, Archaic and Modern Economies: Karl Polanyi's Contribution to Economic Anthropology and Comparative Economy', in June Helm (ed.) *Essays in Economic Anthropology*. Seattle: University of Washington.
—— 1990. 'Writings that Clarify Theoretical Disputes over Karl Polanyi's Work', in Kari Polanyi-Levitt (ed.) *The Life and Work of Karl Polanyi*, pp. 161–70. Montreal: Black Rose Books.
Davis, Mike. 2000. 'The Bullshit Economy', *Village Voice Literary Supplement* September.
Dicken, Peter. 1998. *Global Shift: Transforming the World Economy*. New York: Guilford.
Dirks, Nicholas. 2001. *Castes of Mind: Colonialism and the Making of Modern India*. Princeton, NJ: Princeton University Press.
Dixit, Praveen M. 1995. *Economic Reform in Nepal: A Cursory Assessment*. College Park, MD: University of Maryland.
Doniger, Wendy. 1991. 'Introduction', *The Laws of Manu*. New York: Penguin Books.
Dorling, D. and M. Shaw. 2002. 'Geographies of the Agenda: Public Policy, the Discipline and its (Re)"turns" ', *Progress in Human Geography* 26(5): 627–46.
Douglass, Michael and John Friedmann (eds) 1998. *Cities for Citizens: Planning and the Rise of Civil Society in a Global Age*. Toronto: John Wiley and Sons.
Dreyfus, Hubert L. and Paul Rabinow. 1982. *Michel Foucault: Beyond Structuralism and Hermeneutics*. Chicago: University of Chicago Press.
Drèze, Jean and Amartya Sen. 1995. *India: Economic Development and Social Opportunity*. Oxford: Oxford University Press.
Dumont, Louis. 1970. *Homo Hierarchicus: The Caste System and Its Implications*. Chicago: University of Chicago Press.
Dwyer, C. and Philip Crang. 2002. 'Fashioning Ethnicities: The Commercial Spaces of Multiculture', *Ethnicities* 2(3): 410–30.

Eagleton, Terry. 1991. *Ideology: An Introduction*. London: Verso.

The Economist. 2001. 'Globalisation and Its Critics: A Survey of Globalisation', *The Economist* 29 Sept.: 3–28.

'The End of the Carpet-induced Boom? 1994', *Eco-News* 5(4): 20–3. [USAID, Nepal.]

Escobar, Arturo. 1995. *Encountering Development: The Making and Unmaking of the Third World*. Princeton, NJ: Princeton University Press.

—— 2001. 'Culture Sits in Places: Reflections on Globalism and Subaltern Strategies of Localization', *Political Geography* 20: 139–74.

Evans, Peter. 1996. 'Government Action, Social Capital and Development: Reviewing the Evidence on Synergy', *World Development* 24(6): 1119–32.

Ferguson, James. 1990. *The Anti-politics Machine: 'Development,' Depoliticization, and Bureaucratic Power in Lesotho*. Cambridge: Cambridge University Press.

Fine, Ben. 2001. *Social Capital Versus Social Theory*. London: Routledge.

Florida, Richard. 2000. 'The Economic Geography of Talent', Working Paper. Pittsburgh, PA: Carnegie Mellon University.

—— 2002. *The Rise of the Creative Class*. New York: Basic Books.

Foley, Michael W. and Bob Edwards. 1999. 'Is it Time to Disinvest in Social Capital?', *Journal of Public Policy* 19: 141–73.

Foucault, Michel. 1977. 'Nietzsche, Genealogy, History', in D.F. Bouchard (ed.) *Language, Counter-memory, Practice: Selected Essays and Interviews with Michel Foucault*. Oxford: Blackwell.

Fraser, Nancy. 1989. *Unruly Practices: Power, Discourse, and Gender in Contemporary Social Theory*. Minneapolis: University of Minnesota Press.

—— 1995. 'From Redistribution to Recognition? Dilemmas of Justice in a Post-socialist Age', *New Left Review* 2(2): 68–93.

Friedmann, J. 1987. *Planning in the Public Domain: From Knowledge to Action*. Princeton, NJ: Princeton University Press.

Fukuyama, Francis. 1992. *The End of History and the Last Man*. London: Hamish Hamilton.

Gardner, Kate and David Lewis. 1996. *Anthropology, Development and the Post-modern Challenge*. London: Pluto Press.

Geertz, Clifford. 1973. *The Interpretation of Cultures*. New York: Basic Books.

Gellner, David. 1992. *Monk, Householder and Tantric Priest: Newar Buddhism and its Hierarchy of Ritual*. Cambridge: Cambridge University Press.

—— 1995. 'Low Castes in Lalitpur', in *Contested Hierarchies: A Collaborative Ethnography of Caste among the Newars of the Kathmandu Valley, Nepal*, pp. 264–97. Oxford: Clarendon Press.

—— 1997. 'Caste, Communalism, and Communism: Newars and the Nepalese State', in David N. Gellner, Joanna Pfaff-Czarnecka and John Whelpton (eds) *Nationalism and Ethnicity in a Hindu Kingdom: The Politics of Ethnicity in Contemporary Nepal*, pp. 151–84. Amsterdam: Harwood Academic Publishers.

George, Susan. 1999. *A Short History of Neoliberalism: Twenty Years of Elite Economics and Emerging Opportunities for Structural Change*. On-line. Available www.tni.org/george/talks/bangkok.htm (Accessed 24 August 2002).

Gertler, Meric S. 1995. ' "Being There": Proximity, Organization and Culture in the Development and Adoption of Advanced Manufacturing Technologies', *Economic Geography* 70: 1–26.

—— 1997. 'The Invention of Regional Culture', in Roger Lee and Jane Wills (eds) *Geographies of Economies*, pp. 47–58. New York: Arnold.

Gibson, Katherine, J. Cameron and A. Veno. 1999. *Negotiating Restructuring: A Study of Regional Communities Experiencing Rapid Social and Economic Change.* On-line. Available svc177.bne117v.server-web.com/download/wkpap_11.pdf (Accessed 30 July 2003).

Gibson, Katherine and J. Cameron. 2001. 'Transforming Communities: Towards a Research Agenda', *Urban Policy and Research* 19(1): 7–24.

Gibson-Graham, J.K. 1996. *The End of Capitalism (As We Knew It): A Feminist Critique of Political Economy.* Oxford: Blackwell.

Godbout, Jacques T. 1998. *The World of the Gift*, trans. Donald Winkler. Montreal: McGill University Press.

Goetz, Anne M. and Rina Sen Gupta. 1996. 'Who Takes Credit? Gender, Power, and Control Over Loan Use in Rural Credit Programs in Bangladesh', *World Development* 24: 45–63.

Goody, Jack and Stanley J. Tambiah. 1973. *Bridewealth and Dowry.* Cambridge: Cambridge University Press.

Goonewardena, Kanishka. 2002. 'Planning and Neoliberalism', *Planners Network* 152: 29–31.

Graeber, David. 2001. *Toward an Anthropological Theory of Value: The False Coin of Our Own Dreams.* New York: Palgrave.

Gregory, Derek. 1994. *Geographical Imaginations.* Cambridge, MA: Blackwell.

Gupta, Akil and James Ferguson. 2002. 'Beyond "Culture": Space, Identity, and the Politics of Difference', in J. Inda and R. Rosaldo (ed.) *The Anthropology of Globalization: A Reader*, pp. 65–80. Oxford: Blackwell.

Guru-Gharana, Kishor K. 1996. 'Structural Adjustment: Concept and Practices with Reference to South Asia', in Ananda P. Shrestha and Nav Raj Dahal (eds) *Structural Adjustment Program in Nepal: Impact on Workers*, pp. 12–31. Kathmandu: Nepal Foundation for Advanced Studies.

Haaland, Anne. 1988. *Bhaktapur – A Town Changing.* Kathmandu: GTZ.

Hamilton, F.B. 1986 [1819]. *An Account of the Kingdom of Nepal and the Territories Annexed to this Dominion by the House of Gorkha.* New Delhi: Asian Educational Service.

Hammersley, Martyn and Paul Atkinson. 1989. *Ethnography: Principles in Practice.* New York: Routledge.

Harriss, John. 2001. *Depoliticizing Development: The World Bank and Social Capital.* London: Anthem Press.

Harriss-White, Barbara. 1996. *A Political Economy of Agricultural Markets in South India: Masters of the Countryside.* New Delhi: Sage.

—— 1998. 'Female and Male Grain Marketing Systems: Analytical and Policy Issues for West Africa and India', in Cecile Jackson and Ruth Pearson (eds) *Feminist Visions of Development: Gender Analysis and Policy*, pp. 189–214. New York: Routledge.

Harvey, David. 1989. *The Condition of Post-modernity.* Cambridge: Basil Blackwell.

Hayek, Friedrich von. 1944. *The Road to Serfdom.* London: George Routledge and Sons.

Herod, A. 1997. 'Notes on a Spatialized Labour Politics: Scale and the Political Geography of Dual Unionism in the US Longshore Industry', in R. Lee and J. Wills (ed.) *Geographies of Economies*, pp. 186–96. London: Arnold.

HMG. 1969. *The Physical Development Plan for the Kathmandu Valley.* Kathmandu: Ministry of Housing and Physical Planning.

—— 1996. *Economic Survey, Fiscal Year 1995–96.* Kathmandu: Ministry of Finance.

—— 2001. *Population by Caste/Ethnic Group and Sex*. On-line. Available www.cbs.gov. np/pop/Webpage/html/tab16.html (Accessed 12 April 2003).

Hodgson, Brian H. 1971 [1874]. *Essays on the Languages, Literature and Religion of Nepal and Tibet*. Varnasi: Bharat-Bharati Publishers.

Höfer, András. 1979. *The Caste Hierarchy and the State in Nepal: A Study of the Muluki Ain of 1854*. Innsbruck: Universitätsverlag Wagner.

Holmberg, David. 1989. *Order in Paradox: Myth, Ritual and Exchange among Nepal's Tamang*. Ithaca, NY: Cornell University Press.

Honneth, Axel. 1995. *The Fragmented World of the Social: Essays in Social and Political Philosophy*. Albany: State University of New York Press.

Hutt, Michael (ed.) 1994. *Nepal in the Nineties: Versions of the Past, Visions of the Future*. Oxford: Oxford University Press.

Inda, Jonathan Xavier and Renato Rosaldo. 2002. 'Introduction', in J. Inda and R. Rosaldo (ed.) *The Anthropology of Globalization: A Reader*, pp. 1–34. Oxford: Blackwell.

Isard, Walter. 1956. *Location and Space Economy*. Boston: MIT Press.

Jackson, Bruce. 1987. *Fieldwork*. Chicago: University of Illinois Press.

Jackson, Peter. 1989. *Maps of Meaning*. London: Routledge.

—— 1992. 'The Racialization of Labour in Post-war Bradford', *Journal of Historical Geography* 18: 190–209.

—— 2002a. 'Commercial Cultures: Transcending the Cultural and the Economic', *Progress in Human Geography* 26(1): 3–18.

—— 2002b. 'Commodity Cultures: The Traffic in Things', *Transactions of the Institute of British Geographers* 24(1): 95–108.

—— 2002c. 'Introduction: The Social Question', in Kay Anderson, Mona Domosh, Steve Pile and Nigel Thrift (eds) *Handbook of Cultural Geography*, pp. 37–42. London: Sage.

Jeffrey, C. 2001. ' "A Fist is Stronger than Five Fingers": Caste and Dominance in Rural North India', *Transactions of the Institute of British Geography* 26(2): 217–36.

Jessop, Bob. 1990. *State Theory: Putting the Capitalist State in its Place*. Cambridge: Polity Press.

—— 1994. 'Post-Fordism and the State', in Ash Amin (ed.) *Post-Fordism: A Reader*, pp. 251–79. Cambridge: Blackwell.

Jest, Corneille. 1993. 'The Newar Merchant Community in Tibet: An Interface of Newar and Tibetan Cultures', in Gerard Toffin (ed.) *Nepal, Past and Present*, p. 160. New Delhi: Sterling Publishers.

Jones III, John Paul, Heidi Nast and Susan Roberts. 1997. 'Thresholds in Feminist Geography: Difference, Methodology, Representation', in John Paul Jones III, Heidi Nast and Susan Roberts (eds) *Thresholds in Feminist Geography: Difference, Methodology, Representation*, pp. xxi–xxxix. New York: Rowman and Littlefield.

Joshi, Satya Mohan. 1992. 'Guthi', *An Anthology of Short Stories of Nepal*. Kathmandu: Foundation for Literature.

Kabeer, Naila. 1994. *Reversed Realities: Gender Hierarchies in Development Thought*. New York: Verso.

Kandyoti, Deniz. 1991. 'Islam and Patriarchy: A Comparative Perspective', in Nikkie R. Keddie and Beth Baron (eds) *Women in Middle Eastern History: Shifting Boundaries in Sex and Gender*, pp. 23–42. New Haven, CT: Yale University Press.

Katz, Cindi. 2001. 'On the Grounds of Globalization: A Topography for Feminist Political Engagement', *Signs: Journal of Women in Culture and Society* 26(4): 1213–34.

Kelly, Philip. 1999. 'The Geographies and Politics of Globalization', *Progress in Human Geography* 23(3): 379–400.

Killick, Tony. 1993. *The Adaptive Economy: Adjustment Policies in Small, Low-income Countries*. Washington, DC: The World Bank.

Kirkpatrick, Colonel. 1986 [1811]. *An Account of the Kingdom of Nepaul*. New Delhi: Asian Educational Services.

Kosambi, D.D. 1965. *The Culture and Civilisation of Ancient India in Historical Outline*. London: Routledge and Kegan Paul.

Laidlaw, James. 1995. *Riches and Renunciation: Religion, Economy, and Society among the Jains*. Oxford: Oxford University Press.

Lal, Deepak. 1983. *The Poverty of 'Development Economics'*. London: Institute of Economic Affairs.

Lall, Keshar. 1991. *Folk Tales from the Himalayan Kingdom of Nepal: Black Rice and Other Stories*. Kathmandu: Ratna Pustak Bhandar.

Landon, Perceval. 1993 [1928]. *Nepal*. New Delhi: Asian Educational Services.

Lash, S. and J. Urry. 1994. *Economies of Signs and Space: After Organized Capitalism*. London: Sage.

Lawson, Vicky. 1995. 'Beyond the Firm: Restructuring Gender Divisions of Labor in Quito's Garment Industry Under Austerity', *Society and Space* 13: 415–44.

—— 1999. 'Tailoring is a Profession, Seamstressing is just Work! Resisting Work and Reworking Gender Identities among Artisanal Garment Workers in Quito', *Environment and Planning A* 31: 415–44.

Lee, R. and J. Wills (eds) 1997. *Geographies of Economies*. New York: Arnold.

Lerche, Jens. 1993. 'Dominant Castes, Rajas, Brahmins and Intercaste Exchange Relations in Coastal Orissa: Beyond the Façade of the Jajmani System', *Contributions to Indian Sociology* 21(2): 237–66.

Leve, Lauren. 2000. *Contested Nation/Buddhist Innovation: The Politics of Piety in Theravada Buddhism in Nepal*. PhD diss., Princeton University.

Levy, Robert. 1990. *Mesocosm*. Berkeley: University of California Press.

Lewis, Todd. 1993. 'Himalayan Frontier Trade: Newar Diaspora Merchants and Buddhism', in Charles Ramble and Martin Brauen (eds) *Anthropology of Tibet and the Himalaya*, pp. 249–57. Zurich: Ethnological Museum of the University of Zurich.

Li, Tanya. 1999. 'Compromising Power', *Cultural Anthropology* 14(3): 295–322.

Liechty, Mark. 1995a. *Fashioning Modernity in Kathmandu: Mass Media Consumer Culture and the Middle Class in Nepal*. PhD diss., University of Pennsylvania.

—— 1995b. 'Media, Markets and Modernization: Youth Identities and the Experience of Modernity in Kathmandu, Nepal', in Vered Amit-Talai and Helena Wuff (eds) *Youth Cultures: A Cross-Cultural Perspective*, pp. 166–201. London: Routledge.

—— 1997. 'Selective Exclusion: Foreigners, Foreign Goods and Foreignness in Modern Nepali History', *Studies in Nepali History and Society* 2(1): 5–68.

—— 2003. *Suitably Modern: Making Middle-class Culture in a New Consumer Society*. Princeton, NJ: Princeton University Press.

Low, Setha M. 2001. 'The Edge and the Centre: The Discourse of Urban Fear', *American Anthropologist* 103(1): 45–58.

Lundvall, B. (ed.) 1992. *National Systems of Innovation: Towards a Theory of Innovation and Interactive Learning*. London: Pinter for Royal Institute for International Affairs.

MacKenzie, Suzanne and Dameris Rose. 1983. 'Industrial Change, the Domestic Economy, and Home Life', in J. Anderson, S. Duncan and R. Hudson (eds) *Redundant Spaces in Cities and Regions*, pp. 155–200. New York: Academic Press.

Manandhar, Thakur Lal. 1986. *Newari–English Dictionary: Modern Language of Kathmandu Valley*. Delhi: Agam Kala Prakasham.

March, Kathryn S. 2003. *If Each Comes Halfway*. Ithaca, NY: Cornell University Press.

Marcus, George and Michael Fisher. 1999. *Anthropology as Cultural Critique: An Experimental Moment in the Human Sciences*, 2nd edn. Chicago: University of Chicago Press.

Marriott, McKim. 1976. 'Hindu Transactions: Diversity without Dualism', in Bruce Kapferer (ed.) *Transactions and Meaning: Directions in the Anthropology of Exchange and Symbolic Behavior*, pp. 109–42. Philadelphia, PA: Ishi Press.

Marx, Karl. 1843/1975. 'On the Jewish Question', in L. Colleti (ed.) *Karl Marx: Early Writings*, trans. R. Livingstone and G. Benton. London: Penguin.

Maskell, Peter and Anders Malmberg. 1999. 'Localized Learning and Industrial Competitiveness', *Cambridge Journal of Economics* 23: 167–86.

Massey, Doreen. 1992. 'Politics and Space/Time', *New Left Review* 196: 65–84.

—— 1994. *Space, Place, and Gender*. Minneapolis: University of Minnesota Press.

—— 1999. 'Spaces of Politics', in Doreen Massey, John Allen and Philip Sarre (eds) *Human Geography Today*, pp. 279–94. Oxford: Polity Press.

Mauss, Marcel. 1925/1990. *The Gift: The Form and Reason for Exchange in Archaic Societies*, trans. W.D. Walls. London: Routledge.

Mayer, Peter. 1993. 'Inventing Village Tradition: The Late Nineteenth-century Origins of the North Indian Jajmani System', *Modern Asian Studies* 27(2): 357–95.

Mayoux, Linda. 1995. *From Vicious to Virtuous Circles? Gender and Mirco-enterprise Development*. Geneva: UN Research Institute for Social Development.

McDowell, Linda. 1983. 'Towards an Understanding of the Gender Division of Urban Space', *Environment and Planning D: Society and Space* 1: 59–72.

—— 1997. 'A Tale of Two Cities? Embedded Organizations and Embodied Workers', in Roger Lee and Jane Wills (eds) *Geographies of Economies*, pp. 118–32. New York: Arnold.

—— 2000. 'Feminists Rethink the Economic: The Economics of Gender/The Gender of Economics', in Gordon Clark, Maryann Feldman and Meric Gertler (eds) *The Oxford Handbook of Economic Geography*, pp. 497–517. Oxford: Oxford University Press.

McMichael, Philip. 1995. 'The New Colonialism: Global Regulation and the Restructuring of the Interstate System', in David A. Smith and József Böcz (eds.) *A New World Order? Global Transformations in the Late Twentieth Century*. Westport, CT: Greenwood Press.

McMichael, Philip and David Myhre. 1991. 'Global Regulation vs. the Nation-state: Agro-food Systems and the New Politics of Capital', *Capital and Class* summer: 83–105.

Mies, Maria. 1982. 'The Dynamics of the Sexual Division of Labor and the Integration of Rural Women into the World Market', in Lourdes Beneria (ed.) *Women and Development: The Sexual Division of Labor in Rural Societies*, pp. 1–28. New York: Praeger.

Miller, Sarah. 1992. *Twice-born Tales of Kathmandu: Stories that Tell People*. PhD diss., Cornell University.

Mines, Mattison. 1994. *Public Faces, Private Voices: Community and Individuality in South India*. Berkeley: University of California Press.

Mintz, Sidney. 1986. *Sweetness and Power: The Place of Sugar in Modern History*. New York: Penguin Books.

Mitchell, Don. 2000. *Cultural Geography: A Critical Introduction*. Oxford: Blackwell.

Mitchell, Katharyne. 1998. 'Reworking Democracy: Contemporary Immigration and Community Politics in Vancouver's Chinatown', *Political Geography* 17(6): 729–50.

—— 2001. 'Transnationalism, Neo-liberalism, and the Rise of the Shadow State', *Economy and Society* 30(2): 165–89.

Mittleman, James H. 1996. *Globalization: Critical Reflections*. Boulder, CO: Lynne Reinner.

Moffat, Michael. 1979. *An Untouchable Community in South India*. Princeton, NJ: Princeton University Press.

Moore, H. 1988. *Feminism and Anthropology*. Minneapolis: University of Minnesota Press.

Morduch, Jonathan. 2000. 'The Microfinance Schism', *World Development* 28(4): 617–29.

More Questions than Answers. 2000. On-line. Available www.nepalnews.com.np/contents/englishweekly/spotlight/2000/jan/jan28/national7.htm (Accessed 30 June 2003).

Mukerji, Chandra. 1983. *From Graven Images: Patterns of Modern Materialism*. New York: Columbia University Press.

Munn, Nancy. 1986. *The Fema of Gawa: A Symbolic Study of Value Transformation in a Massim (Papua New Guinea) Society*. Cambridge: Cambridge University Press.

NACLA (North American Congress on Latin America). 2001. 'Introduction to Special Issue, The Body Politic: Gender in the New World Order', *Report on the Americas* 34(5): 12–45.

Nagar, Richa. 2000. 'Religion, Race and the Debate over Mut'a in Dar es Salaam', *Feminist Studies* 26(3): 661–90.

Nagar, Richa, Victoria Lawson, Victoria McDowell and Susan Hanson. 2002. 'Locating Globalization: Feminist (Re)readings of the Subjects and Spaces of Globalization', *Economic Geography* 78(3): 257–84.

Narotzky, Susana. 1997. *New Directions in Economic Anthropology*. London: Pluto Press.

Nepali, Gopal Singh. 1965. *The Newars: An Ethno-sociological Study of a Himalayan Community*. Bombay: United Asia Publications.

NHDR. 1999. *Nepal Human Development Report*. Kathmandu: Nepal South Asia Centre.

Nussbaum, Martha. 2000. *Women and Human Development: The Capabilities Approach*. Cambridge: Cambridge University Press.

O'Brien, R. 1992. *Global Financial Integration: The End of Geography*. London: Pinter for Royal Institute for International Affairs.

Ohmae, Kenichi. 1990. *The Borderless World*. London: Collins.

Oldfield, Henry Ambrose. 1974 [1880]. *Sketches from Nipal*. New Delhi: Cosmo Publications.

Ong, Aihwa. 1987. *Spirits of Resistance and Capitalist Discipline: Factory Women in Malaysia*. Albany: State University of New York Press.

Ortner, Sherry. 1984. 'Theory in Anthropology since the Sixties', *Comparative Studies in Society and History* 26(1): 126–66.

Painter, Joe. 1997. 'Local Politics, Anti-essentialism and Economic Geography', in Roger Lee and Jane Wills (eds) *Geographies of Economies*, pp. 98–107. New York: Arnold.

Panday, Devendra Raj. 1999. *Nepal's Failed Development: Reflections on the Mission and the Maladies*. Kathmandu: Nepal South Asia Centre.

Parish, Steven. 1997. *Hierarchy and its Discontents: Culture and the Politics of Consciousness in Caste Society*. Delhi: Oxford University Press.

Parry, Jonathan. 1980. 'Ghosts, Greed and Sin: The Occupational Identity of the Benares Funeral Priests', *Man (n.s.)* 15: 88–111.

—— 1989. 'On the Moral Perils of Exchange', in Jonathan Parry and Maurice Bloch (eds) *Money and the Morality of Exchange*. Cambridge: Cambridge University Press.

Peake, Linda and D. Alissa Trotz. 1999. *Gender, Ethnicity and Place: Women and Identities in Guyana*. London: Routledge.

Peck, Jamie and Adam Tickell. 1994. 'Searching for a New Institutional Fix: The After-Fordist Crisis and the Global–Local Disorder', in A. Amin (ed.) *Post-Fordism: A Reader*, pp. 280–315. Oxford: Blackwell.

Phillips, Kevin. 1990. *The Politics of Rich and Poor: Wealth and the American Electorate in the Reagan Aftermath*. New York: Random House.

Pigg, Stacy Leigh. 1990. *Disenchanting Shamans: Representations of Modernity and the Transformation of Healing in Nepal*. PhD diss., Cornell University.

—— 1992. 'Inventing Social Categories through Place: Social Representation and Development in Nepal', *Journal of Comparative Study of Society and History* 34(3): 491–513.

—— 2001. 'Languages of Sex and AIDS in Nepal: Notes on the Social Production of Commensurability', *Cultural Anthropology* 16(4): 481–541.

Piore, Michael J. and Charles F. Sabel. 1984. *The Second Industrial Divide: Possibilities for Prosperity*. New York: Basic Books.

Polanyi, Karl. 1944. *The Great Transformation*. Boston, MA: Beacon Press.

—— 1966. *Dahomey and the Slave Trade: An Analysis of an Archaic Economy*. Seattle: University of Washington Press.

Portes, Alejandro and Patricia Landolt. 1996. 'The Downside of Social Capital', *The American Prospect* 7(26): 18–23.

Prakash, Gyan. 1990. *Bonded Histories: Genealogies of Labor Servitude in Colonial India*. Cambridge: Cambridge University Press.

Pratt, Geraldine. 1999. 'From Registered Nurse to Registered Nanny: Discursive Geographies of Filipina Domestic Workers in Vancouver, BC', *Economic Geography* 75(3): 215–36.

Pred, Allan and Michael Watts. 1992. *Reworking Modernity: Capitalisms and Symbolic Discontent*. New Brunswick, NJ: Rutgers University Press.

Putnam, Robert. 1993. *Making Democracy Work: Civic Traditions in Modern Italy*. Princeton, NJ: Princeton University Press.

Quigley, Declan. 1985. 'Household Organization among Newar Traders', *Contributions to Nepalese Studies* 12(2): 13–44.

—— 1993. *The Interpretation of Caste*. Oxford: Clarendon Press.

—— 1995. 'The *Guthi* Organizations of Dhulikhel Shresthas', *Kailash – A Journal of Himalayan Studies* 12(1–2): 5–62.

Raheja, Gloria Goodwin. 1988. *The Poison in the Gift: Ritual, Prestation, and the Dominant Caste in a North Indian Village*. Chicago: University of Chicago Press.

Raheja, Gloria Goodwin and Ann Grodzins Gold. 1994. *Listen to the Heron's Words: Reimagining Gender and Kinship in North India*. Berkeley: University of California Press.

Rana, Madhukar S.J.B. 1992. 'An Open Letter to the Minister', *Himal Himalayan Magazine* 5(2): 5–7.

Rankin, Katharine N. 1999. 'The Predicament of Labor: *Kamaiya* Practices and the Ideology of Freedom', in H. Skar (ed.) *Nepal: Tharu and Tarai Neighbors*, Vol. 16, pp. 27–45. Kathmandu: Biblioteca Himalayica Series III.

—— 2001a. 'Governing Development: Neoliberalism, Microcredit and Rational Economic Woman', *Economy and Society* 30(1): 18–37.

—— 2001b. 'Planning and the Politics of Markets: Some Lessons from Financial Regulation in Nepal', *International Planning Studies* 6(1): 89–102.

—— 2002. 'Social Capital, Microfinance, and the Politics of Development', *Journal of Feminist Economics* 8(1): 1–24.

—— 2003. 'Cultures of Economies: Gender and Socio-spatial Change in Nepal', *Gender, Place and Culture* 10(1): 111–29.

Regmi, D.R. 1960. *Ancient Nepal*. Calcutta: Firma K.L. Mukhopadhyay.

—— 1966. *Medieval Nepal: A History of the Three Kingdoms from 520 AD to 1768 AD*. Calcutta: Firma K.L. Mukhuoadhyay.

Regmi, M.C. 1971. *A Study in Nepali Economic History, 1768–1846*. New Delhi: Manjustri Publishing House.

—— 1978. *Land Tenure and Taxation in Nepal*. Kathmandu: Biblioteca Himalayica.

—— 1988. *An Economic History of Nepal, 1846–1901*. Varansi: Nath Publishing Company.

Regmi Research Collection. (n.d.). 'Stone Contract Land Assignment in Sankhu', Vol. 11, reel E24131. Kathmandu: Nepal National Archives.

—— 1786 [1843 V.S.]. 'Ijaara Granted to Ghana Shyam Upadhyaya for Revenue Collection in Sankhu', Vol. 25. Microfilm. Reel E2432, p. 117. Translated from Nepali. Kathmandu: Nepal National Archives.

—— 1794 [1851 V.S.]. 'Payment of Salary to Mahendra Khawas from Revenues of Customs Duties on Trade with Tibet', Vol. 24. Microfilm. Reel 2431, p. 440. Translated from Nepali. Kathmandu: Nepal National Archives.

—— 1796 [1853 V.S.]. 'Order to the *Hulaaki* in the Area surrounding Sankhu', Vol. 23. Microfilm. Reel E2431, p. 218. Translated from Nepali. Kathmandu: Nepal National Archives.

—— 1799 [1856 V.S.]. 'Order Regarding Supply of Charcoal to Magazine from Sankhu', Vol. 24. Microfilm. Reel E2431, p. 111. Kathmandu: Nepal National Archives.

—— 1812 [1869 V.S.]. 'Check Post Officials and Others in Areas between Sankhu and Falam Sangu Ordered to Provide Necessary Facilities to Lamas Returning from Kathmandu to Lhasa', Vol. 39. Microfilm. Reel 2453, p. 558. Translated from Nepali. Kathmandu: Nepal National Archives.

—— 1833 [1890 V.S.]. 'Unpaid Labor Impressed in Sankhu for Gunpowder Factory', Vol. 29. Microfilm. Reel E2433, p. 461. Translated from the Nepali. Kathmandu: Nepal National Archives.

Riles, Annelise. 1998. 'Infinity within Brackets', *American Ethnologist* 25(3): 1–21.

Rimal, Bishnu. 1996. 'Structural Adjustment Programme: Impact on Workers', in A.P. Shrestha and N.R. Dahal (eds) *Structural Adjustment Program in Nepal: Impact on Workers*, pp. 89–101. Kathmandu: Nepal Foundation for Advanced Studies.

Roberts, Susan. 2003. 'Global Strategic Vision: Managing the World', in R. Perry and B. Maurer (eds) *Globalization under Construction: Governmentality, Law, and Identity*. Minneapolis: University of Minnesota Press.

Robson, Elsbeth. 2000. 'Wife Seclusion and the Spatial Praxis of Gender Ideology in Nigerian Hausaland', *Gender, Place and Culture* 7(2): 179–99.

Rodman, Margaret C. 1992. 'Empowering Place: Multilocality and Multivocality', *American Anthropologist* 94: 640–56.

Rosaldo, Renato. 1989. *Culture and Truth: The Remaking of Social Analysis*. Boston, MA: Beacon Press.

Rose, Leo E. and Margaret W. Fisher. 1970. *The Politics of Nepal: Persistence and Change in an Asian Monarchy*. Ithaca, NY: Cornell University Press.

Roseberry, William. 1989. *Anthropologies and Histories: Essays in Culture, History, and Political Economy*. New Brunswick, NJ: Rutgers University Press.

Rosser, Colin. 1966. 'Social Mobility in the Newar Caste System', in Christoph Fürer-Haimendorf (ed.) *Caste and Kin in Nepal, India and Ceylon*. Bombay: Asia Publishing House.

Rouse, Roger. 1995. 'Thinking through Transnationalism: Note on the Cultural Politics of Class Relations in the Contemporary United States', *Public Culture* 7: 353–402.

Ruddick, Sue. 1996. *Young and Homeless in Hollywood: Mapping Social Identities*. New York: Routledge.

Sahlins, Marshall D. 1981. *Historical Metaphors and Mythical Realities: Structure in the Early History of the Sandwich Islands Kingdom*. Ann Arbor: University of Michigan Press.

Sanwal, B.D. 1965. *Nepal and the East India Company*. New York: Asia Publishing House.

Sassen, Saskia. 1998. *Globalization and its Discontents*. New York: The New Press.

Saxenian, Annalee. 1994. *Regional Advantage: Culture and Competition in Silicon Valley and Route 128*. Cambridge, MA: Harvard University Press.

Sayer, Andrew. 1985. 'The Difference that Space Makes', in D. Gregory and J. Urry (eds) *Social Relations and Spatial Structures*, pp. 49–66. London: Macmillan.

—— 1999. 'Bourdieu, Smith and Disinterested Judgement', *The Sociological Review* 47(3): 403–31.

Scott, Allen. 2001. *The Cultural Economy of Cities*. Beverly Hills, CA: Sage.

Sekelj, Tibor. 1959. *Window on Nepal*. London: Robert Hale Ltd.

Sen, Amartya. 1981. *Poverty and Famines: An Essay on Entitlement and Deprivation*. Oxford: Clarendon Press.

—— 1990. 'Gender and Cooperative Conflicts', in Irene Tinker (ed.) *Persistent Inequalities: Women and World Development*, pp. 123–49. Oxford: Oxford University Press.

—— 1999. *Development as Freedom*. Oxford: Oxford University Press.

—— 2000. *Culture and Development*. On-line. Available www.worldbank.org/poverty/culture/book/sen.htm (Accessed 24 August 2002).

Servon, Lisa J. 1998. 'Credit and Social Capital: The Community Development Potential of US Microenterprise Programs', *Housing Policy Debate* 9(1): 115–49.

Sharma, Shalikram. 2003. *The Development of Formal Microfinance Sector in Nepal and their Role in Poverty Alleviation*. Kathmandu: self-published.

Sharma, Shankar Prasad. 1997. 'Market-led Development Strategy in Nepal', *Developmental Practices in Nepal*, pp. 53–68. Kathmandu: Tribhuvan University.

Shrestha, Bal Gopal. 1999. 'The Newars: The Indigenous Population of the Kathmandu Valley in the Modern State of Nepal', *Contributions to Nepalese Studies* 23(1): 83–117.

—— 2002. *The Ritual Composition of Sankhu: The Socio-religious Anthropology of a Newar Town in Nepal.* PhD diss., University of Leiden, The Netherlands.

Shrestha, Bijaya L. 1993. 'Cry Wolf in Kathmandu', *Himal: Himalayan Magazine* 6(5): 30.

Shrestha, B.P. 1990. *The Nepalese Economy in Retrospect and Prospect.* Kathmandu: Himalayan Booksellers.

Shtrii Shakti. 1995. *Women, Development, Democracy: A Study of the Socio-economic Changes in the Status of Women in Nepal (1981–1993).* Kathmandu: Shtrii Shakti.

Slusser, Mary. 1982. *Nepal Mandala: A Cultural Study of the Kathmandu Valley.* Princeton, NJ: Princeton University.

Smith, Gavin. 1989. *Livelihood and Resistance: Peasants and the Politics of Land in Peru.* Berkeley: University of California Press.

—— 1999. *Confronting the Present: Towards a Politically Engaged Anthropology.* New York: Berg.

Smith, Neil. 1993. 'Homeless/global: Scaling Places', in J. Bird, B. Curtis, T. Putnam, G. Roberson and L. Tickner (eds) *Mapping the Futures: Local Cultures, Global Change*, pp. 87–119. London: Routledge.

Steed, Guy P.F. 1982. *Threshold Firms: Backing Canada's Winners.* Ottawa: Science Council of Canada.

Steedly, Mary Margaret. 1993. *Hanging Without a Rope: Narrative Experience in Colonial and Post-colonial Karoland.* Princeton, NJ: Princeton University Press.

Stiell, Bernadette and Kim England. 1997. 'Domestic Distinctions: Constructing Difference among Paid Domestic Workers in Toronto', *Gender, Place and Culture* 4(3): 339–59.

Stiglitz, J. 1998. *More Instruments and Broader Goals: Moving Toward the Post-Washington Consensus.* Helsinki: 1998 WIDER Annual Lecture.

Stiglitz, J. and K. Hoff. 1999. *Modern Economic Theory and Development.* Dubrovnik: Symposium on Future of Development Economics in Perspective.

Stiller, Ludwig. 1975. *The Rise of the House of Gorkha: A Study in the Unification of Nepal.* Kathmandu: Ratna Pustak Bhandar.

Storper, Michael. 1995. 'The Resurgence of Regional Economies, Ten Years Later', *European Urban and Regional Studies* 2(3): 191–221.

Storper, Michael and R. Walker. 1989. *The Capitalist Imperative: Territory, Technology, and Industrial Growth.* Oxford: Blackwell.

Strathern, Marilyn. 1988. *The Gender of the Gift: Problems with Women and Problems with Society in Melanesia.* Berkeley: University of California Press.

Swyngedouw, Erik. 1997. 'Neither Global nor Local: "Glocalization" and the Politics of Scale', in Kevin Cox (ed.) *Spaces of Globalization: Reasserting the Power of the Local*, pp. 137–66. New York: Guilford.

Taylor, Peter J., Michael J. Watts and R.J. Johnston. 1995. 'Global Change at the End of the Twentieth Century', in R.J. Johnston, P.J. Taylor and M.J. Watts (eds) *Geographies of Global Change: Remapping the World in the Late 20th Century*, pp. 1–10. Oxford: Blackwell.

Tickell, Adam and Jamie Peck. 1995. 'Social Regulation after Fordism: Regulation Theory, Neoliberalism and the Global–Local Nexus', *Economy and Society* 4(3): 357–86.

Tiwari, Ashutosh. 1992. 'Planning: Never without Aid', *Himal Himalayan Magazine* 5(2): 8–10.

Toffin, Gerard. 1977. *Pyangaon: Une communauté Newar de la Vallée de Kathmandou.* Paris: CNRS.

Tomlinson, John. 1999. *Globalization and Culture*. Chicago: University of Chicago Press.

Tsing, Anna. 1993. *In the Realm of the Diamond Queen: Marginality in an Out-of-the-Way Place*. Princeton, NJ: Princeton University Press.

—— 2000. 'The Global Situation', *Cultural Anthropology* 15(3): 327–60.

Turner, Ralph Lilley. 1931. *Dictionary of the Nepali Language*. New Delhi: Allied Publishers.

Uprety, Prem R. 1980. *Nepal–Tibet Relations, 1850–1930: Years of Hopes, Challenges and Frustrations*. Kathmandu: Puga Nara.

Vajracharya, Dhanavajra. 1972. ' "Gumvihara" (The Forest Monastery)', *Madhuparka* 22(5).

—— 1973. 'Licchivikalaka Abhilekha (Licchivi Period Inscriptions), 320–35, 382–3, 508–10'. Kathmandu: Institute of Nepal and Asian Studies, Historical Collections Series, no. 6. Tribhuvan University.

Valeri, Valerio. 1984. *Kingship and Sacrifice: Ritual and Society in Ancient Hawaii*. Chicago: University of Chicago Press.

van der Veen, Klaas W. 1992. 'The Brahmin, the Individual and the Poisonous Gift', in A.W. van den Hoek, D.H.A. Kloff and M.S. Oort (eds) *Ritual, State and History in South Asia: Essays in Honour of J.C. Heesterman*, pp. 695–716. Leiden: E.J. Brill.

Visweswaran, Kamala. 1994. *Fictions of Feminist Ethnography*. Minneapolis: University of Minnesota Press.

Wade, Robert. 1996. 'Japan, the World Bank, and the Art of Paradigm Maintenance: The East Asian Miracle in Political Perspective', *New Left Review* 217: 3–36.

Wehnert, Ulrich and Roshan Shakya. 2003. 'Microfinance and Armed Conflict in Nepal: The Adverse Effects of the Insurgency on Small Farmer Cooperatives Ltd. (SFCLs)', Kathmandu: Agricultural Development Bank of Nepal and German Technical Cooperation.

Weiner, Annette. 1992. *Inalienable Possessions: The Paradox of Keeping-While-Giving*. Berkeley: University of California Press.

Wilk, Richard R. 1996. *Economics and Cultures: Foundations of Economic Anthropology*. Boulder, CO: Westview Press.

Williams, Raymond. 1977. *Marxism and Literature*. Oxford: Oxford University Press.

—— 1983. *Keywords: A Vocabulary of Culture and Society*. New York: Oxford University Press.

—— 1994. 'Selections from Marxism and Literature', in N.B. Dirks, G. Eley and S.B. Ortner (eds) *Culture/Power/History: A Reader in Contemporary Social Theory*, pp. 585–608. Princeton, NJ: Princeton University Press.

Williamson, J. 1990. 'What Washington Means by Policy Reform', in J. Williamson (ed.) *Latin American Adjustment: How Much has Happened?*, pp. 5–20. Washington: Institute for International Economics.

Willis, S. 1991. *A Primer for Daily Life*. London: Routledge.

Wolf, Eric. 1982. *Europe and the People without History*. Berkeley: University of California Press.

Wolfe, David A. and Gertler, Meric S. 1998. 'The Regional Innovation System in Ontario', in H.-J. Braczyk, P. Cooke and M. Heidenreich (eds) *Regional Innovation Systems: The Role of Governances in a Globalized World*, pp. 99–135. London: UCL Press.

Wood, Ellen Meiksins. 1995. *Democracy Against Capitalism: Renewing Historical Materialism*. Cambridge: Cambridge University Press.

Woolcock, Michael. 1998. 'Social Capital and Economic Development: Toward a Theoretical Synthesis and Policy Framework', *Theory and Society* (27): 151–208.

—— 1999. *Managing Risks, Shocks and Opportunity in Developing Economics: The Role of Social Capital.* On-line. Available www.worldbank.org/poverty/scapital/library/woolcock.pdf (Accessed 30 July 2003).

World Bank. 2002a. *Social Capital for Development.* On-line. Available www.worldbank.org/poverty/scapital/ (Accessed 24 August 2002).

—— 2002b. *Culture and Poverty: Learning and Research at the World Bank.* On-line. Available www.worldbank.org/poverty/culture/overview/index.htm (Accessed 24 August 2002).

Wright, Daniel. 1958 [1877]. *History of Nepal*, trans. Munshi Shew Shunker Singh and Pandit Sri Gunanand. Calcutta: Susil Gupta (India) Private Ltd.

Zanen, Sj. M. 1986. 'The Goddess Vajrayogini and the Kingdom of Sankhu (Nepal)', *Purusartha* 10: 125–66.

Zukin, Sharon. 1991. *Landscapes of Power: From Detroit to Disney World.* Berkeley: University of California Press.

—— 1995. *The Cultures of Cities.* Oxford: Blackwell.

INDEX

market-led approach to, 17–18, 30, 74,
  189, 190, 205n2
and planning, 35–9, 196–203, 204n1
and progressive politics, 205n6
development agencies, 17
development banks, 189, 218n1
dharma (religious obligations), 125,
  126–7, 214n38
Ḍhikuṭi (bidding game), 111
dialectical tacking, 62
Dibya Upadesh (nationalist treatise), 94
digu dyo guthis (lineage group
  associations), 122–3, 138, 148–9,
  213n31
disciplines, academic, and globalization,
  41–3, 58, 66
'dividualism', 160
domination, 71, 142
  and Bourdieu, 34–5, 36, 37, 202–3,
    206n13
dowry wealth *see kvasah*
doxa, 35, 51, 202
duāre (functionary), 112–13, 114, 212n17
Dumont, Louis, 130–3, 134–6

East India Company, 93–4, 95
'eating the land', 112–13
economic anthropology, 27
economic competitiveness, 29, 31–2, 60
economic domain, vs. political, 19, 23,
  101, 199–200
economic forms, non-capitalist, 27, 31,
  33–5, 71, 195
economic liberalization, 167–73
economic opportunity, 30, 176, 184, 191
economic policy, of Asian Tigers, 18, 21,
  205n2
economics
  normative commitments in, 26
  of practice, 32–5, 36, 37, 39, 127–8,
    206n13
  theoretical relevance, 206n8
economy
  and culture, 20, 23, 29–32
  and society, 27, 29–32, 198–9
education, 81, 184
egalitarianism, 16
emancipatory social change, 162, 203
engagement gifts, 178

Enhanced Structural Adjustment, 168
essentialism, 71
ethnic consciousness, 79–80
evil (*pāp*), 124–5, 126–7, 133–4, 214n38
exchange rates, 209n17, 211n4
exports, 170–2
extended families, 115–16, 117–19,
  213n27

factionalism, political, 80
false consciousness, 36, 202
families, 115–16, 117–19, 191, 213n25,
  213n27
fashion, 180
feasting, 120–2, 177, 213n26, 213n30,
  217n7
feminist geography, 29–30, 59–60, 61–2,
  65
festivals, 110–11, 125, 137–8, 143, 144
  see also Vajrayogini
Finance Company Act (Nepal), 168
First World, 205n5
'footloose' industries, 61
foreign aid, 166
foreign trade, 167
formalist anthropology, 27–8, 35–6,
  206n8
freedom, 16, 26, 198
Freirian consciousness-raising, 202
functionaries, 112–13, 114, 138, 212n17,
  212n19, 215n5
Funeral Priest caste (Bhā), 134

Gangetic plains, 76, 86
garment sector, 171–2
gender
  and commoditized regimes of value,
    180–4, 185–6, 192
  critical consciousness, 155, 160–2
  and development, 30, 188
  and *guthis*, 148–9
  and habitus, 152–4
  ideology, 147–51, 184, 191
  and labour, 149–50, 175, 183–4, 211n5
  and male migration, 183, 196, 211n5
  and Newars, 2, 204n2
  and space, 59–60, 196, 216n17
  see also aṅgsa
genealogy, 74

Tibeto-Burman ethnic groups, 77, 211n1
topographical geography, 62, 63
tourist industry, 167, 172
trade
    balance of, 95
    and *desa* (sacred realm), 94–5
    post-Second World War, 165–73,
        217n2
    routes, 75–6, 77, 86, 87, 88, 95, 97
    trans-Himalayan, 75–6, 90–5, 96–101,
        105
Trade and Commerce Treaty, 167, 171
tradition, 195
transactional orders, 104, 128
transport, 81, 100–1, 211n44
tvaḥ (neighbourhood centres), 81

udhāro (commercial credit), 111
United Marxist-Leninist government,
    45
United Nations Development Programme
    (UNDP), 197, 199
Untouchable caste (Po), 134, 142, 173,
    179, 214n3, 214n35, 215n8
untraded interdependencies, 60
urban space, 136–7

Vajracharya (Buddhist Priests), 210n28,
    214n37
    and Hinduism, 89, 100, 132, 134,
        209n22
Vajrayana Buddhism, 83, 84–6, 89,
    214n37
Vajrayogini (goddess and festival), 83,
    84, 85, 89, 209n22
    and *guthis*, 122, 138, 213n32

Vajrayogini (temple), 83, 85, 89, 209n27
    Tibetan monks and, 92
    wealth of, 91
value *see* regimes of value
Village Development Committees, 80,
    208n9
violence, symbolic, 34–5, 36, 140, 193,
    199

Washington Consensus, 17–18, 21, 23
    post-Washington Consensus, 21–3,
        26–7, 31, 38, 190, 194, 197
wealth
    global distribution of, 18–19
    Hindu attitudes towards, 106
    see also kvasah
wedding feasts, 177
Williams, Raymond, 47
women
    accumulation by, 192
    and commoditization, 174–5, 180, 192
    and education, 184
    and fashion, 180
    hierarchy among, 154, 189
    and households, 147–51, 154–60, 191,
        216n18, 216n24, 216n25
    market access by, 192
    and opportunity, 184
    and property, 149, 157–160, 161,
        216n19
    seclusion of, 148, 191, 196, 216n17
    and subordination, 160–2, 191–2,
        193–4
World Bank, 21, 38, 168, 199, 206n15,
    206n17
World Trade Organization, 45